Lady Friends

The Anthropology of Contemporary Issues

A SERIES EDITED BY

ROGER SANJEK

A full list of titles in the series appears at the end of this book.

Lady Friends

HAWAIIAN WAYS AND THE
TIES THAT DEFINE

Karen L. Ito

Cornell University Press

Ithaca and London

Portions of articles by Karen L. Ito published in *Culture, Medicine and Psychiatry*: "Hoʻoponopono, 'To Make Right': Hawaiian Conflict Resolution and Metaphor in the Construction of a Family Therapy," 9(2)(1985): 201–217, copyright © 1985 by D. Reidel Publishing Co., and "Illness as Retribution: A Cultural Form of Self-Analysis among Urban Hawaiian Women," 6(4)(1982): 385–403, copyright © 1982 by D. Reidel Publishing Co., are used here with the kind permission of Kluwer Academic Publishers.

Portions of Karen L. Ito's chapter "Affective Bonds: Hawaiian Interrelationships of Self," in *Person, Self, and Experience: Exploring Pacific Ethnopsychologies*, ed. Geoffrey M. White and John Kirkpatrick, copyright © 1985 by The Regents of the University of California, are used with the kind permission of the University of California Press.

Portions of Karen L. Ito's chapter "Emotions, Proper Behavior (*Hana Pono*), and Hawaiian Concepts of Self, Person, and Individual," in *Contemporary Issues in Mental Health Research in the Pacific Islands*, ed. Albert B. Robillard and Anthony J. Marsella, copyright ©1987 by the Social Science Research Institute, University of Hawaii, are used with the kind permission of the Social Science Research Institute.

First published 1999 by Cornell University Press
First printing, Cornell Paperbacks, 1999

Library of Congress Cataloging-in-Publication Data

Ito, Karen L. (Karen Lee), 1947–
Lady friends : Hawaiian ways and the ties that define / Karen L. Ito.
p.   cm. — (The anthropology of contemporary issues)
Includes bibliographical references.
ISBN 0-8014-2636-7 (cloth : alk. paper). — ISBN 0-8014-9939-9 (pbk. : alk. paper)
1. Hawaiians—Social life and customs. 2. Women, Hawaiian. 3. Hawaiians—Ethnic identity.
I. Title. II. Series.
DU624.65.I76   1999
306'.09969—dc21   99-17552

Printed in the United States of America

Cornell University Press strives to use environmentally responsible suppliers and materials to the fullest extent possible in the publishing of its books. Such materials include vegetable-based, low-VOC inks, and acid-free papers that are recycled, totally chlorine-free, or partly composed of nonwood fibers. Books that bear the logo of the FSC (Forest Stewardship Council) use paper taken from forests that have been inspected and certified as meeting the highest standards for environmental and social responsibility. For further information, visit our website at www.cornellpress.cornell.edu.

Cloth printing   10 9 8 7 6 5 4 3 2 1
Paperback printing   10 9 8 7 6 5 4 3 2 1

To my husband, Robert B. Edgerton,
who makes all things possible,
and
Katharine Luomala, in memory
of her meticulous scholarship
and the warmth of her friendship,
both of which are deeply missed

Contents

Preface

This book focuses primarily on Hawaiian culture as I saw it lived in six urban Hawaiian households. The six households were part of an original sample of eleven families chosen in 1974 for ethnographic home studies by the Kamehameha Early Education Project (KEEP), an experimental demonstration project in Kalihi, a neighborhood of Honolulu. KEEP was funded by the prestigious Kamehameha Schools, established in the 1880s by the will of Princess Bernice P. Bishop for the education of children of Hawaiian ancestry. Difficult entrance examinations, high tuition, and a long waiting list limit the number of Hawaiian children who are able to attend. KEEP was established in 1972 as part of "Kam" Schools' outreach program to extend its resources to more Hawaiian children and to develop culturally appropriate learning programs and curricula for Hawaiian children.

The sample families were chosen to reflect the school population, based on the sociodemographics of Hawaiian households in Kalihi. That summer of 1974, four of the eleven families were unavailable because of travel or other obligations. When I returned in 1975 for a new research project independent of the KEEP program, six of the seven remaining families consented to work with me.

I knew and interacted with all members of the household and their extended families and the families of friends, but my primary associates were the mothers of the households, for three reasons. First, Hawaiian families are strongly matrifocal, characterized by a pattern of matrilaterality, uxorilocal residency after marriage, residential proximity of female siblings and their children to their mothers, and the greatest frequency of dyadic interaction between women and their mothers. Second, mothers are the mainstays of the family unit as keepers not only of the hearth and children but of cultural traditions and interpretations. Third, it would be culturally inappropriate and sexually provocative for me as an unaccompanied woman to "talk story" alone with husbands, other male relatives, or male friends of my lady friends. To have done so would have severely compromised or even destroyed my relationship with the women. But I often talked story with men at *lūʻaus*, family gatherings, meals, outings, and shopping trips, while playing cards, or when they joined their wives, daughters, sisters, or female cousins in a talk story session.

One of the terms Hawaiian women use to describe their women friends is "lady friends." While I am sure not all the women I worked with would consider me their lady friend, I found that for my part, I was so affected by their concerns that I consider them mine.

My greatest debt of gratitude is to the people of Hawaiʻi, who taught me so much, gave to me with *aloha* and heart, hospitality and humor. In particular, I owe a very special debt to the families and women of Honolulu who are the core of this book. If I have misunderstood their teachings, it is not from their lack of effort or sincerity of intent.

To Robert B. Edgerton, who is responsible for introducing me to research in Hawaiʻi and has made such research possible, I owe more than can be comprehended. He has been a gentle, steadfast guiding light throughout the years and now more than ever. To him I owe my gratitude for the opportunity to conduct this research and for his constant faith and encouragement to complete the book. Next I must thank Jill E. Korbin, who was there at the beginning of my Hawaiʻi fieldwork (quite literally, as she greeted my plane when I first arrived in Hilo, on the Big Island) and still mysteriously remains a friend after I have tortured her with every version of anything I have written on Hawaiʻi. Geoffrey M. White and David T. Takeuchi have been stalwart supporters and audiences. David has been my special source for things I desperately needed and for thoughtful responses to my often crazed questions. I think Geoff has heard or read so many versions of parts of this book that he could have written it himself, and a great deal faster. To Geoff, Wimal Dissanayake, David Wu, Robert Hewitt, and the East-West Center staff, my thanks for an appointment as a Fellow as well as office space in the Institute of Culture and Communication during the fall of 1988. I am also grateful to the Honorable Yasutake Fukushima and the late Mrs. Helen Fukushima for their generous housing and kindness during the same period. Thank you to Lynette Paglinawan for her tireless and open-hearted discussions with me about *ho'oponopono*. My appreciation goes to the former Kamehameha Early Education Project and its staff, particularly to Ronald Gallimore, Sharon Omori, Violet Mays, and Sherlyn Chun for introducing me to the Kalihi families and for their advice and counsel. To Ronald Higashi, Executive Director of the Susannah Wesley Community Center, and Douglas Oshiro of the Hawai'i State Department of Business, Economic Development, and Tourism, thank you for sociodemographic information about the Kalihi-Pālama area.

Financial support for the original research period was generously provided by the Carnegie Foundation and a National Institute for Mental Health Pre-Doctoral Traineeship from the University of California, Los Angeles, Behavioral Anthropology Program.

This book would not be a reality if it were not for the faith and encouragement of Roger Sanjek and Peter Agree of Cornell University Press. They have been patient and steadfast editors of insight and acumen.

There are others, I regret too numerous to list, who have helped along the way. My apologies for not naming you individually, but do know my appreciation and gratitude are no less.

All Hawaiian place names follow the diacritical standards in Pukui, Elbert, and Mookini (1976), unless they are in a direct quote or citation title. Note that in citations, Hawai'i is spelled both with and without the diacritic for a glottal stop (called an *'okina* in Hawaiian which is a left single quote mark or upside down comma). It is written as it appears in titles and publishers' names at the date of publication. At times, the *'okina* may appear in the title but not the publisher's name. This is not an inconsistency of proofreading but an accurate representation of that publication.

Royalties from this book will be donated directly to Alu Like, Inc., a private, nonprofit community-based organization dedicated to Hawaiian economic and social self-sufficiency.

KAREN L. ITO

Los Angeles, California

Lady Friends

Introduction

Hawai'i is a wonderfully accessible place for Americans. It offers a tropical climate, lush vegetation, and beautiful beaches, all with the tease of the exotic and the reassurance of the domestic. It requires no passport, no language concerns, no worries about the water or changing money, only a plane or boat ticket and some summer clothes. While Hawai'i is accessible, its indigenous people are not. Who they are and what they are about are of little concern to the multitudes of tourists who pass through their land. They exist only as a friendly, ever-present backdrop, indistinguishable to visitors from other amiable local people as Filipino, Japanese, and Samoan Americans.[1]

[1] The term "local" has a complex meaning that has never been adequately explored since Okamura's early and frequently cited piece (1980) and a more obscure earlier work by Yamamoto (1979), which focused more on Japanese Americans. In its simplest definition it refers to people born and raised in Hawai'i, but it is permeated by class distinctions, lifestyle preferences, speech patterns, and affective styles. It is used to distinguish nonwhites born and raised in Hawai'i from whites (*haoles*) as a group, yet individual whites can be considered local *haoles* (Okamura 1980:128). Usually *haoles* who are wealthy or upper-middle-class longtime residents from socially prominent white families (often descended from the earliest white missionaries in Hawai'i, who may have intermarried with Hawaiian nobility) are referred to as *kama'āina* (literally "child of the land" but more commonly "native born") (Whittaker 1986:80; Pukui and Elbert 1986). Linnekin (1985) used this term to refer to individuals of Hawaiian ancestry. Technically it does mean native born; a more recent term in the literature is *kānaka maoli* (Blaisdell and Mokuau 1991; Hasager and Friedman 1994). Trask has referred to "locals as both Hawaiian and non-Hawaiian long-time residents of Hawai'i" (1994:20) but also distinguishes "locals" from people of Hawaiian ancestry and concludes that "only Hawaiians are truly children of the land" (1994:30). As Okamura noted, "local" is a term used in oppositional distinction, "a means of distinguishing between [locals] and non-locals" (1980:132). "Non-locals" are usually immigrants, people from the mainland, whites (*haoles*), landed gentry, tourists, developers, foreign investors, or big business representatives.

[1]

This serene, composed scene belies the turbulent struggles by Hawaiian activists for cultural and economic preservation and revitalization. Hawaiian activists have been waging legal and social battles to regain lost land and traditional livelihoods. The culture they are striving to preserve and revitalize has little to do with the tidbits visible in tour *lū'aus*, the flashy Kodak hula show, or the staged re-creations at the Polynesian Cultural Center; it is a viable and overt amalgam of values, relationships, and meaning. This movement has become known as the Hawaiian Cultural Renaissance.

The Hawaiian Cultural Renaissance began in the 1970s. It was the outgrowth of two social developments, one on the U.S. mainland and one in the state of Hawai'i. The mainland influence was twofold: the federal programs that grew out of the civil rights movement and the ethnic power movements (McGregor-Alegado 1980), particularly the Native American activities (Trask 1984–85). Locally the battles against land developers in rural communities led to an increased focus on the relationship of Hawaiian land tenure, traditional agricultural land use, and cultural activities. Rural Hawaiian communities that still cultivated taro, fished, and had strong interpersonal ties were viewed as repositories of what was left of Hawaiian culture. Eventually rural Hawaiian community members became self-conscious about their role as the maintainers of Hawaiian traditions (Linnekin 1983, 1985). An interest arose, particularly among the student and political activists, in reviving traditional arts and craft forms: traditional *hula* (Buck 1993), chanting, *lei*making, canoe building, fish ponds. Interest revived in having a working knowledge of the Hawaiian language and traditional subsistence methods, particularly taro cultivation and fishing. These elements were all inextricably linked to interpersonal values and structures such as the extended family (*'ohana*), kinship relations, and the emotional ties that bind kin together. All these elements condensed into the idea of *aloha 'āina*, or love of the land. Landownership and reparations have become the linchpin of the political and cultural movement known as the Hawaiian Cultural Renaissance. Subsequent political developments have resulted in a sovereignty movement in which various groups have joined to call for self-government by the indigenous population and reparations both in money and in land (Trask 1993; Hasager and Friedman 1994).

Because Hawaiians took their sustenance from the land, their daily activities—planting, fishing, building, even eating—expressed spiritual as well

as physical aspects of being. This understanding of life as a relationship between the spirit of the land and the people of the land, between material
survival and cultural expression, between work and a respect for the won-
drous and varied bounty of nature—all this shaped Hawaiian philosophy,
music, art, dance, language, and, indeed, structured the core of Hawaiian
kinship, the extended family or *'ohana*. The gradual re-learning of this cultural heritage led activist Hawaiians to demand what their nineteenth century counterparts had demanded: a land base for the practice and transmission of their culture, especially taro cultivation and religious
observances. (Trask 1984–85:120)

This is a self-conscious search for cultural authenticity and meaning
through political action and personal rediscovery.

But what of the Hawaiians who live in the cities: those without
land, without access to specialized education; those who do not participate in these struggles or in the rural lifestyle; or those of the middle class who do not identify with the political agendas of either the
Hawaiian Renaissance or the various sovereignty movements? Have
these people lost their culture? Their Hawaiianness? If one lives in
public housing in Honolulu or in a single-family ranchhouse in the
suburb of Hawai'i Kai, if the only land one cultivates is a family garden, if one goes fishing only on weekends or during a vacation at the
beach, if one lives far from one's immediate relatives, if one speaks no
Hawaiian and knows little of traditional crafts, is one without Hawaiian culture? What if one does not know the family history well enough
to claim with certainty a specific percentage of Hawaiian blood?
Hawaiian activists feel that indeed these city people have lost their
traditional heritage, their culture. They are wage earners, unskilled
workers, welfare recipients, Hawaiians alienated from their land and
their cultural connections. Because Hawaiian activists hold that their
culture arises out of direct material and spiritual relations with the
land—subsistence activities are intended to feed not merely the body
but the individual soul and cultural vitality as well—then urban
Hawaiians, who lack this basic connection, are without cultural
grounding. According to Hawaiian activists, this is evidenced in their
less than vanguard position in the recent Hawaiian cultural and political movements: "Now while most Hawaiians live in urban areas, they
are not the activists calling for an independent land base and a cultural revival" (Trask 1984–85:127).

And in fact most of the urban Hawaiians I worked with in the 1970s
did not understand and sometimes ridiculed the political activities of

[3]

Hawaiian activists. One of those women, June Kamakau,[2] did not approve of the ALOHA organization, an early Hawaiian activist group, (the acronym stands for Aboriginal Lands of Hawaiian Ancestry). She said that "it was meant to be" that Hawaiians should not own the land. She noted that no one had owned it before, and the Hawaiians were just lucky to have been the first to come here: "If we had a right to it, we wouldn't have lost it to the *haoles* [whites].[3] Just like the Indians, huh?" She had a niece who was involved in the Waiāhole-WaiKāne community fight to prevent evictions of tenants and farmers whose leased land was slated for commercial development in 1974,[4] and June had argued with her: the niece and her friends were being foolish; they were wasting their time and energy with their demonstrating. The "papers" had already been signed and "Honolulu Water" would be laying pipes soon for the new development. An extension of the leases granted by the landowners was only a courtesy, and the battle had long been lost. The protesters, June told me, should be praying to soften the developers' hearts so they would be more receptive rather than holding demonstrations that hardened their hearts against them. Another Hawaiian lady friend I worked with, Ellen Kam, laughed at the first group of Hawaiian activists who landed on and attempted to reclaim the island called Kaho'olawe, long used by the navy as a bombing target. She thought they looked foolish, particularly because she considered the island meaningless—after all, it was a bombing target. So the concerns of activists seem warranted: urban Hawaiians are disfranchised from the land and the understanding of the need to reclaim it. But are they alienated from their culture?

Indeed, how can these people, without any formal enculturation system, without any subsistence ties to the land or sea, without Hawaiian language or crafts—how can they claim Hawaiian culture, let alone maintain or sustain it? Perhaps the answer is that they do so by merely living it. These people are un-self-consciously creating, changing, discarding, using Hawaiian culture and its components. They live their lives unconsciously but at the same time powerfully manipulate their cultural heritage and "the contexts and processes that actually produce shared identifications during the course of everyday social life" (White

[2] All the names of people I worked with are pseudonyms, but they retain the qualities of the original names, such as the ethnicity of a surname or the type of nickname.
[3] Though *haole* is now used to refer to whites, originally it referred to anything or anyone foreign.
[4] The land in question was on O'ahu's Windward side, owned by the prominent McCandless Estate.

1991:6). How they do so and what they have to say about it is the subject of this book.

June's discussion of putting love in another's heart, not hardening it, has traditional cultural roots that have developed into a contemporary cultural understanding of meaning. The details of "heart" and the emotional transference from one person to another are discussed in Chapters 2 and 3. Hawaiian culture is manifest as unconscious, nonreflective, contemporary, lived. It resides in the quotidian social interactions and emotional relationships among Hawaiians and the shared meanings of those interactions and relationships. Much of those cultural elements are uncodified but familiar, unspoken but shared, unconscious but known. These individuals have not taken the phenomenological turn of knowing what they know and how they know it. But they do live it and recognize that there is something that binds them together. Listen to Evelyn Michaels, one of my lady friends, when I asked her what it means to be Hawaiian.[5]

> Oh, in way [*sic*] we relate. It's like—a common thing. . . . You feel comfortable. Like this is way I mean by Hawaiians. When you 'round them, to mean, I feel you comfortable and you guys all have similar ways and, and it's accepted. You know the ways. It's like Hawaiians they have this certain way about 'em. You don't have to draw a picture but it's there. . . . Like let's say me and my old man, and get[6] about five different couples. And we're invited to one party. And get one Japanese and different nationalities. Now, if one, if somebody does something to one of the couples, the one Hawaiian couples, all of the Hawaiian couples would notice the offense. It's unusual. They [the Hawaiians] all going notice. And they going know—exactly how that person, who was offended, let's say the husband was offended or the wife was offended, they know how the person going to react. It's unusual.

Evelyn's words indicate cultural ideals of manners and proper behavior, cultural interpretations and emotional understandings, and from there a collective sense of being Hawaiian in how they "relate."

---

[5] Transcriptions are in the local dialect known as pidgin English, which has many subforms. Characteristic phrases and forms are "da kine" (the kind), which can be used as a noun or a verb; "tell" for say; and "wen'" plus a verb, as in "I wen' go to the park" or "You wen' see da guy?" Also nouns that refer to collectivities are sometimes pluralized: "stuffs" and "junks." Carr's work (1972) is still the definitive work in explanation and examples. There are also comic glossaries of pidgin that are humorous as well as instructive (Simonson et al. 1981, 1982). Island literature has captured the richness of pidgin (Maruyama 1988; Yamanaka 1996, 1997).

[6] The use of "get" for "have" is another characteristic of Hawaiian pidgin.

But what exactly is culture? This descriptively elusive but powerful definer of humanness has been much discussed, maligned, disregarded, and renewed. The most dynamic and clearheaded examination of culture theory is the volume edited by Richard A. Shweder and Robert· A. LeVine (1984), where they develop "a symbols-and-meanings conception of culture." For LeVine, culture is "a shared organization of ideas that includes the intellectual, moral and aesthetic standards prevalent in a community and the meanings of communicative actions" (1984:67). The key element for LeVine is "the meanings of communicative actions": the contexts, interpretations, and rationales that define the meanings and the standards that make certain acts meaningful. These meanings are not unorganized but ordered in some culturally significant way. In that regard, I would append the modifier "patterned" to "meanings," so the phrase would read "and patterned meanings of communicative actions." Further, I would add to LeVine's definition of culture as "a shared organization of ideas" the word "negotiated," for it is the constant use and challenge between culture members that keeps culture from being a static, artifactual body of mere information. In addition, a culture has a body of knowledge and interpretation that can be called ethnopsychology. As Catherine Lutz (1985) explains, ethnopsychology concerns a people's organized theories of motivation, behavior, intent, consciousness, self, and standards of morality or proper behavior and emotions.

This book focuses primarily on the Hawaiian culture observed primarily in a neighborhood of Honolulu called Kalihi and to a lesser degree in South Kona, on the Big Island of Hawai'i. I examine "the patterned meanings of communicative actions" through Hawaiian interpretations of motive, judgments of proper behavior (etiquette), ideas of self and other—both in their idealized forms and in their failings—and the central communicative role of emotion. It is through these systematic interpretations that Hawaiian culture will be explored, as it is used and maintained in an urban setting, by people without formal enculturation, traditional rural lifestyles, or fluency in the Hawaiian language.

Metaphor

Hawaiians use metaphors in a wide variety of ways that illustrate social relationships, interpretations of motive, and constructions of self and other. Hawaiians express, create, and retain their culture-as-lived through their use of metaphor. Metaphors demonstrate a cultural coherency across several systems: a moral system of retribution and responsibility (Chapter 2), cultural understandings of self, person, and individual (Chapter 3), and methods for conflict resolution (Chapter 4).

However, this book is not about the analysis of tropes or metaphor. Rather it is about the culture behind the metaphor as it appears and is manipulated in everyday life. Metaphors arise from cultural conceptualizations of patterned, shared meanings that allow understanding and communication between members of a culture (Quinn 1991). George Lakoff and Mark Turner explain the power of a conceptual metaphor: "It is automatic, effortless, and generally established as a mode of thought among members of a linguistic community" (1989:55). In other words, it is shared, usually unconsciously used, and assumed to be valid—an accepted convention.

Metaphors frame situations by giving them paradigmatic definitions. In addition, they create an understanding of the dynamics of a situation as well as the solutions (Schön 1979). If a social problem is referred to as a "cancer," the term defines the situation as an internal, spontaneously occurring problem. The dynamics are of a growing deterioration or increasing chaos, and the solution is the excision or bombardment of the problem. In this way metaphors reveal a perspective on the world and a proper method of action. In this sense, they imply a moral system.

The Hawaiian use of metaphors about interpersonal relationships reflects the structure of those relationships, their dynamics, the moral implications of correct or incorrect behavior and intent, and remedies for transgressions.

An important Hawaiian metaphor for problems in interpersonal relationships is expressed in the word *hihia*, literally "entanglements." *Hihia* is used to refer to interpersonal conflicts that entangle individuals in escalating hostile and hurtful emotional exchanges. These entanglements of negative affect and intent can lead to misfortune, illness, even death. The solution or cure suggested by the entanglement metaphor is to have some way of unraveling the conflict to clear the way for positive emotional exchanges. In Chapter 4, the methods for "loosening" (*kala*) and "cutting" (*'oki*) the negative affect are described as part of a conflict resolution method called *ho'oponopono* (to correct or make right). Further, Hawaiians use *'oki* for a variety of actions taken to stop the ramifications of bad feelings or intent; they speak, for instance, of the need to *'oki* or sever the adverse affect of a disturbing dream by telling it to another person immediately upon awakening. No doubt these metaphors have origins in the concepts of *kapu* (in its meaning of "bound") and *noa* (in its meaning of "free, or unbound"). This indication of the entangling quality of negative emotions or intent is discussed in Chapter 4.

The metaphors of entanglements, loosening, and cutting suggest that Hawaiians think of interpersonal relations as ties or bonds. The fact that they can be tangled or untangled, closed or open, binding or free, indicates a dynamic malleability of the emotions that mark relationships. Relationships are both like nets binding people together and like paths linking them. When there is *hihia*, people will say that "things come all jam up," implying a blockage caused by emotional entanglements that prevents the proper exchange of loving, kind, generous emotions. People do many things to clear the "way" or path of possible entanglements to ensure a positive outcome. Traditional formal clearing-the-way prayers and path-clearing ceremonies are directly linked to the path/way metaphors. Today people commonly refer to the need for "the way to be open" and the need "to open" or be honest, confessional to others. To open is also to release something; you can open the lights (turn them on or release the electrical current) or open your slippers (take them off or release your feet from confinement); all suggest the *kapu/noa*–bound/free metaphors and the *kala* (loosening) and *'oki* (cutting) metaphors of *ho'oponopono* remediation. Further discussion of the social implications of these metaphors of entanglements, binding nets, connecting paths, and "to open" (to release) are discussed in Chapters 2 and 4.

Obviously the emotional tenor of relationships is important, but what types of emotions are proper and improper? Appropriate and inappropriate emotions are not spoken of metaphorically but are referred to quite directly. Proper emotions are those associated with *aloha*: love, generosity, affection, hospitality, empathy, warmth. Also sincerity of intent is important and is referred to as "heart," derived from the Hawaiian *na'au*, literally intestines but figuratively mind, heart, affections. Conversely, improper emotions are antisocial, hurtful ones of coldness, unkindness, jealousy (*lili*), stinginess, and insincerity. These emotions (and behaviors that lead to an emotional response) are central to Hawaiian lives.

They are also important elements of Hawaiian ideas about self, other, and person (the topic of Chapter 3). Four primary complexes of emotion are involved in defining self and other: the expansive qualities of *aloha* (love, generosity, empathy, affection); the small, retentive qualities of stinginess and jealousy (*lili*); the shame and guilt one feels when one fails to express an *aloha* spirit and hurts another; and the hurt and anger one feels when one is the object of some unkind act or intent. Personhood is a culturally defined social status of a mature, responsible person. For Hawaiians, such a person displays an even temper, generosity, reliability, protective or justifiable anger, and an active social engagement with others. Thus the quality and quantity of one's social relationships are ties that define one's self, the person, and the other.

At the heart of Hawaiian culture is emotional exchange. Emotional exchanges, the quality of the emotions and of the emotional responses, define the nature of one's interpersonal relations and in turn one's self. A major portion of daily discussion is about others: their attitudes, the quality of their sincerity, their nature or personality, how one was made to feel by another; in other words, the emotional tenor of social interactions.

Hawaiians require emotional engagement and social commitment from culture members. Even outsiders are not exempt. It is not possible to be dispassionate observers or tentative participants. As I bartered and negotiated at the insider-outsider edge of Hawaiian culture, I was socialized to that imperative very quickly; and through these sometimes quite direct lessons in proper behavior or cultural meanings I was taught important elements of Hawaiian culture. Since it is in these border negotiations that an ethnographer learns about another culture, Chapter 4 demonstrates the interactive ways we negotiate and are negotiated into a kind of cultural understanding.[7]

Proper Behavior, Nosy Questions, and Talk Story

My initial fieldwork was done in South Kona, on the Big Island of Hawaiʻi, in 1973. Almost immediately I was taught an important Hawaiian rule of behavior.

I came out of the teacher's cottage with two other fieldworkers. We went to the nearby basketball court to watch a game between the male teachers and the seventh-grade boys. One fieldworker went off to play in the game and another joined a group of onlookers, leaving me alone on the sidelines. Quickly three seventh-grade girls came to join me and began good-natured, often mock-serious baiting and teasing. Could I remember their names, two of which were quite similar, Marlene and

[7] Rosaldo (1989) argues that "borders" and "border crossings" are the porous, dynamic, creative areas where cultures intermix, sometimes becoming another culture altogether, but he is not speaking of them as the places where ethnographers gain their understandings. See Alvarez for an excellent review of "the development of an anthropology of borderlands" (1995:447).

Lorene? Did I have a boyfriend? Was I for the students or the teachers? We bantered and jousted for awhile and sometimes even watched the game. The girls shouted encouragement at the boys, yelled to insert comments in other conversations, usually ignored inquiries of mine, and demanded responses to their own. We engaged in a long commentary about each other's toenails and bare feet.

After a long silence, Marlene asked if I knew what *nīele* was. I didn't understand and said, "What?" and all three repeated the word and asked if I knew what it was. When I was finally able to discriminate the word and repeat it, they all said, "Yes, yes!" I said I didn't know what it meant and they said, "You ask too many questions." Slightly offended, I said, "What?" and they repeated: "You ask too many questions." I just looked puzzled and said, "*Nīele*?" and they said, "Yah, *nīele* means you ask too many questions." "Oh!" I said. I repeated the word and the definition and they tolerantly said, "Yes."

Marlene said I should remember that word and what it means. I asked if they had heard the word a lot. All emphatically replied, "Sure!" Marlene elaborated: "My mother always tell that to me, '*Nīele!*' when I ask too many questions." Lorene concurred. I asked what kinds of questions she asked too many of and Marlene grinned. "Like, 'Where you going?' She say, '*Nīele!*'" Marlene accompanied her rendition of her mother's admonition with a look of distaste and a brush of her hand to the side. The girls continued to watch the game. I repeated the word several times in the hope of remembering it, and the girls couldn't resist mocking me: "You say '*Nīele. Nīele. Nīele.*'" When I said, perhaps too piously or didactically, that I repeated it so I could remember it because it was a new word, they took in my explanation but did not reply and continued to watch the game.

I had been given a valuable lesson in Hawaiian etiquette. For Hawaiians, proper behavior (*hana pono*) is to be respectful of boundaries: physical, emotional, social, psychological. To breach those boundaries is a violation, an error, a failure (*hala*). The *hala* can set in motion a back-and-forth (*hukihuki*) exchange of entangling retaliations (*hihia*) between the violator and the wronged individual and often among other family members and friends.

The nosy question, the improper probe, the insistent, aggressive inquiry can result in opprobrium from which one will have difficulty recovering. People will no longer meet with you, will ignore you, give you false answers, or simply not be around when you come to visit. *Nīele* applies to a minor breach; *maha'oi* applies to an offensively persistent or grossly invasive act or question. Welfare workers are often described as *maha'oi* with their persistent personal questions and surprise visits. Mothers laughingly talk of hiding from their "worker" when she or he come to call.

One of my Honolulu lady friends, Evelyn Michaels, explained the distinction between the two words: "*Maha'oi* is inquisitive. Like you don't know me that well but you have a tendency to keep askin' me questions that are personal. You know."

I ask, "Is that like *nīele*?"

·Evelyn replies, "*Nīele*—same thing: curious. *Nīele* is less. *Nīele* is more nice way of saying—curious. You see, curiosity gets the best of you. You only want to go look only again. But *maha'oi*—when they say that—is rougher. They say, '*Ooo, maha'oi!*' Means you don't belong over there or you go over somebody's house you don't belong. You ask questions that don't even pre-tain to you. Kind stuff."

Another Honolulu lady friend, June Kamakau, defined *maha'oi* a bit more explicitly as the kind of probing intrusions of which ethnographers are guilty: "*Maha'oi* is my neighbor. You know, just barges in on you. Just opens the door and walks right in. You know, turns the stove on. That's *maha'oi*. Nosy. Somebody that like to . . . be always find out what's happening. And just come right out and . . . That's *maha'oi*."

I inquire, "Get a good example of this?"

Junie says, "It's um . . . [laughs] like [laughs] like I wen' call *you maha'oi* [laughs] because you asking me so many questions! [Laughs.] You know. People they, if they, if they, they didn't have the understanding I have, they wouldn't answer your questions. Plenty people come over here, I tell 'em, 'Oh, I'm sorry. I'm busy.' Then when they turn their back, I going call them plenty *maha'oi*." Then she laughs again and adds, "To myself."

Direct questions not only invade personal boundaries but uncomfortably place an individual in the spotlight. One may suffer the embarrassment of performance failure or "shame" of an improper, incorrect, or foolish response. People who are sensitive to others and have good manners avoid the direct question that calls for a specific response.

A third problem with asking direct questions is that they interrupt the flow of the storyteller's discourse. You have taken control of the talk by interrupting and possibility changing its direction. Your questions are a selfish usurpation of the social setting. Naturally, if you are an outsider, they are even more disruptive.

Even with longtime lady friends who understood that I would be asking for clarifications, at times a question so disrupted the speaker that she stopped talking. She seemed to be either avoiding an incorrect response or annoyed because I had ruined her story line.

Fortunately, there is an appropriate forum for hearing information. It is called "talk story." Talk story is a relaxed, rambling, sometimes intense commentary or conversation. This form of communication most likely derives from the vast and rich oral tradition of Hawaiian culture. Traditionally skills in reciting myths and telling stories (*moʻolelo*), making speeches (*haʻi ʻōlelo*), telling riddles and parables (*nane*), singing and chanting (*mele*), and reciting the long genealogies of the *aliʻi* (Hawaiian royalty) were treasured. The clever raconteur and the adept at the multiple wordplay possible in Hawaiian were and still are popular people. Puns and riddles are enjoyed by Hawaiians of all ages. People repeat long and intricate plots of movies, books, and television shows with all the attendant sounds, facial expressions, and details. Daily happenings and encounters take on a theatrical intensity in the retelling.

The accuracy of the details, however, is less important than enjoyment of the social interaction. The point of talk story is not an accurate transfer of information but a social exchange, affective enjoyment of one another's company. Some aggressive individuals will challenge another's veracity or demand clarifications, but they are publicly demonstrating dominance by confrontation. Most listeners forgo clarification rather than break the speaker's rhythm. It was never clear to me if it was unimportant to understand certain details (who was involved, when the incident took place) or if this lack of specificity was confusing only to me, not to the other participants. Or did they find it confusing, too, but not important enough to disrupt the social interaction? I do know that if I asked other listeners about some detail later, they would say they did not understand either, often with a slightly embarrassed shrug, although it cannot be discounted that they understood but did not want to tell me.

The proper way to find out something that interests you or arouses your curiosity is to muse aloud about it. This can occur directly after a speaker has spoken, but out of her earshot or sometime later, perhaps in the middle of a walk or doing a shared chore. Hawaiians are acutely sensitive and perceptive. Once an interest has been expressed, it does not have to be repeated. If someone knows about the topic, she will speak about it if and when she wishes. Or later you may be introduced to someone who is knowledgeable about your area of interest. The person who introduces you will mention your interest in the area of the other person's expertise. The key is not to be aggressive but willing to wait until the next meeting or even several meetings later to find out more about the topic or incident. This strategy gives control of the dialogue to the respondent rather than the questioner. Direct and dogged questions will only label you *nīele* or the more pejorative *maha'oi*, and your contact will be diminished or truncated. In an urban setting, it is extremely difficult to gain access to information or even to observe your subjects if no one answers your knock. Or if you surprise someone by arriving early, they may courteously say that they have an appointment, grab their car keys, and determinedly speed off.

Once researchers are accepted, they are given some latitude to ask direct questions, but they must take care not to be too formal or to ask a long series of questions. What I usually did at an interview session was to give a short introduction to my topic and perhaps ask an initial question to clarify something I had heard about. I came prepared with additional questions and topics to be inserted in the conversation as we moved to a talk story format or engaged in some other social activity, such as eating, watching television, or playing cards. Everyone knew I was there to find out about Hawaiian culture, but it was important to conduct my work with some semblance of a Hawaiian social interaction and not a research one. As in most social interactions, the tone varied with the individual. Some women preferred to let me ask questions and did not take much initiative in developing the discussion; others were more comfortable leading the conversation and resented intrusive questions. In a creative adjustment to my questions, Elizabeth Nohi Nacimiento, another Honolulu lady friend, surprised me when, after giving a long description of something, she remarked, "Then you going to say how I know that? When I first see this kine [kind]? What it mean to me?" She would then either answer my obviously well-worn litany or not, depending on her knowledge or preference. This recitation eventually became a standard part of our talk story interaction.

It was only in the very last interviews that I was able to use the direct interview format about daily activities, sociodemographic background, income source, length of residence, and so forth. These interviews were introduced with apologies. I explained that this was information I had to have to complete my studies in Hawai'i. At this point in our relationship, people were quite open and willing to sit for a long list of direct questions, as a favor to me, to help me with my own questioners back at the mainland university. But it was not the preferred mode of interaction.

For Hawaiians, talk story is a central forum for the negotiation of meanings. It encompasses social exchange, narrative, teamwork, challenge and counter, sometimes moral lessons in the narrative, creativity, and just good fun.[8]

Emotions and Fieldwork

Another lesson I learned was the importance of expressing proper emotions. Anthropological work on emotions has focused on cultural definitions, interpretations, and configurations of affect and words about affect (Briggs 1970; Levy 1984; Lutz 1985, 1988; Lutz and White 1986; Rosaldo 1984; Solomon 1984; White 1985). But one learns directly about cultural affect less in the socially removed, researcher role than as a participant in social interactions with people. The ethnographer's proper display of emotions is essential to establish what used to be referred to as "rapport."

Emotional bonds and intensity of emotional expression are important aspects of Hawaiian culture, and anyone who wants to understand Hawaiians and the basis of their core interpretations of meaning cannot be an impassive observer. Hawaiians find individuals who are reserved or too agreeable difficult to be around. They feel uncomfortable and vaguely suspicious that the person is trying to hide something. They also find it annoying. A lack of emotional engagement or intensity indicates an aloofness, a setting apart of the person from the group; it is interpreted as a demonstration of feelings of superiority. Not that Hawaiians are madcap Dionysians, teetering at the edge of an abyss of passion, but they do feel strongly about feeling strongly.

Three incidents taught me the importance of emotions in Hawaiian culture. The first involved humor, the second an expression of anger, the third sentimentality and tears.

It is important not to take oneself or one's task too seriously. To be relaxed enough to laugh or make jokes, to lighten a tense moment with humor, to be willing to be or to make oneself the object of a joke is to display both interpersonal engagement and group solidarity.

Of course, you cannot play the fool, either. If you are too ingratiating, too amicable, people are suspicious about what real feelings you may be hiding. Early in my Honolulu fieldwork I was talking story with a *haole*

---

[8] See Boggs and Watson-Gegeo 1979, Watson 1975, and Watson-Gegeo and Boggs 1977 for excellent analyses of children's "talk story" that has many of the elements of the adult form.

woman who had married into a Hawaiian family. She was a nice middle-class midwestern woman of liberal tendencies who had come to Hawai'i as a volunteer with VISTA (an early federal domestic version of the Peace Corps) and met her Hawaiian husband on the outer island where she was stationed. She said she tried hard to be a "good daughter-in-law" and was friendly and ever helpful to her mother-in-law, cheerily taking orders and ignoring slights and overt hostility; but one day when her mother-in-law criticized her stew, she finally blew up. Her mother-in-law did not reply to the anger but merely said that now she could begin to treat her as if she were "real." Hawaiians, the daughter-in-law explained, "they want you to be real."

Anger also has an important place in response to a challenge. During a talk story session my Honolulu lady friend Ellen Kam, suddenly challenged my use of the tape recorder. I had been taping our discussions for months. During this session, the tape had been running for a while when she appeared to become self-conscious about the taping; not about the topic but her understanding of the use of her taped words. She became agitated and asked me if I listened to the tape later. I said sure, I used the tape to write down what we'd talked about. She asked if others heard the tape. I said no, only I listened, and I reminded her that I had told her that before. She got angry and denied that I had ever told her I was taping our talk story. The tape recorder was not in the best working condition; setting it up took some time, because a rubber band had to be pulled around the switch to keep the machine running. Then at forty-five minute intervals this maneuver had to be repeated when I turned over the tape or inserted a new one. It was hardly a clandestine operation. She had always waited patiently while I set up the tape recorder or changed a tape and had spoken without hesitation while it ran. I became angry and said that that was not true, she knew that I taped our sessions, I had explained it to her before. She had the right to tell me she did not want a session taped or to stop the tape at any time. I had told her that in the beginning and she had agreed to it. She smiled, sat back on the sofa, and said, " 'At's right." We continued the session and the rest of the fieldwork with no further discussion of the tape. I, of course, was fuming from my outburst for some minutes, but she was now calm and as forthcoming as always.

Lady friends issued challenges about other issues, but if they were unjustified and I replied with the appropriate indignation, they were satisfied. I had shown myself to be real enough not to accept unjustified criticism docilely or to pretend I was not offended or angry.

Both humor and appropriate anger play their parts in the negotiation of meaning between ethnographer and informant. By participating in cultural interactions, one learns cultural lessons. One does not become a member of the culture but one learns a great deal about being a member.

Another emotional exchange in Hawaiian culture that is essential for rapport is the ability to let oneself go enough to be sentimental and empathetically sad. Until I had done fieldwork in Hawai'i, I was not overtly sentimental. One day my Honolulu lady friend Iris Nakasone was telling me about how her father-in-law would walk from one side of the island to the other to visit them. Often he was picked up by the police for walking along the busy Likelike Highway that bisects the island and family members would be called to pick him up at the police station. On those occasions when he was not picked up, he would be found patiently waiting at their home. In either case, the family would scold him about taking unnecessary risks. She suddenly became overwhelmed by sadness as she recalled that now that he was dead, he would never walk across the island again. She also regretted the numerous scoldings they had given him when all he had wanted to do was be with them. Iris, an outgoing woman, usually hearty and jovial, now had tears running down her face. Suddenly I found that I was crying too. We said nothing, just sat there awhile looking out the window, and eventually pulled ourselves together to continue a more muted discussion. But an important emotional exchange had occurred. I was no longer the outsider observing her and listening impartially and impassively, if pleasantly, to her talk story. I had become a social other engaged in a human and a cultural interchange. It would be nice to say that after that we grew wonderfully close, but in fact our relationship continued to be slightly formal, though congenial. But this important lesson of being able to feel sentimental, sad, a sense of loss (the Hawaiian words, I found out much later, are *pohō* and *minamina*), served me well—not just in fieldwork but in my own life as well. I was learning to become more real.

It was through these lessons that I was able to comprehend the centrality of emotions and intent in Hawaiian lives. In gratitude for those lessons, this book is a "payback," as Nohi would say, to demonstrate how very real, complex, and vital Hawaiian culture remains, even among some of the most seemingly disfranchised. And it is being passed on so that even young girls can explicitly teach an outsider an important rule of *hana pono* (proper behavior).

[16]

[1]

Lady Friends and
Their Island Home

Evelyn Michaels, twenty-seven, is a robust, passionate, opinionated, strong-willed, stubborn woman. She prides herself on being a good cook, housekeeper, and mother. She is a self-indulgent, strong personality with a quick tongue and ready retort. As she says, she "don't take no shits" from anyone. The youngest of four children, she is close to her second-oldest sister, Emily, affectionately known as 'Uala (sweet potato). 'Uala is married and has three children. She lives in a suburb eight miles from Honolulu, but the two sisters spend a great deal of time together, meeting for lunch or breakfast several times a week at a neighborhood café near their mother's house in a public housing project called Queen Emma (pseudonym),[1] where they grew up. Queen Emma is known as one of the oldest and roughest public housing developments. Both women are close to their mother, Beverly Rosario (married to her fourth husband, James Rosario).

Evelyn aptly describes Mrs. Rosario's two-bedroom cinder-block apartment "the Grand Central Station—for everybody." Indeed, friends and relatives gravitate to Mrs. Rosario's to socialize, look for others who might be there, buy the ginger Mrs. Rosario grows in her yard, or just to sip beer, watch TV, and talk story. The apartment, with its old but well-kept furniture, has a relaxed, comfortable air. Something is usually either on the stove or in the process of being made. It is dark and breezy, with lots of places to sit, put down a cold drink, and enjoy the company.

---

[1] Names of institutions, housing projects, and businesses directly associated with the lives of the families in this book are pseudonyms.

All three women are forceful, strong-willed individuals who frequently clash. But Evelyn has a great deal of admiration and respect for her mother and in fact models herself after her:

> My mom was a very strong person. And she not only took care of her four, she took care of my cousin, Bradley-them, seven of them, and all of my other stray cousins come in, running away, you know, from their homes and staying with my mom. And my mom used to go, you know, take care of all of us. So—seeing this and being married, a few times, she must have had some flair. My mother had personality. She made friends a great deal with her personality. The way she is—very outspoken. Yet—she used to grumble, but she always gave.

Evelyn also opens her house to lost souls, other people's children, old and recently made friends. She is a sensitive, generous, and loving person of tremendous loyalty and affection. But her maternal largess is unhampered by sentimentality.

"But you know the strength my mom had. It wasn't easy, Karen. I seen many times when my mother used to drink and I used to wonder why. And today I know why my mother used to drink. Well, shit. It used to be so hard before. So like, it wasn't easy for my mom so I think she, she influenced me a great deal and in many ways I'm like her. And if you put me, 'Uala, my mother together, we all talk alike and act alike."

Evelyn succinctly describes how they are alike: "Nuts. And, you know, we use terms like that. You know, 'nuts' and 'crazy.' Loosely. Cuz it ain't no big deal. But no let anybody else call us that!"

Another way Evelyn and Emily model their mother is in their household cleanliness and care: "[My mother's] very clean. Her and 'Uala is alike. They very immaculate. . . . Her house is so neat, Karen, it make my house look like one slum. I'm not kidding. My sister's house is so clean. She take after my mother."

But Evelyn's two-bedroom apartment in a new high-rise cooperative of individually owned low-cost, government-subsidized units also is carefully arranged and decorated. Often when I arrived I found Evelyn vigorously washing the rug or vacuuming. She has Oriental-style plaques and porcelain artfully placed on the walls and shelves. The living room furniture is stylish and the couch and love seat are a matched set. The *lānai* (balcony) offers a breezy vista of the green Ko'olau Mountains. Evelyn also has a TV, a stereo, a wall unit of display shelves, and a dinette set. She has decorated the room of her oldest daughter, Millicent, with a colorful quilt on the bed, wall hangings, and plants. Her own bedroom is crowded with her younger daughter's crib and baby things, but the items are well chosen. Like Mrs. Rosario's, this place is an expression of its occupant. It has tasteful, orderly touches as well as a relaxed, homey atmosphere.

She has defiantly kept her own family surname through two pregnancies, preferring her independence rather than to depend on the fluctuating virtues of the girls' fathers. For Evelyn, marriage and motherhood are not necessarily bound together. She feels that not being married should not preclude being a mother.[2]

Evelyn, along with Emily and their mother, Mrs. Rosario, form the core unit of their family, bringing in husbands, boyfriends, children, and friends. Hawaiian women are the linchpins of their families and of their society. The actual roles and statuses of women in Polynesia (particularly those of the Society and Hawaiian Islands) have been obscured by the often rapturous hyperbole used to describe their physical charms. The women of Polynesia have been immortalized in the prose of early European explorers and writers:

> Travelers and residents alike have pronounced the Polynesians to be one of the finest races of the world, and many do not hesitate to describe the women as perfect types of feminine beauty, of their child-like simplicity, and have told of their eyes, shining like lustrous stars beneath the deep fringed lids; of their skin of the tenderest olive, the olive that has a shade of gold in it, like a honeycomb that has entangled a sunbeam, and is therewith transfigured; of heads turbaned with glossy ropes of hair casting a twilight shade over brows of purest olive; of full ripe lips parting in a smile, disclosing teeth that are in themselves a smile. (Hingston 1908:37)

These European representations of Polynesian women as mythical sexual creatures reflected projections of European society and culture but left few records of note about male and female Polynesians and their sociocultural realities.

Between the raves about the beauty and charms of Polynesian women, however, some writers have given hints of their important roles and statuses in Hawaiian society. Among the commoners (*maka-*

---

[2] After the initial research period, however, Evelyn married twice. She joined her last name to her first husband's with a hyphen, *hānai*-ed (adopted) his three girls, and had a son with him. When she married her second husband, she not only changed her last name but got him to change his to a different surname in his family that she preferred and claimed was their rightful name. She had two more children with him and they remain a stable, amiable couple.

'āinana), for example, men did the cooking and *poi*-making (pounding of the cooked taro corm) while the women manufactured the valuable *kapa (tapa)* cloth, wove fine mats, and made salt (Malo 1971; Stewart 1970; Handy and Pukui 1972).[3] Whether the women were in charge of the distribution of these goods as well as of their production is not clear. David Malo, however, notes that matmaking was "a source of considerable profit; so that the women who engaged in it were held to be well-off, and praised for their skill" (1971:49–50). Women may well have obtained income directly from the sale of those items, or at least from their mats. Jocelyn Linnekin (1990:46) notes that the Hawaiian evidence for income from mats and *tapa* cloth is inconclusive but not contradicted. Postcontact evidence indicated that "Hawaiian women, both chiefly and common, owned moveable property . . . which they could distribute as they wished. Moreover, Hawaiian women could and did use material and sexual gifts as instruments to influence the behavior of others" (Linnekin 1990:55).

Polynesian women's participation in the public domain of politics was limited to the upper class and influenced by primogeniture, descent types, genealogical sanctity, and the theme of the male as sacred (*kapu*) and the female as *noa* (common or free from *tabu*) (Goldman 1970; Rogers 1977; Hecht 1977). It was in the highly stratified Society and Hawaiian Islands that primogeniture and genealogical sanctity outweighed gender.

This right of power and authority for *ali'i* Hawaiian women carried "the awesome privileges of sanctity equally with men" (Goldman 1970:217). The *kapu (tabu)* was sometimes so strong that some Hawaiian women had what was called *'ūhā kapu* (sacred lap). This *kapu* reflected the dual nature of the concept in Hawaiian: *kapu* means both a prohibition and sanctity. A woman with *'ūhā kapu* could kill or cripple her child by her mere presence because of the power of her sanctity, so she was prohibited from picking up and carrying her infant. The prohibition was intended to protect the mother's sanctity from defilement if the child urinated or defecated on her as well as to protect the incontinent child from the fatal wrath of the mother's *'aumakua*, or guardian spirit (Handy and Pukui 1972:49).[4]

In contemporary Hawaiian society, a woman's role in her family is piv-

---

[3] Women in Samoa (Deihl 1932) and Tahiti (Oliver 1974) also were known as fine mat-makers.

[4] Male chiefs could also have *'ūhā kapu* (Handy and Pukui 1972).

otal.[5] As Alan Howard (1971) documented in a suburban area of Oʻahu, Hawaiians have a strong tendency for matrilaterality and uxorilocal residence after marriage. Sylvia J. Yanagisako notes that matrifocal groups in general are characterized by "patterns of co-residence, residential proximity, and mutual aid, and in the frequency of interaction and the strength of affective ties among kin" (1977:208), primarily among female kin. These conditions, compounded by the importance of the maternal role over the conjugal, places Hawaiian households among the classically matrifocal. Yanagisako (1977) summarizes Raymond T. Smith's definition of this domestic situation as including the primacy of the mother-child relationship over the husband-wife, an early decline of the husband-father's authority, and an increase in the mother-wife's authority in the family, particularly in economic matters, as the family matures. Howard (1974) uncovered a changing Hawaiian domestic pattern in extended households as the years pass and the numbers of children increase. Wives increasingly use confrontational tactics and decreasingly avoid conflict with their husbands. For husbands, there is the converse movement from confrontational behavior to conflict avoidance. Howard attributed this change to the increasing authority women gain from the role of mother. At the beginning of a domestic relationship, the woman and her young child must compete with the social and economic demands of the man's peer group. A woman's role of mother often precedes her status as wife. In these early, unstable years, a woman "has the most to lose by disruptive conflict. . . . As a marriage progresses, two significant changes generally occur to alter these circumstances" (Howard 1974:122). First, home life becomes more appealing to men as more children are born. Children are highly prized by both men and women and are even more powerful an attraction when they are one's own. A woman is much more valued and respected as a mother than as a wife. Robert H. Heighton (1971:52–55) discusses how females move from child to "mother-in-training" to "mother" in the Hawaiian Homestead community of Nānākuli; motherhood is a favored status and desired role from both male and female perspectives. Men become increasingly committed to their wives as "the mothers of their children." Second, the male peer group begins to disintegrate as more men devote time and money to

---

[5] Linnekin further posits, "In the Hawaiian perspective women are still active, authoritative, and instrumental. Given the numbers of Hawaiian women who exercise personal and political leadership today, 'inside' as I use it here [within the Hawaiian community] is empathically not the same as the 'domestic domain' " (1990:228).

their families. "By the time this shift has been completed, it is men who stand to lose the most by domestic conflict, and women the least" (Howard 1974:122). Furthermore, the husband is unlikely to withhold financial support, for to do so would be to deprive his children and to impugn his reputation as an adequate provider.

For Hawaiian women, however, a matrifocal society does not necessarily mean a privileged life. Ellen Kam is shy and sensitive but covers it with a rough-tough tomboy bravado. She is small and heavy, with sad eyes in a worn face, but she sometimes flashes a mischievous childlike smile. One can see reflections of her youth in the playful, softly rounded faces of most of her eight children. A few of her children are slim and sharp-featured like their father, Richard.

Richard had a construction job for a while, but most of the time he is unemployed. He is a tough, wiry man with piercing eyes. He has an explosive temper and has been known to throw things in fits of anger. Once when they lived in a high-rise public housing building he threw the kitchen table off the *lānai*.[6] But he is capable of great charm and boyish enthusiasm. One day he decided to take me on a tour of the island and we jumped into their broken-down car, the three of us packed into the front seat. We bounced around the island with Richard giving an endless commentary. His charm was evident when he stopped along a stream. We all got out and sat beside it while he picked wild ginger blossoms for me, Ellen hollering and teasing him all the while. As we drove up the busy Pali Highway, Richard suddenly stopped by the side of the road and picked a huge bouquet of ginger blossoms for Ellen which she sniffed until the fragile flowers wilted and turned brown. When we got to the famous cliffs called the Nu'uanu Pali, he gleefully told me of one of his tourist scams. The wind that whips up the cliffs is said to be so strong that when Kamehameha I fought the final battle for consolidation of his power here, the bodies of vanquished warriors falling from the cliffs were blown back

---

[6] This was not a habit peculiar to Richard; so many large and small items were tossed from the many *lānais* and often onto unsuspecting pedestrians below that the management put iron grates over all the *lānais*. But smaller items such as flowerpots and used disposable diapers still find their way off the *lānais*; sometimes purposely tossed, at other times mindlessly dropped. I was warned to walk close to the wall so that the many people who had antipathies toward Japanese Americans would not use my head as a convenient target for various missiles of choice. Once when I knocked at a door of an absent lady friend, I noticed a policeman knocking at a door a few doors down. He looked incredulously at me and said, "What? You no scare?" With bluffed bravado I said, "No." He looked astounded. "No? Me, I scare [when] I come here!"

up. The ever-helpful Richard tells tourists that if they toss a penny over the cliff, it will be blown back up to them just like the bodies of the slain Hawaiian warriors. In their enthusiastic haste to dig into pockets and purses for a penny, chuckles Richard, the tourists fail to notice that bills of various denominations also are liberated from their confines, tossed into the air by the wind, and make their way into Richard's waiting hands.

Richard and Ellen have a roughhouse life. Ellen talks to Richard in a baiting, aggressive way. Richard exudes a threatening air of violence and has a hair-trigger temper. Ellen is not afraid to confront his temper with her own challenge. Both are strongly physical in their communication of almost any emotion—joy, anger, tenderness, hostility—demonstrated by punches or open-handed slaps. Ellen's missing two front teeth are evidence of Richard's dictum "No fight, no love," a saying that Ellen does not dispute.[7] In spite of the edgy quality to their interactions, they enjoy each other's company and pass time together, playing cards, socializing with others, even having a rare outing such as going to dinner, the auto races or bowling.

Richard is an incorrigible womanizer, and that angers Ellen. She has effective ways of ending the affairs she discovers. If she can find out where the woman lives, she gathers her eight children and shows up on the doorstep to shame the woman. She tells the woman, "Look how many kids he get!" The woman usually is so shocked that she has a fight with Richard, and the affair is over. Another method also uses the children. Ellen threatens Richard with divorce and tells him that she will not allow him to see the children. This maneuver is so upsetting to Richard that he temporarily halts his philandering.

As Howard (1974) observed, the domestic draw is the increasing number of children a man has with his wife. For all his unreconstructed ways, Richard is very fond of their eight children, particularly the young ones. He misses them if they are not home when he arrives. This does not mean he indulges them, however. He seems to ignore the young ones and is strict with the older ones. He enforces discipline with a rough physical emphasis. But at the same time, it is clear that he is proud of

---

[7] Domestic violence in Hawaiian households has only recently been addressed as a social problem, and data are poor (Furuto 1991). In 1987 a state report (cited in Furuto 1991) noted that shelters for battered women received more than 4,700 calls for assistance, and requests for restraining orders against batterers rose from 164 in 1980 to 1,720 in 1987. The increase is most likely the combined result of greater public awareness, more available services, and improved data tracking. See also Hawai'i State Commission on the Status of Women 1993.

their accomplishments, and he does exhibit a certain softness toward them.

Richard definitely feels that having children is an important display of a successful marriage and his own masculinity. Howard interprets a man's desire for many children as public evidence of his competence as a provider (1974:141). Richard also sees it as a demonstration of affection and love for Ellen. After the eighth child, Ellen said she did not want any more. She was tired of having children. She had married at seventeen and had her first child at eighteen, and the seven others had been born over the next ten years. (She had her ninth a few months after I first left the field.) But Ellen has a sort of boastful public pride in this procreative demonstration of Richard's affection. One day a visiting lady friend complained about her husband's neglect, leaving her at home alone with three children, never paying any attention to her. Richard threw Ellen a look that could be described only as *kolohe* (mischievous, lecherous, roguish). The sexual implications of the look were obvious. Ellen noted the look, appeared to ignore it, then said, "Yeah, he pays attention to me—too much! That's *why* I get eight kids!" Richard laughed. Ellen appeared cynically resigned, but her resignation had an undertone of pride in Richard's continued sexual interest in her.[8]

The burden of Ellen Kam's life hangs heavily on her rounded shoulders. The constant need to struggle with limited funds and escalating household needs often leaves her in despair: "Sometimes I feel like I just like trip out, you know?"

I offer sympathy. "You'd like to leave, huh?"

"Yeah—I wish I could if I knew how. If I never had kids—I would. Just, you know—trip out. When you get kids, you have to think of them. You want to go and leave but you cannot go because who going take care of the kids! See what I mean? Whu-u-u! Just like I get problems up my geeks, you know. . . .

"I like go, go, go [and do things for fun] but no more time! You know, get too many things to do. By time get finished, you so beat. By time get some work done, gotta turn around do the same thing. The same routine.

[8] Ellen and I had a conversation about birth control that revealed her understanding of a woman's role and her lack of power. She asked me how I kept from having children. When I explained about using birth control, she looked fearful and said, "You husband know?" When I said yes, her expression immediately changed and she said, "Oh, poor ting," her face filled with sadness and pity. Clearly a woman's reproductive life was not within her control; either I was courting trouble by hiding my contraceptive method or he was forcing me not to have a child by insisting that I use it.

And then gotta make sure the small ones eat and make sure the big ones *pau* [finished]. And make sure she [the latest baby] eats, takes a bath, and then she have to eat again. Then she say, 'Nuff, *pau*,' and it lasts through the night. Oh, boy."

In comparing her own duties with her husband's, she finds little solace. "I hate it when he's home, say, 'Oh, I work, you know. I work all day, hard.' I go, 'Oh, really? Well, me too. I work twenty-four hours a day. I still not through.' That's the truth! As soon as you get the house clean by the time you get kids—the house dirty."

I respond, "Yeah?"

"Yeah! And if I clean upstairs, get the rooms clean, get everything all set up, do my vacuuming—by the time my kids come home from school, dirty already. See what I mean? And then when I through upstairs, it's dirty. I'm stay in the kitchen cleaning and cooking, by the time I reach the parlor—dirty. Oh, boy. Too much, too much."

Indeed, it is almost too much for her. Her place is always filthy. The cement floors are sticky and dirty, the furniture is stained and ripped. There is the damp odor of urine from children's accidents and undisciplined pets. Many of the household items are broken; the cabinets in the kitchen are grimy with dirt. The children's clothes, especially the preschoolers', have ground-in dirt that washing will not get out. And all the children wear clothes that are either too large or too small.

But her home has touches of grace and care. Ellen has floral centerpieces made from brightly colored feathers, Hawaiian display dolls, and crocheted doilies that are placed carefully under framed photos of the children, as well as a framed snapshot of Richard and Ellen on an anniversary night out at a Waikīkī nightclub. A large tapestry of resting lions on a rich blue field hangs on the wall. Ellen constantly rearranges the furniture, even moving a heavy freezer.

Whenever Ellen invites me over for lunch, she makes it a special occasion. She carefully sets a lovely table with place mats, two matching glasses, a colorful centerpiece, and two matching plates and flatware. It is an odd oasis in the disarray and dirt of the rest of the kitchen which has included a litter of frisky puppies—all unhousebroken—in the closet next to the kitchen table. Nevertheless, we would sit, eat our egg salad sandwiches, and "talk story" about anything that came into our minds as if we were in the most tranquil, elegant setting.

Ellen rarely gets out of the house; Richard usually takes the car, and his schedule is unpredictable. She often is overcome by her confinement and sometimes "gets terrible headaches," sleeping for long periods, leaving the cooking and caretaking to her two oldest girls, Coradine (nine years old) and Geraldine (eight). She laments her lack of preparedness for a job and expresses a yearning for something meaningful to do: "I really wanna work. I wanna do something with my hands, you know. But, but seems like—how I gonna work, Karen?

"Babies, small babies. Gotta work nighttime, I work daytime: babysitting kids! Cleaning the house: working. But I like to work [at a paid job]. I like to do something that I can keep my hands busy. You know like—I, you know, for do something. You know. Even if—you know, I go to school and pass out [paper, supplies], do some paperworks, you know. Maybe, I don't know. I not that smart but, you know, I can learn."

I protest: "You are smart. Not true."

"It is. I not that smart, Karen! I can *learn* but I'm not really—the only thing I really can do is, uh, maybe bake or help with the kids or something."

Ellen does try to overcome her situation and sometimes thinks of things to make and sell to children as after-school snacks. Once it was frozen juice cubes made from a sugar concentrate (Malolo syrup) with a "cracked seed" (preserved salted plum) in the middle. They were very popular, and kids crowded around the back door before and after school to purchase them. But, she sold them for so little that she probably did not even recover her costs. Yet clearly she enjoyed making them, selling them, and the bustle that surrounded both activities. It gave her a connection to an external social life and a sense of creativity and value.

June "Junie" Kamakau, too, had domestic difficulties, but she has taken a different course of action. She has been married for seventeen years and has six children, the oldest fourteen, the youngest seven. Her first child, who died either during or shortly after birth, would have been fifteen. The marriage has been difficult. Her husband, Vincent, is a philanderer, a heavy drinker, and an undependable provider although he holds a civil service job. Junie herself is hot-tempered and quick-tongued: "Yeah, like me, I'm a very forward person. You know. I, I can read people off and I can tell them where to go in a minute. One of my famous problems is my mouth."

June is about 5'2", a stocky, rugged woman with a raspy voice. Solid and compact with short, sturdy limbs, she has a determined, firm look to her face and in her step. Yet vulnerability sometimes appears in her speech when she affects a childlike, submissive tone. Perhaps this is a result of an unhappy childhood. When June was young, her mother, a schoolteacher, was in poor health and had died. June, the second youngest of five children, was adopted by a couple, even though her father, a policeman, was still alive. The couple eventually also adopted June's niece (her only sister's child), who was eleven years younger than June. While June always refers to her adopted parents as her mother and father, once when explaining her relationship with her siblings she said, "And being that I was adopted *out of* the family, I guess *my own* family— resented me. Because they didn't understand *why* I had to go live with my auntie and uncle." She did not mean the adopting couple were actual kin; "uncle" and particular "auntie" are also used to refer to fictive relationships, to designate an affective bond, or as a term of respect. In Hawaiian culture (and throughout Polynesia [Carroll 1970]), adoption is very different from adoption practices in the larger American society. This practice is called *hānai* and children are usually adopted by family members or close friends. As Howard and his colleagues deftly describe it, "In contrast to the ideal, middle class, mainland pattern, which stresses the severance of ties between an adopted child and his natural parents, Hawaiian ideology stresses the reverse. It is regarded as not only desirable for the child to know his natural parents but for him to maintain intimate contact with them as well" (1970:33). They identify three contemporary forms of Hawaiian adoption: "legal adoption; *hānai*, a Hawaiian term designating 'an agreement to transfer primary parental rights over a child'; and fosterage, which involves the taking care of a child without a transfer of primary parental rights" (Howard et al. 1970: 21; see also Beaglehole 1937; Handy and Pukui 1972; and Pukui, Haertig, and Lee 1972.) Many adoptive parents are childless or have no children living nearby to care for them in their declining years. It is not unusual, however, for a couple with children to adopt a child. If a child's birth parents are still alive, relationships are not severed, but the *hānai* parents are referred to by maternal and paternal kin terms without qualification. Only when one distinguishes between one's "real" parents or siblings and one's *hānai* parents or siblings will "my *hānai* mother" or "my real father" be used. Howard has found adoption in Hawaiian households to be relatively common and widespread. In a survey of 1,000 Hawaiian households (with 681 respondent households) in four Hawaiian Homestead communities on Oʻahu, almost 28 percent reported one of the three forms of adoption. In Nānākuli, Howard's team found that 32.5 percent of the households had an adopted child (Howard et al. 1970, Howard 1974). They observed all forms of adoption, from the informal "fosterage" to *hānai* to formal, legal adoption. A grandmother may formally adopt a grandchild whose parents are unable to care for their child; a woman may foster her husband's children from a former marriage and care for them even after her marriage with their father has ended, or, as in Junie's case, a couple close to her parents who were without children *hānai*–ed her.[9] Junie's was not a happy adoption. She bluntly says, "They never showed me any love." Her parents made her do all the housework, and by the third grade she knew how to wash, starch, and iron clothes. Her father, a fireman, beat her regularly, slapping her for infractions such as not speaking in a polite enough tone. She began to run away from home, cut classes, and hang out in a downtown shopping area called Castle Street to escape the beatings and housework. Junie became more embittered toward her parents after they adopted Cheryl, her older sister's child, whom they favored and spoiled. It is a Hawaiian tradition to have a favorite child, who is called a "pet," and people are said to pet certain children. Traditionally it was customary to designate such a child *punahele*, or favored child. Usually the firstborn, the child was given special treats, foods, mats to sleep on. But he was also trained to become the family leader, to learn genealogies, family chants, and other family knowledge. In contemporary times, however, "many parents or grandparents give *punahele* treatment to one child, yet that child is in no way destined or being trained to become the family's responsible, decision-making senior. *Punahele* treatment without *punahele* obligations then results in *lili* (jealousy) and sibling rivalry" (Pukui, Haertig, and Lee 1972:190). The favored treatment of Cheryl has continued into adulthood; their father pays Cheryl's bills, bought two houses for her, and showers her with affection. Cheryl is married to a truck driver who makes good money by working overtime. Apparently he recently had a psychotic episode, for according to June, "And my brother-in-law was running around crazy, you know. Takin' off his clothes and . . . was sitting in the mud eating all the spiders and eating that crawling beetle that was crawling around this [old] house." Eventually he was confined in the state hospital a month. After his release, he joined a Hawaiian church in which Junie's extended family is prominent and has become an active member. No further psychological problems were mentioned.

Although she says she and Cheryl are now close, June "really resented" her sister as they were growing up and cannot recall any happy childhood times. Junie wants her own children to recall only happy times, so she

[9] In colloquial Hawaiian or pidgin, it is a common to attach an English tense to a Hawaiian verb, such as *hānai*-ed, rather than to use the proper Hawaiian conjugation.

tries to be very loving toward them. Junie's birth father was hospitalized in Wailani Hospital the last ten years of his life. By then married and with her own children, she still visited him regularly and tended to him while her children stayed downstairs in the waiting room. Perhaps it is not a co-incidence that June is now a practical nurse at Wailani.

Her own six children are highly protective of her and sometimes chide her as if she were the child. When twelve-year-old Teresa arrived home from school, and saw the house in disarray, she said sternly, "What? How come you no clean the house?" Junie laughed sheepishly, ducked her head, and said softly, as if to disarm Teresa, "I was waiting for you to come home." Teresa, not disarmed, eyed her mother steadily, then turned and marched upstairs. Nine-year-old Lisa once tried to stay home from school to "tell off" their social worker because she thought "the worker" was coming to give her mother a hard time. Even after June got Lisa off to school, she discovered her later sitting on a stone wall, waiting for "the worker."

June and Vincent eventually divorced. Junie sometimes refers to Vincent as "my ex-husband," but usually she still refers to him as her husband. Her main reason for divorcing Vincent, she said, was his poor financial support for his family. Although gainfully employed with a union job, he spent the money carousing in nightclubs and on gifts for girlfriends. The primary role of a husband-father is as a provider. Neglect of that role is considered a justifiable reason for a woman to seek a divorce (Heighton 1971; Howard 1974).

After her separation, June began dating Rocky, a former Honolulu policeman, who liked to take her to nightclubs, and parties. Junie, who had dropped out of school and married when she was sixteen, after her painful childhood of emotional and material neglect, took to this new lifestyle with a vengeance. She spent a lot of money on clothes, makeup, and wigs. She would go out with Rocky and leave her children alone, and sometimes stayed out until the pre-dawn hours. She would come home drunk and vomiting. She still feels bad that her children had to witness this drunken behavior. She says she never slept with Rocky and always drove her own car to meet him at a bar. She always came home by herself, never went with him to a hotel. Junie is glad she never went to bed with Rocky because now she has no children by him and he respects her. Even though they broke up years ago, he still sends her flowers and a card every Valentine's Day and on her birthday. June smiles a lot when she talks about Rocky. They dated for about six years.

Junie has tried to reconcile with her husband, but the marriage has not

[29]

recovered, although their relationship is now more cordial, even friendly. Vincent still visits and sometimes provides her with money and household appliances such as a washing machine (which immediately was stolen from the open back porch of June's public housing unit). At one point he moved back with her, unbeknownst to "the welfare."[10]

Since the divorce, Junie's life has been hard. To provide not only for her six children but also for a niece and the niece's newborn, she took continuation classes in the morning for four hours to get her high school equivalency diploma (she confessed that she did not know how to add, subtract, or multiply), then worked at Wailani Hospital for four hours as a nurse's aide in the afternoon and cleaned an office building at night. The night job was, ironically, to pay off one of her husband's debts, for which she had cosigned. When she obtained her GED, she passed a certification test to become a practical nurse and worked a day shift at Wailani until she found that she could earn $42 more a month if she worked from 11 P.M. to 7 A.M. That would make her total monthly income $551 to support a household of nine.

Like Ellen Kam, she sometimes finds the pressures are too much. Recently she spent two weeks in a psychiatric ward for "a mental breakdown and depression." She had been going to school mornings, working two jobs, and getting only a couple of hours of sleep a night. A precipitating event was when she went to her "worker" for assistance and said the worker was brusque with her. She had extended herself in a needy, vulnerable condition and was devastated when she felt her worker had rejected her. Junie "just gave up, just wanted to give it all up." While she was in the hospital, however, she received a letter from a friend, another janitor, whom she had helped through a lot of problems. The woman had moved to the mainland and continued to clean offices. In gratitude for Junie's support, she had managed to save $700 and sent it to her, asking her to bring her kids for a visit. Junie was so touched that she "just cried and knew I had to get out [of the hospital]." She asked her doctor to release her. He was reluctant, but he reconsidered when she said she was worried about her kids, "Well, if you are starting to worry about your kids, then you must be well enough to leave." So she was released.

Being *hānai*-ed is not always as painful an experience as Junie found it. Jane "Pua" Kahana (*pua* means flower or blossom,) had a happy child-

---

[10] Ten years later, Junie and Vincent reconciled, and they live in a Hawaiian Homelands house in Nānākuli. They seem to have worked out their differences and live a stable and pleasant suburban life.

hood growing up in the then rural Honolulu neighborhood of Kalihi. Her birth mother died when she was only a few years old. She was *hānai*-ed shortly thereafter into a family of six children and became the fourth oldest child in her new family. She remains close to all of her brothers and sisters, in particular her oldest sister, on whom she relies for advice and aid.

Pua thinks of her *hānai* mother as her own and has tremendous respect and admiration for her. She was a kind, loving, and patient parent. When she had to work late, she left "cracked seed" under her children's pillows. Pua's voice softens. "I like be like her."

Her *hānai* parents separated but remained close. The father came over every Sunday to cook a huge family dinner and he always remembered birthdays and holidays with generous gifts of money.

Pua was also very attached to her birth father, who spoiled her and indulged her every whim. He was killed in a car crash when Pua was in high school. Her eyes still fill with tears when she recounts his death.

Her childhood was filled with love and fun. She talks of walking from Kalihi to downtown Honolulu, playing in streams along the way, sneaking out late at night to gossip with girlfriends next door, getting dressed up in Sunday clothes to go to church followed by breakfast at a local diner and a movie, or just sitting by the road drinking Kool-Aid with girlfriends, talking story and counting the few cars that ambled by. Many times Pua said, "I wish I could live my childhood again."

Pua is now thirty-five years old, with five children aged seven to seventeen and a dependable if erratically employed husband named Emery. She is a stolid sort who never seems to move in or from her easy chair. At 5'3", she is stocky with a thick neck and heavy upper arms and thighs. Her smooth oval face and round unblinking eyes remain expressionless unless she is suddenly taken by something on the constantly playing television set or as she retells some movie she has just seen. Sometimes her blank, immobile face suddenly lights up and she breaks into a girlish giggle. Equally surprising is when she abandons her matronly aloofness to toss off girlish, coquettish glances to accompany her high-pitched giggle.

The Kahana family lives in the Moanaluna low-rise public housing project, where the apartments have a half bath downstairs and four bedrooms and a full bathroom upstairs. The front and back yards are basically common areas for the residents of the six apartments in the building.

Pua is an avid bowler and classifies her days as "bowling days" and "other days." She belongs to two bowling leagues and spends most of her time at the local bowling alleys. Emery, too, is a bowler, and as testimony to this devotion, they have bordered a small flower garden in the front yard with old bowling pins. Bowling trophies line the shelves in their living room. Their collection is beginning to be supplemented by trophies won by some of their children.

Their home is comfortably furnished with a nice stereo, two TVs in varying states of repair, and throw rugs covering the concrete floors. Carefully framed photos of children and relatives are everywhere, with the requisite crocheted or plastic *lei* draped over them. Neither Pua nor her husband has a regular job; they are "under the welfare." Sometimes they take temporary jobs. Emery has worked as a mechanic and bus driver. Pua types or does odd jobs such as delivering free product samples from door to door. Of course, they also sometimes make money working off the books at the bowling alley: Pua at the desk, Emery fixing the pin setters. They sometimes sell things at a local swap meet, but Pua is embarrassed to be seen selling some of their possessions to make money.

Her husband is a quiet, friendly man who fishes and dives for seafood to supplement their diet. Emery also collects coral on his dives and makes decorative plaques that are intermixed with the bowling trophies and family photos. Emery's nickname, Pelo, is a play on words. It is a unique shortening of the name for a common local fish called 'ōpelo. *Pelo* mean fishermen's tales or tall stories. Although Emery has a Hawaiian surname, his father was part Chinese. His mother was full Hawaiian. Pua explained that Emery's father took a Hawaiian surname because he so thoroughly adopted a Hawaiian lifestyle, "living country," meaning the family resided on the rural Windward side of the island, fishing and raising fruits and vegetables, living with an ever expanding and contracting extended family.

Pua complains bitterly that the welfare system makes it impossible for them to get off it. Thus Hawaiians commonly speak of this oppressive system as "living under the welfare." Her husband has often taken jobs with the intention of becoming self-sufficient, but when they begin to accumulate a savings account, their public housing rent is raised and their welfare payments are reduced. They find themselves back with no reserves, so they give up and stay on welfare, trying to make nonreportable cash on the side.

The most middle class of the six households belonged to Iris and Jack Nakasone. Iris Nakasone is a hearty, good-natured woman with a bluster that hides deep emotions. She is the only one of my lady friends who regularly reads a newspaper and several popular women's magazines. At thirty-two she is a strapping 5'9" tall, solid with broad shoulders and a husky upper torso, and has a rapid-fire way of speaking punctuated with bursts of laughter. She speaks so quickly that one seems to comprehend her meaning without understanding any of the individual words.

Iris was born and raised in Kalihi, and her mother still lives in the single-family house in which she and her nine brothers were raised. The only girl in a family of boys, Iris was particularly close to her father, who died in 1974, one year before I met her.

"I'm the only one really spitting image of my father. 'At's why, when my father had that stroke at the park [attending her son's baseball game], and when we took him to the hospital, my brothers, my mother and I. And when the doctor walk [in] and he said, 'I'm sorry but he's—' Look down, you know. Think I broke down more than my mother cuz she took it strong, you know cuz I guess the doctor prepared her for it. Tell [her] if my father had one more stroke—he might not make it. Cuz he had several stroke [sic] before that." When she speaks of him she still breaks down in tears. "When my father died, it just was like I lost everything." Iris still will not go to the ballpark where he had his fatal stroke.

Since her father's death, she has become increasingly close to her mother. "I'm up my mother's house, every day. Everybody comes to my mother's house, you know. Those who live far come every weekend or every other weekend. And us who live around the area that's near, we're always at my mother's every weekend, you know. Like we, they come down there after work, you know. Time we get tired eat[ing] dinner at home, we just pack our dinner, go down mama's and all of us eat our dinner together." Since her mother's home is near the children's school, they go to their grandmother's after school and their father picks them up there when he finishes work.

Jack and Iris seem to have a comfortable rapport and do a lot of joking. Iris says, "Marriage is fifty-fifty. If forty-sixty, I take sixty, you take forty." If it's the other way around, she tells her husband, "Take it out in trade, honey," and laughs uproariously.

Jack is an electrician and has always held a steady, well-paying job. A Japanese American, he ran away from home as a teenager on Moloka'i and lived with a Hawaiian family. Although he seems to have endured a lot of teasing about being Japanese, he obviously identifies and revels in the Hawaiian lifestyle of close family and socializing—including nights out drinking. Bar culture and drinking are important aspects of Hawaiian socializing for many men and women.

[33]

Iris has worked for many years as a dispatcher and union leader. She works the night shift two nights, from 11:30 P.M. to 7:30 A.M., and three days she works the day shift. On her days off, she still keeps a busy pace. During the summer she takes her husband to work so she can use his truck to take their kids and friends to the beach. She has a wide network of friends: "So many all over. My friends around—up dis road, all my friends! I get friends live—Waimānalo, Nānākuli, Hale'iwa. Yeah! All around the island! I just go here and there. All my kids. Just pack my kids in the car and weekends, if I get off."

Even though both Jack and Iris work forty hours a week, and some-times more, they find time to chauffeur their six children to *hula* classes, baseball and basketball practice and games, parents' meetings, potluck dinners: "I think only time we get rest is time for sleep," Iris joked. Both Iris and Jack feel committed to this frenetic pace as a way to "keep 'em busy." They see the alternative for their children as too much spare time and too much opportunity to get into trouble.

This flurry of coordinating work and children's activities leaves little time for housekeeping or yardwork. They rent a small house in Kalihi Valley. The house is constantly in some new form of disarray, and the yard has a rural quality of benign neglect, in spite of a chore chart for the kids (dishwashing, feeding the dog, cleaning their rooms, washing clothes) and Iris's love of plants. Within the yard's seeming disorder are lovingly cared-for anthuriums, orchids, and roses. Iris always makes time to visit her mother and socialize with a favorite lady friend.

"Then usually, on one day a week, or every other week, I have lunch with my girlfriend who works for the water company. Pick her up. But she has lunch hour, eleven o'clock or twelve. That's one of my best girl-friends. Then we go down Ala Moana Park. I make something at home, and then go pick her up and then go Ala Moana Park, sit down, have lunch, and talk, you know." Adds Iris, "Oh, yeah, then pack my son [the youngest, age two], you know. And my neighbor's baby. Take to the park, let 'em run around. Yeah, usually have about twice a month I usually spend that time my girlfriend, about, while she have her lunch hour. Pick her up eleven to twelve, have lunch, talk story. See what new and who's seeing who and who's married and all that." Iris gives one of her big chuckles.

Elizabeth Nohi Nacimiento is an animated delight with no teeth, an unruly mop of hair, and shapeless clothes that drape over an ample body (evidence of fourteen children and thirty years of childbearing).[11] She is a lively and enthusiastic person with an earthly forthrightness that is entertaining and often immensely touching. She enjoys talking and thinking about Hawaiian culture.

Nohi is an exceptional woman on many counts. Nohi is one of the 10,000 residents of the state who is pure Hawaiian. She grew up in the then tiny community on Maui which she refers to as Hānatown. Now a tourist attraction with an elegant hotel at the end of a long two-lane switchback road, in her childhood it was an isolated plantation town, more often reached by sea than by road. She met her Filipino husband, Roberto Nacimiento, forty years ago, when she was fourteen. She became pregnant with their first child at fourteen and gave birth at fifteen. Since she was underage, she was sent to Honolulu to give birth at the Salvation Army Booth Memorial Hospital, and Roberto spent some time in the local Maui jail. When she returned to Hāna with their baby girl, she said, her eyes welled to see Roberto and her mother and stepfather waiting for her—her family. Nohi lost only one child, her fourteenth, in a miscarriage. Their children range from thirty-seven years to eight years. She sometimes cares for a toddler grandson called Roman, a beautiful boy with large dark eyes, and adopted her granddaughter when she was ten years old, an irrepressibly lively and pretty girl named Kalena.

Their lives have been difficult, for Roberto was often without work. Currently they live on Roberto's social security payments and public assistance. He was once a boxer, but during the early years of their marriage he was primarily a cane cutter on the local plantation. Their life has been "plain this, plain that. Bare. Bare." Seven years ago they moved to Koʻolau Valley Housing, built alongside a valley. It is one of the older and larger public housing developments and shows the wear and tear of the years. It is considered one of the more dangerous projects, particularly after dark, as the unlit hillsides hide a multitude of nefarious individuals and misdeeds.

The Nacimientos live in a tiny four-bedroom, one-bath apartment. The unit is smaller than the newer ones of Pua, Ellen, and Junie. Anywhere between two and six of their children live with them, at any one

[11] Nohi once said that it wasn't having children that made one's body "come old" but raising them. She told me about an elderly Hawaiian neighbor who had had twelve children and *hānai*-ed all of them. Nohi often helped Mrs. Ward dress, and in a hushed whisper of awe she revealed that Mrs. Ward's body was still young. Not like her own, she added, breaking into raucous laughter. Nohi kept and raised all fourteen of her children, and several grandchildren besides.

time. Two of the youngest children, Bartlett (eight) and Ben (ten) are still living at home. Their youngest daughter, Marissa (fourteen) comes and goes, living sometimes at home, sometimes with her boyfriend, Russell; sometimes they both live with the Nacimientos. The next daughter, Donna (seventeen), also lives there sporadically with her two-year-old son, Roman. And finally, sometimes their granddaughter, Kalena, stays there when she is not living with her mother. Kalena's mother is the Nacimientos' fourth child, Clarrisa, about thirty now. At one point, all these people, including Clarrisa and her boyfriend, Matthew, were staying with the Nacimientos.

There is a pack-rat quality to the place. Nohi has filled every space with chairs, coffee tables, sofas, bookcases, end tables, hooked rugs, chests of drawers, mattresses piled several layers high in the bedrooms to accommodate the varying number of family members and associates. On the tables, the bureaus, and the backs of sofas are carefully placed framed photos of the Nacimiento children in various graduation and school poses, each carefully draped with a shell or woven *lei*. Other spaces are filled with plaster dolls, displayed books, certificates of merit and awards, crocheted doilies, Hawaiian quilted pillows, Hawaiian gourd instruments, crocheted hats with beer-can crowns, religious statues, and other artifacts of their lives. The walls are covered with taped snapshots, religious items and sayings, more school awards and mementos, a clock shaped like a cut apple, a tapestry rug portraying John and Robert Kennedy, and countless other items. Nothing, however, is sloppily done. Despite the clutter, each item's placement and maintenance shows order and care. Nohi keeps the place clean and neat despite the plethora of people and things. Each piece has special meaning for Nohi; each an historical catchment.

"I keep this for many, many years, you know. 'At's twenty-two years some things over here I keep. Yeah. Since I arrived from my Hāna. Then they [other people] throw away, eh? So I pick 'em up, I keep. See? I take, keep until now. I, I love my stuff."

Outside, in front of the apartment, is an amazing lush jungle of plants. Tenderly nurtured by Nohi, the plot is a narrow strip of dirt about ten-by-five feet. The cool green foliage makes a pleasant screen over the living room window, blocking out the harsh sun and the blazingly bright view of decay and rubbish. On the hill behind the unit Roberto has built a coop for his "chickens" (fighting cocks) and Nohi grows vegetables and medicinal plants.

Nohi is about 5'1" tall and weighs over 250 pounds. She favors worn-out, "broke clothes." In a remarkable transformation, when she is dressed to go out, wearing a nice *muʻumuʻu* or pantsuit, her hair combed, makeup on, and dentures in, she is almost unrecognizably handsome.

She prefers, however, to cultivate the appearance of a bumbling old Hawaiian lady who is a bit forgetful and simple. This pose belies not only her bright and lively mind but a remarkable memory. She says she knows "plenty things," and indeed she is knowledgeable and capable in many ways, but she prefers to let people think otherwise so they will not burden her with requests and unwanted responsibilities. She can give an artful imitation of how she cocks her head, looks perplexed, and almost closes her eyes in incomprehension when someone asks her to do something she does not want to do.

Nohi's eyes are remarkable. They sometimes seem to darken and sink into her face so that she almost appears blind, her head slightly tilted forward, eyes averted, as she is speaking to you. She will startle you as she suddenly turns and fastens you with a look that is clear and penetrating. This often is a random thing, unrelated to what she is saying and done with no break in her story. More meaningful is the hooded gaze she slyly rolls your way to punctuate what she is saying.

Nohi and Roberto have a close, tumultuous relationship. Both can be harsh and rejecting of the other but there is a loyalty and love built on the memories and years that bind them. Nohi recounts one of their major recent arguments and her words to Roberto:

" 'You think you better than me? And I think I better than you. Cannot be,' I tell like that. 'Us two gotta be same. 'Ats why we must not think like that. We must love one another, like keep. Because—you and me— we wen' get fourteen children together, you think we can forget the kind? You think, how look like [to] our children? If you would think of, uh, uh, fight, divorce and go away. Us old already. Who the hell like us?!' I tell like that to him. 'No. You keep me, and I keep you.' I tell him that, you know. 'For the sake of our children, you know. Cuz they young, they like, maybe like somebody else. But you and me—ah, no can. Hard to part.' I told him."

"Too many years, huh?" I remark.

"Yeah. Thirty-eight years this year. 'Ats why, I tell him. And uh, you know, I told him, 'I remember all the past years that we had lived together. The hard times we get together.' I told him, 'And our, the hard times and the good time,' I told him. 'So that no can, uh, no can be patch. You know. It remains in our heart forever. Not only remains in our hearts forever—cannot, uh, depart.' I just tell him like that."

[37]

The ties that bind are in one's heart, one's *na'au*; ties of memories, of history, of hostilities, and of love. One cannot patch or cover over the emotions intensely shared. One cannot depart.

Hawai'i

I first visited Hawai'i in 1972 as a tourist. On O'ahu, I marveled at the steep cliffs of the Nu'uanu Pali and those that surround Kailua-Kāne'ohe. I gawked at the fish as I snorkled around the fish preserve of Hanauma Bay. I could not believe the dazzling blooms of the aptly named shower trees along the streets of Honolulu and the fragrance of the countless plumeria trees. I struggled around the fifty-seven turns to Hāna, Maui, and gasped for breath on Haleakalā, the huge dormant volcano whose highest point is over ten thousand feet. I was mesmerized by the Halema'uma'u fire pit of Kīlauea, on the Big Island of Hawai'i, and struck by the contrast between the lush Windward side of Kaua'i and the barren Leeward side.

When I returned, beginning in 1973 and continuing over the next twenty-five years as a researcher, I realized how very little of Hawai'i and its people I had experienced. But the intense images of my first visit still resonate and I often think of them when I think of Hawai'i or even while I am there. This illustrates the power of Hawai'i as a tourist mecca.[12] It delivers on its promise of a tropical clime with lush, heady flora and wonderful beaches with white sand and clear blue water. The local people tourists meet in their controlled environments are always warm and friendly. Hawai'i lures with the exotic but reassures with domestic familiarity. Almost 56 percent of the 6.1 million tourists who visited Hawai'i in 1993 were from other states (State Department of Business, Economic Development, and Tourism [DBET] 1993–94:169). Hawai'i is an accessible dream place for Americans. It requires no passports; the people speak English, but a unique pidgin English; the water is safe to drink; and the money is U.S. currency. Of course, many Americans often forget that Hawai'i is part of the United States. But that is an important part of the artifice.[13]

[12] See Buck 1993; Farrell 1982; and Kent 1983 for both cultural and political critiques of the tourist industry.
[13] A report in a Honolulu newspaper was headed "Loss of Identity Called Tourist Threat." The concern was that Hawai'i needed to maintain an exotic difference from the U.S. mainland to continue to attract tourists from there. The report noted that few resi-

Hawai'i's history is very similar to that of all of the Americas: an indigenous population conquered and displaced by western European capitalists and missionaries. Since 1778, when Captain James Cook first landed, Hawaiians have suffered the consequences of Western exploration and colonization. The most profound effect was the marked decline in the indigenous population after 1778. The earliest population estimates of Hawaiians were made by officers who landed with Captain Cook in 1778 and 1779, which ranged from 242,200 to 500,000; the figure generally accepted is around 300,000 (Schmitt 1968). The earliest estimates were based on known inhabited areas and generalized to other settlements and islands. David E. Stannard (1989) has challenged these assumptions. He estimates an all-island population in 1778–79 from a conservative 478,000–658,000 to 800,000–1 million, with a likely population of 800,000.[14] In 1823, missionaries estimated the islands' population to be a maximum of 150,000. The first two official censuses were conducted by missionaries in 1831–32 and 1835–36: 130,313 in 1831–32, 108,579 in 1835–36. The sociologist Romanzo Adams reanalyzed those figures and revised them to 124,449 in 1832, and 107,954 in 1836. The official census of 1850 (the fourth and thought to be one of the first reliable ones) counted 84,165 Hawaiians. By 1878, one hundred years after the landing of Cook and his crew, only 44,088 pure Hawaiians were left (Schmitt 1968:74), a decline of 85 percent; if Stannard's 1788 figure of 800,000 is used, the decline is a staggering 95 percent. High mortality from disease appears to have been a major factor. Venereal disease, first introduced by Cook's sailors in 1778, spread quickly through the Hawaiian population and affected not only the mortality rates but the fertility rate as well. An epidemic, perhaps cholera or bubonic plague, around 1804 killed between 5,000 and 15,000; it was followed by an influenza epidemic in 1826 and epidemics of measles, whooping cough, diarrhea, and influenza in 1848–49 (Schmitt 1968; Nordyke 1977). It is estimated that 10,000 Hawaiians died in this twelve-month period (Schmitt 1968:37). Social problems such as alcohol abuse, landlessness, forced

---

dents of Hawai'i wear *mu'umu'us* or *aloha* shirts as everyday attire, pidgin is spoken less frequently in favor of standard English, and entertainment does not feature traditional Hawaiian *hula*, locally developed slack key guitar or indigenous sports such as canoeing. A tourism specialist noted: "We must offer more than the climate. If that is all we have, people can go to Mexico or the Caribbean for less money" (Andrade 1988).

[14] See Nordyke 1989b; Schmitt 1989; Hunt 1990; Ramenofsky 1990; Black 1990; Cruz and English 1990; Stannard 1990; and Kirch 1990 for more detailed discussions of Stannard's argument.

labor, and sexual promiscuity added to the decline in fertility and the increase in mortality (Schmitt 1968). Out-migration was a notable if lesser factor in the decline of the Hawaiian population. Hawaiians signed on as seamen to work in fur trading and whaling along the Northwest Coast. Many did not return; either dying or settling outside of Hawai'i, most notably in small Hawaiian enclaves in Alaska, California, and the Northwest Coast. Robert C. Schmitt (1968:39) cites figures from Adams indicating as many as 4,000 out-migrants in 1850, or 5 percent of the total Hawaiian population and 12 percent of the Hawaiian male population above age eighteen. Intermarriage also played a part in the declining numbers of pure Hawaiians. The 1853 census noted 983 part-Hawaiians. The 1896 census reported 8,485 part-Hawaiians and 31,019 "natives" (referring to full Hawaiians) (Schmitt 1968:74). The trend of increasing numbers of part-Hawaiians and decreasing numbers of full Hawaiians has continued to the present. Andrew W. Lind concluded early on: "Far from being a 'dying race,' as they seemed to be during most of the nineteenth century, the Hawaiians are now the Islands' most rapidly expanding ethnic group" (1967:19).

In 1973, when I began my research, there were 10,063 pure Hawaiians, representing 1.2 percent of the state's population. They and the 134,230 part-Hawaiians made up 17.7 percent of the population of Hawai'i. By 1990 there were 8,711 (0.8%) Hawaiians and 196,367 (18.0%) part-Hawaiians (DBEDT 1993, 4:37).[15] In 1984 the Office of Hawaiian Affairs (OHA) found that only 0.04 percent of the Hawaiian population (*N*–8,244) had 100 percent blood quantum and 34.8 percent (*N*–72,709) had between 50 and 99 percent. The majority (127,523, or 61.2%) had less than 50 percent (OHA 1986).

---

[15] There is considerable variation in how ethnic and racial categories are defined in different counts and some have changed their methods over the years, such as the U.S. Census. Methods for classification have ranged from self-report, report of mother's race or ethnicity, and report of father's race or ethnicity. For example, in 1960, descendants of mixed parentage were classified on the basis of the nonwhite parent's background or in the case of individuals with two parents of nonwhite heritage, individuals were classed by the background of the father. This was with the exception of Hawaiians or part-Hawaiians who were tallied separately. In 1970, race of the father was used. In 1980, people were classified on the basis of self-designation. In the case of self-designation, it is difficult to assess the changing role of sociopolitical factors in the readiness or reluctance to identify oneself as belonging to any particular ethnic or racial category. The ethnic and racial breakdowns provided by the state's Health Surveillance Program are usually considered more sensitive and accurate. See OHA 1996:10 and Native Hawaiians Study Commission 1983a:36 for discussions of the differences in U.S. Census data and state figures for Hawaiians.

How and who defines the categories Hawaiian, part-Hawaiian, full Hawaiian, and Native Hawaiian are inextricably linked to political decisions and circumstances (Trask 1993:53-54). Blood quantum is particularly germane. The Hawaiian Homes Commission Act of 1920 (HHCA), passed by the U.S. Congress in 1921, set aside approximately 203,500 acres of public land to be leased for ninety-nine years at $1 per year to persons who were at least 50 percent Hawaiian or "any descendant of not less than one-half part of the blood of the races inhabiting the Hawaiian Islands previous to 1778" (Native Hawaiians Study Commission 1983b:152). Originally the land was set aside to make available agricultural lands for Hawaiians to "enable Hawaiians to return to their lands in order to provide for their self-sufficiency, initiative, and preservation of their native culture" (Hawaii Advisory Committee to U.S. Commission on Civil Rights 1991:1), but within two years Congress amended the act to allow residential tracts. In fact, the majority of requests—57 percent as of June 1993—have been for residential lots (OHA 1994). They are no longer available for $1 a year, but the Department of Hawaiian Home Lands (DHHL) contracts for subdivision development and design and arranges for favorable financing (Hawaii Advisory Committee to U.S. Commission on Civil Rights 1991). The waiting list is long, however, and growing longer: 15,680 applicants were waiting for residential lots and 12,961 for nonresidential lots in 1996, as compared to 10,798 residential and 6,845 nonresidential applicants in 1988 (OHA 1996, 1994).

In 1958 the federal government returned approximately 1.4 million "ceded" acres (land taken after the overthrow of the monarchy in 1883 and ceded to the United States at annexation in 1898)[16] to the state to be "held . . . as a public trust for several purposes, including the betterment

[16] The issue of "ceded" lands is complex and begins with the Great *Mahele* (Division) of 1848 of Hawaiian lands originally held and controlled by the king and managed by his chiefs (*konohiki*). See Kameʻeleihiwa (1992) for a comprehensive discussion of pre-and post-*Mahele* conditions and consequences. The Great *Mahele* divided the lands into thirds—for the king, the chiefs, and the commoners—but in reality the king received two-thirds and the commoners one-third. The king further divided his land into Crown lands held privately by himself and government land held by his government. The Kuleana Act of 1850 gave the commoners (*makaʻāinana*) four years to establish claims to land. See Buck 1993:69–72; Daws 1968:124–28; Kelly 1980. But most of the land was lost to foreigners, who by 1890 owned three out of four acres in Hawaiʻi (Native Hawaiians Study Commission 1983a). In 1895, Crown and government lands were combined into "public" lands, which at annexation in 1898 were ceded to the United States. At the time of statehood in 1959, the United States maintained control of some ceded lands, which were then military bases, parks, the Honolulu airport, and other such government land but turned the rest back to the state.

of the conditions of Native Hawaiians as defined in the HHCA" (quoted in Hawaii Advisory Committee to U.S. Commission on Civil Rights 1991:25). Until 1978, most of the money generated from the ceded lands went to public education and was under the jurisdiction of the State Department of Land and Natural Resources. In 1978, however, the state established the Office of Hawaiian Affairs "to promote the betterment of conditions of Native Hawaiians" by the expenditure of 20 percent of the revenues obtained from the ceded lands.[17] Native Hawaiian was defined as at least 50 percent Hawaiian. All others, though called Hawaiian, have no claim to Homelands or the benefits of revenues from the ceded lands.[18] Currently another federal designation of "Hawaiian" conflicts with the HHCA's. In 1980, congressional legislation to establish a Native Hawaiians Study Commission defined a native Hawaiian as "any individual whose ancestors were native of the area which consisted of the Hawaiian Islands prior to 1778" (Public Law 96-565, 96th Cong., title III, sec. 305, Dec. 22, 1980). The dissenting volume of the Native Hawaiians Study Commission recommended this broader definition, and it is also supported by sovereignty movements (1983b).

In the 1970s, most people of Hawaiian ancestry described themselves as part-Hawaiian or described their often varied heritages if they were not pure Hawaiian. People did not refer to ethnic or racial backgrounds but rather to "nationality," reflecting Hawai'i's history as a sovereign nation.[19] Evelyn Michaels described herself as a "cosmopolitan mix," a designation that no doubt covered her lack of certainty about exactly what elements composed her "mix." During this period, the term "native" was not always well accepted. For Ellen Kam it was a pejorative, the equivalent of "primitive" or "savage." By the mid-and late 1980s, people of Hawaiian ancestry felt less impelled to qualify "Hawaiian" with "part," perhaps reflecting the political changes in the conceptualization of the terms Hawaiian and Native Hawaiian. One's percentage of Hawaiian "blood quantum" has economic ramifications, for it determines one's qualification for Hawaiian Homelands and other benefits such as busi-

[17] Not all revenues for ceded lands are subject to this 20% revenue diversion to OHA. Also, the state legislature has threatened to "suspend, reduce, or redefine moneys received by the Hawaiian agency" (Johnston 1996:1). For a critique of OHA and its policies, see Trask 1994 and three OHA Trustees, Beamer 1996:14, Kealoha 1996:14, and Akana 1996:15.

[18] OHA does use matching nontrust funds obtained from government and private sources to provide services to Hawaiians of less than 50% Hawaiian ancestry.

[19] The state song is actually a national anthem rather than a song of regional accolades. One of its lines translates, "Hawai'i's own, O nation, your great duty strive."

ness loans from OHA. All the Hawaiians I worked with, with the exception of Evelyn, were quite clear on their "blood quantum" of Hawaiian ancestry. Pua reported she was seven-eighths Hawaiian, Junie five-eighths, Iris half, Ellen a quarter, and Nohi 100 percent. Almost all used that blood quantum to apply for and obtain a residential Hawaiian Homelands lot on Oʻahu in the 1980s. In 1976, Iris Nakasone's application had been approved and she was preparing to move from Kalihi to Nānākuli. A few years later Nohi and June also moved to Hawaiian Homelands houses in Nānākuli. The homes are pleasant, new suburban tract houses with big yards and room to add on, as Iris has been doing continuously to accommodate the return of various adult children and their families. Nohi's front and back yards are overflowing with her plants and her husband's animals; Meanwhile June and her husband maintain a pristine lawn in front and back.[20]

Ethnic Population and Geographic Distribution

Hawaiʻi is known for its racially and ethnically diverse population. In mid-1975, the state's resident population was estimated at 864,900, including 58,700 members of the armed forces and 63,700 of their dependents. Nonmilitary ethnic representation from a 1972–74 sample was estimated as follows: Caucasians, 28.6 percent; Japanese, 27.3 percent; part-Hawaiian, 17.4 percent, Hawaiian, 1.0 percent; Filipino, 10.2 percent; Chinese, 4.3 percent, and mixed non-Hawaiian, 7.9 percent. All other groups, such as Korean, Samoan, and Puerto Rican, represented less than 1 percent each (Hawaiʻi Department of Planning and Economic

[20] I lost contact with Pua. A letter written to Ellen in 1988 came back with the word "Deceased" written on it. I was told later by a mutual acquaintance that she had heart problems (Steven Boggs, personal communication). In 1988, I returned to Honolulu to see if I could find my lady friends. While I sent regular notes and cards over the years, and continue to do so, not all would or could respond. Nohi and Ricardo celebrated their fiftieth wedding anniversary in a glorious fashion, returning to Hāna, Maui, to rededicate their vows in 1988. Ricardo was suffering from Parkinson's Disease and was frail but alert. Nohi died in 1996, apparently of a heart attack. Thanks to Steven Boggs for that gracious update. June had discovered a malignancy in her breast and was awaiting the diagnosis when I left in 1988. I have not heard from her. Iris was still driving from Nānākuli to visit her seventy-two-year-old mother every Friday in Kalihi. She still worked at her job as a dispatcher. Jack planned to retire in a few years. Iris sends me a Christmas card every year. Evelyn married and has five children and a successful design business. She still lives in Kalihi in the same two-bedroom place with her husband and all her children, everyone thriving in the close quarters.

Development [DPED] 1976:24). By 1992, the civilian population distribution was Caucasians, 23.2 percent; Japanese, 19.7 percent; part-Hawaiian and native Hawaiian, 19.3 percent; Filipino, 10.5 percent; Chinese, 4.6 percent; and other/unknown, 22.5 percent (based on Hawai'i Department of Health figures as cited in OHA 1996).

Since the late 1800s O'ahu has been the most populous island. In 1975, the state's Department of Planning and Economic Development (DPED 1976) reported that 81 percent of the population lived on O'ahu (704,500) and 40 percent lived in the city of Honolulu (344,000) (DPED 1976). By 1990 O'ahu and Honolulu were still the most populous areas, but the population had spread to other areas and islands: O'ahu now has 75 percent of the state's population and Honolulu City 34 percent (based on figures in Department of Business, Economic Development, and Tourism [DBEDT] 1994:21). The Hawaiian population varies depending on the source (see DPED 1985 for a discussion about the differential categorization and reliability of federal versus various state sources).

Of the Hawaiian–part-Hawaiian population, 76 percent lived on O'ahu and about 46 percent lived in the city of Honolulu in 1971 (Hawai'i Department of Health, Research, and Statistics Office 1973). By 1990, about two-thirds of Hawaiians lived on O'ahu (1990 census and a special tabulation by the State Department of Health as cited in OHA 1994). This reduction of numbers may have been caused by the high cost of urban living, which is characterized by expensive, limited housing and high unemployment. Nevertheless, "most of the Hawaiians live in an urbanized environment" (OHA 1994). Clearly, country living and its romanticized lifestyle are more a nostalgic memory than a reality for most Hawaiians. The problems urban Hawaiians face and their solutions offer a unique opportunity to observe not only cultural innovation and change but cultural resiliency.

Socioeconomic Conditions of Hawaiians

The social problems Hawaiians face are many. They are overrepresented in social service areas such as correctional facilities, public housing, and social service rolls and underrepresented in professional employment.

Hawaiians are disproportionately represented in both the arrest statistics and correctional facilities. During 1972–73, 53.8 percent of the juveniles and 49.6 percent of the adults confined in correctional facilities were of Hawaiian ancestry (Hawaiʻi Department of Social Services, Corrections Division 1972–73a, 1972–73b), although Hawaiians represented less than 18 percent of the population (DPED 1973). In 1990–91, adult Hawaiians constituted 37.6 percent of all sentenced felons (Hawaiʻi Department of Public Safety 1992 cited in OHA 1994) and 33.9 percent of the inmate population, including both prison and jail inmates. By 1993–94, Hawaiians represented 38 percent of the total inmate population, but they represented only 18.8 percent of the state's population in 1990. In 1993, 56 percent of the juveniles in youth correctional facilities were of Hawaiian ancestry (OHA 1994).

In 1976, only 11.4 percent of those arrested were of Hawaiian ancestry: 13.3 percent adults and 7.6 percent juveniles (Hawaiʻi Criminal Justice Statistical Analysis Center 1977). By 1993, Hawaiians represented 23 percent of all the adult Crime Index arrests made and 35 percent of the juvenile Crime Index arrests (OHA 1994).[21]

In 1975 Hawaiians were the largest group in public housing projects: 35 percent of the 5,419 households had at least one Hawaiian household head or parent (male or female) (Hawaiʻi Housing Authority 1974–75). In 1987 Hawaiian household heads (both male and female) were the largest ethnic group (24.1%) in public housing. The next most populous groups were whites with 18 percent and Filipinos with 14.2 percent. Since the mid-1970s in many of the urban housing projects the Samoan population has increased dramatically and in several they now dominate. For example, in the largest public housing facility, Kūhiō Park Terrace, which includes two large multistory buildings and a sprawl of two-story low-rise units, 53.7 percent of the heads of households are Samoan and only 20.4 percent are Hawaiian.[22] In 1975

---

[21] Crime Index offenses are a standardized group of offenses used for national data reporting and include violent crimes (such as murder and forcible rape) and property crimes (such as larceny-theft and burglary). There are several problems in comparing data collected in 1976 with those after 1979 because the classification procedures for juveniles changed in 1979. Before 1979, part-Hawaiians were classed as "mixed" and after 1979 as Hawaiian. Further, as the Hawaiʻi Criminal Justice Data Center cautions, the police collect race and ethnicity data to identify offenders and not for demographic studies. For example, repeat offenders within a year will be counted as many times as arrested. If they give different racial or ethnic identifications, they will be reported as such.

[22] In an attempt to upgrade the neighborhood, Kūhiō Park Terrace was recently privatized and renovated (Ronald Higashi, personal communication). In 1996, there were plans to develop the first two floors for offices and small businesses, but by 1998, this venture was no longer viable. The housing project looked very much as it did twenty years ago, with the exception of several deserted, boarded-up low-rises and a new paint job on Building B.

Samoans were a minuscule portion of the housing population (Hawaiʻi Housing Authority 1988).

Hawaiians were overrepresented on the welfare rolls in the mid-1970s. They represented 17.7 percent of the state's population yet made up 26.5 percent of those on welfare in 1973. On Oʻahu, 17 percent of the population was Hawaiian and 24.7 percent of welfare recipients were Hawaiian. The difficulty of sustaining a rural lifestyle in the fiftieth state is dramatically illustrated by Molokaʻi and Lānaʻi, two of the most rural islands, where in the early 1970s, 33 percent of the population was of Hawaiian ancestry and 50.4 percent of the welfare recipients were Hawaiian (Hawaiian Association of Asian and Pacific Peoples 1974; DPED 1973).[23] In 1993 Hawaiians were the largest ethnic group receiving financial assistance,[24] as well as food stamps. Almost 27 percent of individuals receiving financial assistance were Hawaiians, followed by Caucasians with 15.5 percent, Filipinos, 7.2 percent, Japanese, 1.6 percent, and Chinese 0.7 percent. Hawaiian individuals made up 24 percent of those receiving food stamps, Caucasians 18 percent, Filipinos 10 percent, Japanese, 2.6 percent, and Chinese 1.6 percent (OHA 1994).[25] "In Nānākuli and Waiʻanae, over one-third of Native Hawaiian [Hawaiian ancestry of any blood quantum] households received public assistance. Moreover, Native Hawaiian households in these areas comprised over half of all the households receiving public assistance. Eighty-five percent of households in Waimānalo Beach receiving public assistance were native Hawaiian" (OHA 1994). Nānākuli, Waiʻanae, and Waimānalo are three traditional areas for Hawaiian Homestead Lands on Oʻahu.

The median income of Hawaiians in 1979 was $20,030 per household and $17,841 per family as compared to the state medians of $20,473 per household and $22,750 per family (DBED 1987:49,393). In 1979 9.9 percent of the state's people lived below the poverty level, but 14.6 percent of Hawaiian individuals were below the poverty level (DBED 1987:49,399). The median income of Hawaiians in 1989 had increased to

[23] When I worked with people from the fishing village of Miloliʻi in the early 1970s, most of the residents, while proud of maintaining a traditional fishing lifestyle, counted on welfare payments to sustain their households.

[24] Financial assistance is provided through Aid to Families with Dependent Children (AFDC), Aid to Aged, Blind and Disabled (ABD), and General Assistance (GA).

[25] The category of "Mixed," which includes those individuals of mixed ancestry who do not claim any portion of Hawaiian, had the highest proportion of individuals receiving financial aid, 29%; the "Other" category received 19%. A similar pattern was reported for those receiving food stamps, with the "Mixed" category representing 25.5% of those individuals and the "Other" category representing 18.5%.

$36,135 per household and $37,960 per family as compared to the state's medians of $38,829 per household and $43,176 per family (U.S. Census 1990 cited in OHA 1994). There is a well-defined middle class of Hawaiians in which 19.8 percent of families made between $35,000 and $49,999; 21.2 percent made $50,000 to $74,999, and 13.4 percent earned more then $74,999 in 1989 (U.S. Census 1990 cited in OHA 1994). But 18 percent of Hawaiian families earned less than $15,000, representing about one-fifth of Hawaiian families. A further indicator of low income is the proportion living below the poverty level. In 1989 only 6.0 percent of the state's families lived below the poverty line as compared to 14.1 percent of Hawaiian families. Homelessness was not recognized as a social problem in the 1970s but 1992 figures indicate that Caucasians accounted for the bulk of both the "truly homeless" (49.9 percent) and the "hidden homeless" who live temporarily with friends or family (33.2 percent). Hawaiians ranked second among the truly homeless (20.6 percent), and Filipinos ranked second among the hidden homeless (20.6 percent), with Hawaiians (13.6 percent) and Japanese (13.3 percent) in a tie for third (OHA 1994).

In 1970 Hawaiians were underrepresented in professional, managerial, technical, and sales occupations and overrepresented in construction trades, as operatives, and in service occupations. They were overrepresented in one white-collar occupation: public administration (Lee 1976: 17–18). In 1991 they were still underrepresented in the managerial, professional, technical, sales, and clerical professions and overrepresented as motor vehicle operators, material moving operators, and in the protective services (including police and firefighters) (U.S. Census 1993 cited in OHA 1994).

Kalihi

This research was conducted in Kalihi,[26] which includes the neighborhoods of Kalihi-Pālama and Kalihi Valley. I was introduced to Kalihi in 1974 when I was associated with the Kamehameha Early Education Project. The school drew its students from the Kalihi-Pālama and Kalihi Valley area, and I made every attempt to maintain comparability with the neighborhood public schools' populations.

During the initial research period, Kalihi had the largest percentage of

---

[26] In earlier publications the neighborhood was given the pseudonym of Ka Pumehana.

Hawaiians in any Honolulu neighborhood (15.7%), and it had many of the problems faced by Hawaiians throughout the state (Lee 1976). Hawaiians, however, were not the most populous ethnic group in the neighborhood. Filipinos made up almost one-third of the population (33.1%) and Japanese over a fourth (25.2%) (Lee 1976). The rest of the ethnic representation was Caucasian (16.1%), Hawaiian (15.7%), Chinese (4.9%), and other (5%).[27]

Kalihi is a neighborhood of contrasts. Large modern shopping centers with supermarkets, drugstores, restaurants, and often a bowling alley compete with small old-fashioned grocery stores which have front walls that fold back to make them open-air stalls filled with canned goods, fresh produce, red Coke coolers, and rows of huge glass containers filled with assorted preserved fruits called crack seed. The neighborhood has both the Oʻahu State Prison and the internationally renowned Bishop Museum. Run-down housing projects painted drab institutional colors with rusty outdoor metal stairs and cinderblock walls are only a street or two away from large well-kept middle-class houses and new townhouse complexes. This contrast is reflected in the variability in 1980 income by census tracts: the lowest mean household income for a tract was $9,670 and the highest mean household income for a tract was $37,349. The lowest income tract had the biggest housing project in the state, Kūhiō Park Terrace. Two of the tracts with the top five highest mean household incomes in the neighborhood, $32,421 and $32,722, respectively, were adjacent to each other (U.S. Census 1983). By 1990, little had changed except that the mean household income of $10,343 in the Kūhiō Park Terrace tract had not increased by $1,000 in ten years. The flanking tracts were still among the wealthiest in Kalihi in 1990 with mean household incomes considerably higher than in 1980: $51,762 and $55,013, respectively (U.S. Census 1990). Both those tracts are dominated by Filipino residents while Kūhiō Park Terrace tract is dominated by Samoan residents. Hawaiians continue to be a presence in Kalihi, if still in the poorest tracts: 19.5 percent in the Mayor Wright Housing tract, 18.4 percent in Kūhiō Park Terrace tract, and 17.8 percent in the Mokauea tract. In the Mayor Wright Housing tract 41.7 percent of families were below the

[27] The population has changed considerably, and in the 1990 U.S. Census the neighborhood was composed of 31.3% Filipinos, 21.4% Japanese, 10.2% Hawaiian, 11.4% Caucasian, 13.0% Chinese, 4.5% Samoan, and 8.01% others. The Filipino population continues to grow and the Samoan population is increasing as well, but unlike the Filipino population, which is much more middle class, the Samoan population remains marginal in income levels.

poverty level while in the Kūhiō Park Terrace tract 71.6 percent of families were below the poverty level. In contrast, Mokauea increased considerably in mean household income, from $17,142 in 1980 to $40,094 in 1990, making it one of the higher income tracts in the neighborhood, if also one of its least residential because the Oʻahu State Prison, Kapālama Military Reservation, and many warehouses and businesses dominate the area. The median income for the state in 1990 was $38,829.

Kalihi is known locally as a pocket of old Honolulu. There are wooden storefronts with slat sidewalks, semipermanent lunch wagons that serve plate lunches of rice, macaroni salad, and such island favorites as *shoyu* spareribs, *nishime* (a Japanese chicken and vegetable dish), sweet-and-sour short ribs, and *kalua* pig (Hawaiian-style roast pork). Vegetation aggressively asserts itself wherever dirt is exposed. The atmosphere is a jumble of sights, sounds, smells, people, structural styles, businesses and residences, old and new, honky-tonk bars and family recreation, giving the neighborhood an earthy vitality that is in sharp contrast with the cool orderliness of middle-class Mānoa Valley or the suburban sterility of Hawaiʻi Kai.

Neighborhood landmarks include Tamashiro's Fish Market crammed with native fruits, steamed foods, and a wall-long counter of crushed ice packed with every form of local seafood; the feisty, rough Farrington High School; Dee Lite Bakery, famous for its *haupia* (coconut custard) cake, *lilikoʻi* (passion fruit) and guava creme pies; and Kūhiō Park Terrace, a notorious two-building public housing high-rise, along with five other public housing projects, the most of any neighborhood in the state.

Other Honolulu residents view Kalihi as a rough, crime-filled area. But longtime neighborhood residents feel a scrappy pride in Kalihi; romantic in their childhood memories of playing in the several streams that still run through the neighborhood, buying a big bowl of *saimen* (noodles in broth) for a nickel, eating hot *malasadas* (fried sugar doughnuts) or *manapua* (steamed pork-filled buns), and counting the rare cars that trundled up and down old Kalihi Road, part of which is now a major state highway. According to a feature story written by a local reporter, Kalihi is "an anomaly by anyone's standards, [it] exists in Honolulu with its own identity, the bad child of the City to those who don't live there and a nest of diversity to those who have come to understand it" (Fujii 1974). And it is the home of the six families of this research.

[2]

Comeback and
the Ties That Bind

"Like you spit up in the air, goin' come right back down on you," says Evelyn Michaels. She is always frank and direct: "It's like you do something to me, Karen. And you get away with it. I let you get away with it. Okay? In the end, the same thing will happen to you. Maybe not from me. Somebody else going do it to you. Let's say if you did something really bad to me. Same thing going happen to you. Like you know, the Bible states, yeah? 'Do unto others as you would have them do unto you.' So now what you do to other people eventually will come back to you. See?" With these words, Evelyn encapsulates the core of Hawaiians' understanding of their cultural system of morality and interpersonal obligation, a system of affective ties and emotional entanglements, of retribution and reward.

"Instead of my cousin telling me sorry, everything *pau* right then, no," Evelyn continues.

"Oh, oh, oh." I get a light of understanding. "I see. Like he lie to you."

"Yeah. He lie to me. And yet somebody tell me. And somebody tell me it's so. But he keep telling me no, no, no. Then the feeling is bad already 'cause I know!"

The cousin, Bradley, is sitting with us nodding his head in agreement.

Evelyn takes her explanation a step further: "Let's say we get into an argument. My cousin deny to me. But I know inside my heart he lied to me. And because he's close to me, even though we don't see each other regular because he live country now, but because he's close to me—and for him to hurt me like that—it's going to cause me great hurt. Hawaiians, when they get hurt—they get hurt. And can be something really minor sometime but it's just the principle of the thing or what it represented."

The "principle of the thing" is the lack of sincerity and trust. What it represents is an unkind intent to hurt a person with whom you have an emotional relationship. It means a person's motives are self-serving and selfish, not considering the other's feelings or reactions. This is a serious negation of the other person because the offender does not even care enough to remember the other in his or her actions. Hurt feelings often lead quickly to anger. When you care about someone, when you have an emotional tie to another, you are willing to extend yourself in a manifestation of *aloha* (love, warmth, hospitality). This extension of self leaves you open and vulnerable because you trust the other person not to take advantage of your openness and vulnerability. So when another rebuffs, ignores, or hurts, the pain turns to the anger of being taken advantage of, being made to look foolish.[1] This anger often marks the beginning of the spiral of emotional entanglements called *hihia* that can lead to negative repercussions.

Evelyn explains, "And it going to hurt me and if this thing, let's say, you know it might become, you know, the feeling just going grow—you know the mad or the hurt that going cause us. Somebody going have to pay for that mistake."

Bradley said that whatever the emotions the offended person is feeling, you will also feel, meaning you will suffer the effects of that emotional turmoil. If the other feels bad, so will you.

Evelyn agrees and adds, "If, if you that close, the person, the other person going to feel it—the strong." In other words, the offended person will feel the repercussions of those hurt or angry emotions more forcefully if the offender is a close friend or relative.

Closeness is not a matter of proximity or frequency of interaction. It is defined by the binding emotional ties of affection and history. Evelyn states that even though she does not see her cousin very often because of distance, they remain close. Relationships are not only renewed or kept fresh by direct social interaction or proximity but by memory as well. A recalled wound or slight can cause anger anew. Seeing a special place, hearing a familiar sound, or smelling a certain fragrance refreshes an affection. The memory of the love, anger, loss, vindication, or indifference is like an emotional souvenir that one carries to be dusted off and recalled as experienced before—maintaining the relationship.

[1] See also Howard 1974:33, 105.

Bradley says the *hihia* or entanglements can be solved by the approach and offering of an apology in the form of an explanation or discussion. It is a form of "opening the way" for renewed positive emotional exchanges: "Either he come up and talk to her or something like that, either way."

"Then," continues Evelyn, "he going have to come. See we wouldn't need *ho'oponopono* [a form of conflict resolution]. Like we wouldn't need a priest to help us if he come to me and tell me: 'Hey, cuz. Look. Remember the time you wen' ask me about this thing that I wen' bring the *wahines*[2] [women] up here and I told you I didn't? Well, I did.'

"Okay if you open up and he admit to me and tell me and tell me he sorry, then the feeling is *pau*. And it's gone. And everything is made up. And we make up by, you know, if we going drink or whatever."

Not only does one apologize, but one also returns to the hospitable trust of drinking and eating together. Both of these acts are features of *ho'oponopono*. (*Ho'oponopono* is described in detail in Chapter 4.)

Evelyn also has used a significant metaphor for Hawaiian social relations: "open." It not only means an act of confession and apology but also connotes a relationship unentangled by negative emotions. It is important that relationships be "open" to the exchange of positive affect to allow the extension of self in the form of offering *aloha*.

Of course, there are ramifications in this moral system if one does not confess and apologize. Evelyn warns, "But if he don't [confess and apologize]—if something like, if he gets sick—"

"But if you just hold on," interjects Bradley, "then you know, whoever gets sick—"

Evelyn cuts Bradley off: "And it usually going be him. If he did the wrong, he's the one going get sick. Not me."

"Yeah," confirms Bradley, nodding his head.

"But he going come to me for tell me he sorry or he not going to get better."

Evelyn emphasizes the need for apology to effect a cure for the illness caused by some transgression of affect.

I ask, "How do you know the sick is related to the—"

Evelyn cuts me off: "Because you *know* the trouble you have. Well, it's something like your conscience that tells you."

I persist. "So you feel bad and you get sick—"

" 'Ey!" Evelyn shouts. "You feel bad and sometimes you get sick or you get into an accident."

---

[2] In colloquial usage, Hawaiian pluralization uses the English addition of an "s."

"Right," confirms Bradley.

"Like you get into a freak accident or something happens to you that, right at the time, at that split second that thing wen' happen to you, you know why, this happen to you. Something tells you why it's happening to you and it's telling you, 'Wise up.'

"Right then and there you gotta wise up to what's happening. You gotta either straighten up your mistakes or you the one going pay worse. That's your warning ahead of time."

"You the one going be the patient," notes Bradley.

Ellen Kam, doe-eyed mother of eight and wife of the incorrigible Richard, struggles more painfully than the feisty Evelyn. Ellen is a kind and sensitive soul—emotions and sincerity are important elements in her life. For Hawaiians, sincerity is expressed as doing something "with heart."

I ask Ellen about this. "You know a lot of people talk about things 'coming from the heart.' Like some say a girl will dance with a lot of heart or somebody will do something from the heart—"

"Yeah," Ellen answers quickly. "There is. Like my si—I have one, my sister. When my kids . . . when she give you something she's not giving it from the heart. You know, she's not giving it because she wants to. Actually, she don't want to. So when my sister do thing that . . . we don't take it. Because it might not fall on us but fall on the kids."

"Like what?"

"Well, uh, I don't know how to explain it. The way, like if I going do a favor for you, you see. I not going to do it because I want to, you see? I going do it because my heart is in my friend. Like that. You see what I mean?"

Ellen's act of sincerity is a total empathetic extension of herself in an *aloha* gesture of giving. She places her feelings wholly within her friend; the gift is a gift of herself.

I ask Ellen, "What do you mean it might fall on the kids? Why don't you take what your sister gives you?"

"Like my kids, see? Like pretend, like. Do like now: you're me, see? And I'm my sister. You're playing the part of me. 'Kay, you asking me like you no more food or something: 'Do you have hamburger I can borrow last me till you know come pay you back?' Then I going tell you, 'For what!?' You see what I mean? Then I going say, 'Okay. Okay.' And I go in my icebox. It's like saying, my sister's taking her for dish out for me and she don't want to. 'Cause she going need 'em for her kids too, see? Like that."

[53]

"And then for you," I ask, "she offers you that and you'll say no?"

Ellen affirms, "Yeah. Then I say, 'Oh, no. That's all right.' I won't take it you know."

I ask, "Even if she on her own says, ' 'Ey, do you want?' "

"Yeah. Yeah. Because I always told her, 'You know, if you're going give me something . . . you tell me you giving it from your heart.' I said, 'I don't want to take something and the, and then you know I going regret taking 'em. Because you going bitch.' She going . . . you know, like one tale-like. She goes back, she says, 'Oh, she [Ellen] went [3] borrow. I no like it because she went borrow my last hamburger.' You see what I mean? Just because she taking [giving] the last hamburger for feeding my kids. And then she goes to the next person, she'll tell 'em, maybe she go to my [other] sister, she tell her, 'Oh, Ellen wen' take my last hamburger because she no more food for her kids and I no more too.' You see what I mean? She ask [tells] another one. She never give the hamburger because she wanted to."

Still confused, I ask, "How does it fall on the kids though?"

"While the kids are eating them, it's not . . . it doesn't taste good."

"They can tell?"

"Yeah."

"Do they, they don't—"

"They get sick from it. What I do is I just throw 'em away."

Ellen is attempting to discard the distasteful affect of her sister's begrudgingly given gift.

The social bonds between Hawaiians are protective. They protect individuals from the hostilities and hurt feelings of others. One's social network is like a protective net. Children, however, are referred to as the "weak link" because their protective bonds are less complex and developed, and sometimes they become the victims of conflicts between adults. Elizabeth Nohi Nacimiento, a full Hawaiian long married to her Filipino American husband, Roberto, told me that whenever there was *hukihuki*, or arguments back and forth, a child in the family would become the victim because children are defenseless. She felt they were only a spirit until they were six or seven years old, "when your eyes open. I mean to say, your eyes open and you know. That when the age of six and so forth." E. S. Craighill Handy and Mary K. Pukui (1972:100) note that traditionally a child's life could be stolen by spirits until he or she reached

---

[3] Sometimes Hawaiians and other locals do not use the pidgin pronunciation "wen' " but actually pronounce the last t, as Ellen does in this sentence.

the age of seven. What this may represent is the increasing social networks of a child as they grow older and become more independent of their parents and more the responsibility of sibling or child caretakers, thereby expanding their own emotional and social ties.[4] Not only are children defenseless, but their victimization, signaled by unexpectedly falling ill or having a bad accident, is a warning from God or other spirits for the parents to stop the conflict. Parents say that they are more likely to take notice of such a situation involving their child than themselves.

To illustrate, June "Junie" Kamakau related her own experience, following her divorce from her husband, Vincent, the father of her six children, when she began dating Rocky, a former Honolulu policeman. They lived a fast lifestyle. On her nights on the town, she left her children alone, sometimes staying out until the next day, although she emphatically denies that she ever slept with Rocky. Her youngest daughter, Lisa, suddenly became ill. On three successive occasions, Junie took her to the outpatient clinic of a local hospital where most welfare recipients receive medical care. Each time she was told it was an infection and Lisa was given antibiotics. But Lisa failed to improve. On the fourth visit, the attending physician hospitalized Lisa. June said that the doctor diagnosed "double pneumonia" and possibly spinal meningitis. The spinal tap for meningitis proved negative, but the doctor felt emergency surgery for the pneumonia was imperative or Lisa might die.

Junie grew up in a family that was very involved with a Hawaiian fundamentalist church called the Church of the Living God. She had rejected the church in a teenage rebellion but said that she had prayed before the fourth clinic visit. She said that since she had gone the previous times "without prayer" the diagnoses for Lisa were incorrect. Because she prayed the fourth time, the proper diagnosis was made. Further, before the operation, Junie went to her aunt, who was the church's minister (and the daughter of the church's founder),[5] for prayer, consultation, and interpretation of the meaning of Lisa's illness. Her aunt said that the "double pneumonia" was caused by the "cold heart" between Junie and Vincent. The "double" represented their marriage and joint estrangement. Even though they were divorced, they were still married in the eyes of God. Lisa's illness was a sign of the abuse of and disrespect for that union. To save Lisa's life, Junie would have to give up her boyfriend

---

[4] See Gallimore, Boggs, and Jordan 1974; Gallimore and Howard 1968; and Korbin 1978 for details of this shift from parental caretakers to sibling or other child caretakers.

[5] See Peterson 1975 for details of the political struggle for the control of the church after the founder's death.

and her wastrel lifestyle and try to reconcile with Vincent. A reconciliation would also protect her other children from similar fates of serious illness, accidents, or death. Her aunt said that Junie and Vincent did not have to remarry but that they had to stop the hard feelings between them. It was this *hihia* or troublesome entanglement between the two of them that was the cause for Lisa's illness.

The aunt's interpretation is a complex and subtle use of Hawaiian symbols. The loss of affection is associated with coldness. The location of that coldness is placed in the heart, or *na'au* (literally the intestines but meaning both mind and heart or affections). This symbolic importance of a cold heart is based on Hawaiian conceptualization of the heart as the source of sincerity, warmth (*pumehana*), and love (*aloha*). To do something "with heart" means a person does it openly, lovingly, genuinely, expressively. It also implies an un-self-conscious grace. A compliment about a young girl learning the *hula* would be to say "she dances with heart." Or if someone speaks forcefully about something he or she feels strongly about, and even if the words are angry or hurtful, people will excuse it by saying that he or she spoke with heart. So to have a cold heart is a problem indeed. It means to lack affection, sincerity, or empathy for others. This is why Ellen was so disturbed by her sister's lack of generosity, or heart.

The diagnosis of double pneumonia reinforces the symbolism of coldness and the duality of the couple. A common lay belief is that a cause of pneumonia is prolonged exposure to the cold or a chilly wind or draft. So Lisa's pneumonia was said to be symbolically caused by her prolonged exposure to the cold emotions between her parents. Furthermore, symbolically, there are two "cold lungs," or parents, flanking the "warm heart," or child, threatening the vitality of that child, symbolized by a cold heart. Junie agreed to stop dating Rocky, change her ways, and return to the church. Lisa's operation was a success (most of one lung was removed), and Junie emotionally told me that by changing her ways, she saved her daughter's life.

When I met Junie almost ten years later, she and Vincent had improved their relationship but were still divorced. Rocky remains a thoughtful ex-suitor who still sends flowers for Junie's birthday. Junie remains a stalwart believer in the church and its tenets. Although her life is circumscribed by financial difficulties, she is supported by the protectiveness and devotion of her children.

Jane "Pua" Kahana, a bowling zealot, whose nickname means flower or blossom, related another example that illustrates how coldness is viewed as a retentive tightness, the opposite of a giving, open person of *aloha*. Cancer is used as the metaphor for a friend's coldness and egoism:

"It's like she wants our attention. She wants us only to focus on her. She have—I don't know—something eating away at her, like cancer. Eating up her—heart. She really—cold."

Like Junie's case, the heart is the symbol and site of warmth, love, and self-extension. If one's heart is "eaten," one's generosity of spirit is being wasted, as if by a cancer.[6]

Pua explained the cause of this friend's coldness: "It's jealousy mixed with pride and, uh, with all kinds of junky stuff. That if you don't use it right—it—turns—on you."

Therefore, it is not that the woman has no emotions or has repressed them but that she has improper, antisocial ones. Further, negative emotions, particularly self-interested ones like jealousy (*lili*), can return to the originator, as described by Evelyn and Bradley.

Elizabeth Nacimiento, who now goes by her mother's name of Nohi, which means "bright colored . . . as the rainbow" (Pukui and Elbert 1971), discussed the idea that children are the vulnerable weak link in social relationships, caught between the emotional fighting of adults. She agreed that children are the victims of *hihia* (entanglements) or *hukihuki* (pulling or fighting back and forth) between adults: "Can. Can like that. That's why, you know, it's not so good when you make mistake to other people.

"No come to you—come to the other one. To the family. And that's right. That one, that one never miss, Karen. See, maybe they say like this, 'Okay, maybe I cannot get you but maybe I can get your daughter. Or you son.' Somehow, some way they get it. They going do it. That's why. 'Cause that person—did it. That's why. So they angry. Suppose to be that person get the rap, but no. Go to the other one: daughter, son, or mother, father. I believe that one. And can happen. Some way, somehow. They get it. Revenge. Revenge-like."

Another example of the innocent being affected comes from Bradley, Evelyn's cousin: "My uncle was a nice man, a nice man. But who got hurt? The daughters. The nicest people—he's a nice man—but he must have did something wrong. The son is retarded, the daughter—dying of cancer."

---

[6] The metaphoric link between cancer and the repression or attrition ("eating up") of emotions is not uncommon in Western societies. In spite of Sontag's protest against the impropriety of this metaphor, her 1979 book presents a superb case for the power of this metaphor.

"She's young, she just found out," adds Evelyn.

Bradley explains the reason: "The burden hit on nicer people."

"Why?" I ask.

Evelyn says, "Because they're the weaker."

"The weaker person, that's how it is," reiterates Bradley.

"Oh," I respond blankly.

"See," tries Bradley, "if you're strong—you can fight it back."

"The kids are weaker?" I ask.

"Right," reassures Bradley. "That's my mother's brother."

Evelyn explains, "When he say my uncle did a lot of wrongs before. Like the house my uncle lives in is actually my grandmother's house. See my grandmother used to live there when he moved in, he moved in with my grandmother. When his wife passed away. And then my grandmother died. And he just took over the house—what was hers. You know."

Cancer is again symbolic of the selfish, wrongful retention, a holding in, a holding away from others. In this case, what is physically appropriated is property (a common complaint and the source of many family disagreements),[7] but what is symbolically withheld is the emotional investment, one's regard, one's care. One has disregarded the relational ties of obligation and protection between parent and child.

Evelyn continues: "But, uh, what he's saying is that now, my cousin, Dorie, the oldest girl—all of a sudden—out of the blue now. She goes checkup every six months. She find out she get cancer. It's so bad that she's had two operations. They had her open. Now they had all her tubes draining," motioning to her own abdominal area. Evelyn raises her voice: "Now, Karen! If you go checkup every six months, you know what you have. You know you get something. But now, she only got three months to live. Forty-eight years old."

"So it's sudden," I interrupt.

Evelyn responds, "It's like—it *is* sudden. Now, you know, I cannot explain it, you know. I just feel bad that it is happening to her. I've never been close to that cousin. I don't know the reason."

"Which one?" asks Bradley.

"Dorie. I've only met her once."

---

[7] The supply of housing in Hawai'i is limited and hence the inheritance of homes is often a source of family friction. The ratio of people to homes from 1980 to 1992 remained stable at three to one. Furthermore, the ratio of population to housing is increasing faster in the most desirable location, the city and county of Honolulu, which had 76% of the population but only 71% of the housing in 1992 (OHA 1994).

Bradley adds some personal details: "This one married to 'Japanee.' "[8]

"But what my cousin is saying," continues Evelyn, "is just like for what my uncle—them do—"

"That's right," cuts in Bradley. "She get the burden."

"It falls on her," confirms Evelyn.

Bradley repeats, "It falls on her."

"She was like the perfect example, my sister was telling me," illustrates Evelyn. "I says, 'Why her though?' Because my sister was telling me, 'Well, you know. Her, when she was married—she had a good husband.' "

Bradley adds, "Till today;[9] she still married that husband."

"Till today," continues Evelyn, "she has a good husband. They work hard."

"And now," interjects Bradley, "they taking her life."

"And now," says Evelyn, "you know, she's always had everything going for her. But, uh. But now—nobody can see it. Why she's the one."

I ask, "Because otherwise she's had a good life?"

"She's had a beautiful life, as far as her ways—you know," affirms Evelyn.

"She's a nice-looking woman," adds Bradley. "But the burden fall on her."

"Because there is no explanation for why it's happening to her," says Evelyn.

"That's right," responds Bradley.

"I don't think she drinks or smokes," asks Evelyn.

"She don't smoke. She don't drink," Bradley confirms.

For Hawaiians, there are no innocent bystanders. The phrase "you related" means more than kinship. If you know each other, you are "related": you are engaged in a social, emotional exchange with obligations, benefits, and burdens. Social links are kin ties.

The basis for all social relations is one's kin. An individual is never isolated: "an individual alone is unthinkable in the context of Hawaiian relationships" (Handy and Pukui 1972:75). One is bound through time as a descendant of real and mythical ancestors and as the genitor or genitrix

[8] Local slang for Japanese. Similarly, Portuguese is "Portagee." Chinese, however, are referred to by the Hawaiian word for this nationality, *Pāke*, but it can have derogatory connotations depending on context.

[9] The phrase "till today" does not refer to some past event that continued through the present time but ended recently. It means that it still continues. Carr 1972 notes that it means: "to the time of, up to, until."

of one's offspring and subsequent generations. Every Hawaiian is part of a contemporary matrix of relatives and fictive kin relations. The importance of the kin tie as central to structuring all social relationship is seen in the liberal use of terms such as "auntie," "cousin/cuz," "bra" (brother), "*tūtū*" (grandmother), and "*tūtū*-man" (grandfather) to refer not only to fictive relationships but to include other individuals in one's social network. Hawaiians will sometimes find it so incomprehensible and painful to know someone who *is* truly alone, such as many elderly Filipino men who came over as field laborers in the 1920s and 1930s and were never able to return or marry, that they will insist these men come and live with them. Housing and food are informally exchanged for their domestic help as baby-sitters and cooks.

Social relations include not only humans but also the spiritual and natural worlds. Hawaiians feel direct kinship with these worlds. They do not think of them as separate spheres. Gods and goddesses take form in certain flora and fauna of the land and sea, colors, tools for certain tasks, landforms, and natural events. Each deity has multiple forms called *kino lau*. These are not symbolic manifestations but actual transformations. For example, Pele is the goddess of the volcano. She resides in the Kīlauea crater of Mauna Loa on the island of Hawai'i. Her *kino lau* are visible not only in volcanic activity and fire but also in human forms such as an old hag, a woman dressed in white, a beautiful young woman. She is visible in the red earth, various land formations such as Ka-iwi-o-Pele (meaning the bones of Pele) in Maui, and the small lava pebbles found on the Big Island of Hawai'i which are known as Pele's tears. Residents on the Big Island still encounter Pele as they drive along the roads, particularly in the districts of South Kona, Ka'ū, and Puna, where most of the major volcanic activity and lava flow occur. Children will explain that Pele is in the lava rocks they pick up on the ground (see also Ciborowski and Price-Williams 1982). Pele is temperamental, and contemporary Hawaiians cite her as an ancestor (without genealogical verification) if they themselves have a quick temper: a type of personality *kino lau*. Today it is not uncommon to find Hawaiians who claim an ancestral link to some Hawaiian deity or animal form, such as the gods Kū, Pele, the shark, or the lizard (Mo'o), without any specific genealogical links other than family lore or family origins from a place associated with a particular deity or *kino lau*. Not much was recorded about the *maka'āinana* (commoners), but most likely they were aligned with the spiritual world, not through genealogy but by local or craft affiliation. The *ali'i* (royalty or aristocracy) kept detailed oral genealogies of their descent linking them to various gods and goddesses of Hawai'i and thereby the natural and supernatural worlds.

People respond emotionally to *kino lau* (Handy and Pukui 1972) as if encountering a known person. The emotion depends on the timing and the context of the *kino lau* sighting, although seeing the same *kino lau* does not mean all people exhibit the same affective reaction. Just as seeing a relative or associate does not call up the same feelings each time, one may feel indifference, affection, or anger depending on the circumstances of the meeting or the condition of the relationship.

This emotional response reaffirms the bond between Hawaiians and their ancestors, their spiritual world, their physical environment, and each other. Such affiliations with the natural environment allow Hawaiians to participate in kinship relations even without human companionship. Currently, *kino lau* are less elaborately known or understood among the general population, particularly urban dwellers, whose subsistence involvement with the natural environment is more restricted and genealogical and geographic places of origin are more obscure, but nevertheless there are strong beliefs in the spiritual presence embodied in certain places, in the sea and some of its creatures, the weather, certain foods, and some plants and animals. This generalized belief in the spirituality of all things was traditionally called *mauoli ola*: "meaning that the essence of life is present in every part of the world, th[is] principle still seems to form a basis for understanding Hawaiian behavior" (Heighton 1971:22).[10] And one must act as appropriately with the natural and spiritual environment as with one's interpersonal environment. One's behavior has consequences in relations with all social others, human or otherwise.

Not only can one's improper behavior or intent be dangerous, but words as well can be hazardous for Hawaiians. *Hua 'ōlelo*, which refers to a rash, malicious statement or a broken promise, literally means "fruit

---

[10] These beliefs are not restricted to those of Hawaiian ancestry. Many local residents, influenced by Hawaiian culture, feel and believe in spiritual elements associated with various places and local flora and fauna. For example, a commonly held belief by Hawai'i residents is that you will displease Pele if, even unknowingly, you "take pork over the Pali" (the Nu'uanu Pali) in your car. In her anger, she will cause your car to malfunction. Most likely this belief is based on the legend that Pele has a volatile temper and is easily offended. However, it makes more sense for the pig demigod, Kamapua'a, to be the one to punish this offense. Kamapua'a is himself a pig, who (of course) never eats pork, and his family home is in the Ko'olau Mountains, which bisect O'ahu, so carrying pork over that mountain range where the Nu'uanu Pali is located would be maximally offensive (Kame'eleihiwa 1996). Thanks to Lee Ann Punua and Eugene Ogan for this clarification.

[61]

of word or speech." Words have consequences: "Hawaiian tradition holds that a spoken word becomes an actual entity, an operative agent that can bring about events" (Pukui, Haertig, and Lee 1972:86).

Nohi Nacimiento explains why words have effects. A phrase that I did not understand was said often in response to criticisms of one's children: "Look to your own first. Maybe more worse [yours]." I ask Nohi what this means. She responds, "If you say to me, 'How come you kids always go naked?' Then I say to you: 'Oh, how come you look at my kids. Why no look at yours?' You know that kind talk, yeah? You know, Hawaiians, yeah? They get angry with the kind talk. And you know that kind of talk? Are sharp. You know what I mean by sharp? Uh, hurting. Um hum. That's why sharp." The words cause pain and injury.

"Now, if the answer say like this, 'Oh, uh, how come you no look at your kids before you talk about mine, yeah?' Oh, gotta watch out, though. Because—something going happen, you know. To you."

She continues, "Uh, the Hawaiians says, yeah? The mouth the cause of the trouble. 'Cause what you saying—you always hurt the—When you talk, you hurt, you know. That's why. This kind you gotta watch out."

Criticism of one's children gets a strong response. In addition, the mouth is often cited as the symbolic source of trouble as the origin of critical talk.

When I said to Ellen Kam, "I've heard that when people argue, adults argue—" Ellen cut in, "The mouth, yeah."

"What is that?"

"Your mouth."

"Does it fall on the kids?"

"Yeah."

"Is that true?"

"It is. I find that it's true. Because I have my sister and my brother—they act—one of my brothers and one of my sisters—they cannot see eye to eye. One insists that 'My kids are better than your kids.' I have one and I find it's true. Because no kids are more better than any other kids. That's how I feel. And nobody's perfect. Like if I have something and she comes up and say, 'Oh, where did you get that?' And then, you know, I tell 'em where and this and that and when I get to her house—she has something better than what I have."

"Do her kids and her brother's kids get sick from that?" I ask.

"No. No, they just argue—just the mouth. Like my brother will say, 'Oh, you kids do this and your kids do that,' and you turn around and the kids are doing it. His kids are doing it."

"Oh, his kids. So you mean it falls back on—"

Ellen interrupts and finishes the sentence: "Back on them.

"Yeah. Like I know what my nieces and nephews do. See? But I'm not going say anything because I don't want my kids to do it. Like if I go out and tell, ' 'Ey. You know your kids, they do this and they do that in my house.' And the next thing, turns around, my kids are doing it—to somebody else. See what I mean?"

I try to clarify. "Is that why people say, 'Look to your own kids—' "

Again Ellen jumps in. "Yeah."

I expand a bit. "You know, if somebody criticize—"

"Yeah," Ellen cuts me off. "Before you start criticizing my kids you better look at yours first. Yeah."

"Is that what it means?" We are interrupted by a friend of one of Ellen's children who comes looking for the child and also buys one of Ellen's homemade "ice cakes" of frozen juice with a dried salted plum inside.

After the child leaves, I begin again. "So, I see. So then if you talk bad about somebody else's kids—"

Again Ellen finishes my sentence, "And then it turns on my kids are doing it. See? Doing it when, while my mouth is going through somebody, my kids are turning around and doing it to me. You see?"

Ellen reiterates the idea of the mouth as the source of retributive troubles. She articulates the boomerang effect or "comeback" of one's negative words with the phrases "turns around, my kids are doing it," "it turns on my kids," "my kids are turning around." And she further elaborates the power of words with the phrase "while my mouth is going through somebody." Her words and affect can pierce another's emotional barriers and hurt. They are cutting and "sharp," as Nohi had said.

Evelyn gives another amplification: "It's like when you're pregnant, don't talk about people. Don't say things. 'Cause it, they say it reflects. Just like a mirror, what you say. It reflects back on you."

"Just like a mirror?" I ask.

"A mirror."

A bit confused, I say, "Because you're pregnant?"

"No. Anything. It's like when you talk, it reflects—you personally."

"Oh, anytime."

"Anytime you talk. It reflects you as a person. Like I can look really nice, right? I can look as a really nice person. But when I open my mouth, that's what's going decide what kind of person I really am. See what I mean?"

[63]

I repeat to clarify, "So it's what you say—"

Evelyn interrupts: "It's what comes out of your mouth that is really you because in the Bible it states right? It's not what goes into the body that defiles the body. It's what comes out of the mouth because it comes from the heart."

It reveals one's inner, heartfelt feelings from the *na'au*. And words bear the fruit of retribution, *hua 'ōlelo*, the fruit of a broken promise, a harsh statement. Words come back to you. They reflect who you are, your emotions, your intent. In addition, the symbolic association of the bearing of a child under less than optimal conditions (such as out of wedlock or with a deformity or birthmark) reveals the retribution of one's talk: one's fecund state is associated with the fruit of one's hostile or hurtful words.

Pua Kahana also has strong opinions about the relationship between negative talk and pregnancy.

"I mean, you know like—I had an aunt before, she used to talk so much about my older sisters. See, her, she had my mother's sisters, eh? She used to talk about my sisters. Not to my mother but to other friends. Say, 'Yeah, look. Her oldest daughter have a baby, not even married,' and this and that. You know. 'Kay, fine.

"My mother says, 'Talk. Talk all you want. Just remember one thing, you have girls growing up too.' Like my sister them, she's the first grandchild. So you know, older than the others, eh?

"Then when *her* daughter, was forced to get married—"

I interrupt to clarify: "Oh, this lady. I mean your auntie?"

"Yeah. Yeah, and then she says, uh, her talk was, 'You see, at least my daughter got married,' You know. But then—her daughter got married— five months later, she had her baby. That's about the same thing. Right?

"So my mother says, 'See? You never talk. Happens to you. I'm not wishing anything on you but you never, never talk about anybody like that because sooner or later,' my mother always tell, 'sooner or later—and I'm not wishing it upon you—but sooner or later—something similarly will happen to you because you talk too much about somebody else.' Which is true," Pua concludes.

Pua is not only relating the retributive fruit of her aunt's critical words about having a daughter bear a child out of wedlock but the understanding that even by merely explaining this, by giving a warning, her mother recognizes that her own words could be interpreted as a curse, illustrated by the repeated phrase "and I'm not wishing it upon you."

Whether good things return in kind is a topic less ardently discussed

[64]

than whether bad things are returned. For example, I ask Pua, "Somebody said that if you do something good to somebody, it'll come back to you."

"Right. Right," Pua confirms but does not elaborate.

So I take a different tack: "If there's something bad, it'll come back to you. Not necessarily like if you do something bad to that person, that person will be bad to you."

"Yeah, maybe somebody else. Um hum. That's right. It happens. It does. Okay. Like, like say, you know somebody, comes over and we fight. You know, and maybe I say, you know, like my girlfriend, the other day, she like get in trouble. She say: 'Oh, I curse you. You not going to have this and that.' It happens.

"So okay. So maybe I wish them, you know, bad luck or stuff. My mother always says, it is not good to wish anybody like that because it'll happen to you. But maybe most likely it's not you, but to your kids. 'Cuz like if my kids get sick whereas they don't have a cold. They have nothing that I can think of that is making them sick. My mother would tell us, you know, go to church, forgive yourself, you know, whatever, you did wrong. It come out good. And it does! Yeah, and we believe that if you do anything to somebody, you know, anything bad, wish bad, it's gonna happen to you."

Pua not only refers to actions but intent, "wish bad," as an operative mechanism. I try again with Pua: "I mentioned that earlier we were talking about how bad things come back to you like when you criticize others. But what about good things?"

"Well, I think so—if you do good to others. You know, good things come back to you."

I try to prod her. "What kind of good things do people usually do?"

"Like I mean you know, like, like us for example. We may not be the richest or anything but if anybody came to the door asking for help we would help them. My husband and—well, especially me, the kind that can be our last, you know, we would help them. They really need the help and then maybe we don't get riches and stuff like that but I mean, our kids are healthy—you know. One thing I can say, my kids, they don't get sick too often. If they do get sick, I get panic anyway. So—" and she gives her distinctive girlish giggle.

In this case the absence of something negative is proof of a good life with kind, generous intentions. To confirm I ask, "Yeah, I guess the sickness comes on the children if there's trouble—"

Pua cuts me off and states emphatically: "Yeah. I feel that way too." Then she launches into a long story about her friend who does not share her problems with Pua and other friends, has children who are in poor health ("constantly with running nose and sores"), and feeds her children only "eggs and rice, Spam and rice, hot dogs and rice . . . a lot of soda . . . a lot of pastries." The implication is that the woman's lack of trust in and dependence on her friends—a form of "bad" behavior—leads to her children's poor health.

Obviously the more salient interactions are the negative ones which call up a myriad of responses, whereas the discussions of positive comeback are usually trivial or thin. Nevertheless, while a life of disarray and ill health is powerful symbolic evidence of improper social interactions, a good life filled with health and few misfortunes is evidence of one's righteousness: "One thing I can say, my kids, they don't get sick too often."

Nohi, provides an example of positive comeback in which she uses a metaphor to illustrate how good works and intentions can bear delicious rather than poisonous results. She is talking about not being greedy and taking all the mangos or papayas on a tree.

I ask, "What kind of mangos do you like?"

"Any kind mangos! Don't be choosy. I no like be choosy." She sniffles. "The kind, well, in the store. They selling only Hayden [a variety of mango], right? So I only buy Hayden. But when I go somebody house, and I see mangos, I go ask. She give, you know. 'Cuz she cannot eat 'em all. But I can. 'Cuz I don't take all, right? She can't. All go to waste. I see her throw one [garbage] can out, you know. They spoil, eh? So that's what I mean. When you give out, yeah? And every year when you get your mango, yeah? Always full, come plenty."

" 'Cuz you give?" I ask.

"Right. Give! You give your fruit."

Still a bit unsure, I repeat, "So it pays you back for uh—"

Nohi interrupts: "Yeah. Fruit just like people.'Cuz if you treat, if you give a, uh, a person what you have, so long they ask, I'm sure you going get, going get pay, repay back. Somewhere or somehow."

Not everyone is content to wait until some future time to claim retribution in negative happenings despite a firm belief in retributive comeback. Some take it as a justification for taking matters into their own hands.

Earlier Pua said, " 'sooner or later—and I'm not wishing it upon you— but sooner or later—something similarly will happen to you because you talk too much about somebody else.' Which is true."

She continues: "Like today for example. This morning I had to go to school. My son came home yesterday and said that the teacher yelled at him. I didn't mind the yelling but it's what she said that I didn't like.

"I said, 'Why did she yell at you?' "

Pua gives her son's reply: " 'Oh, the teacher told me to erase Mark's name from the chalkboard, and I did. And then she says, 'Oh, you kids! One of these days, I'm going to kill some of you!' "

"I says, 'What?!'

"He says, 'Yeah, mama'; she says, 'One of these days, I'm going to kill some of you kids.'

"I said, ' 'Ey, man. That teacher gotta go.'

"So I called up the principal. I wanna talk to him tomorrow morning. As soon as school opens, I wanna talk to him.

"And he [my son] says, 'Oh, mommy, and not only that, you know when you and daddy went on the airplane? The next day, the teacher slapped my face.'

"I went, 'What?!'

"Say, 'Yeah, the teacher wen' slap me.'

"I said, 'That's too much.'

"What I called the principal to talk to him.

"So this morning—that's why I, I told you to come about nine—I didn't know how long it would take, I went to talk to him and Mr. Nakano [the principal] from Forest School, he's really understanding. You know, he'll *make* time to talk to the parents if anything with the kids.

"When I went there this morning to talk to him, I says, 'I don't mind the teachers yelling at the kids, you know. But yell in the way where, you know, like says, 'Why don't you listen?!' Or, 'Do things right.' But don't say, 'I'm gonna kill you!'

" 'I mean what's wrong? She get something missing up there (pointing to her head) where she gotta bring out that kind of thing? And that's not even half of it. She slap my son.'

"I told him, 'You know, she's darn lucky that—you know when my older girl, Emmalene, was a little girl going to kindy-garden, first grade, I go straight to the teacher and I slap her back. I did that.' "

"Oh, yeah?" I comment.

"Yeah. At Lāola School. At that time, I mean, being your only child, you know. Oh. It really hurts, you know.

"So when she comes home and tells me that the teacher wen' pull her hair, I went there and I yanked that teacher's hair right back. And I told—and then you know, then they start calling the principal and the

[67]

vice principal and everybody came running. I say, 'Well, if she don't like me do that, then don't do that to my kids.'

"So I told Mr. Nakano, 'You know, this my first boy, you know. He's my oldest boy.'

"And I says, 'I get hurt when anybody hurts him. So—she's just lucky that I'm in a state where I talk first. You know, I come to you, you know, come to you. I talk sense. She's lucky I didn't go to her room.'

"Because I was sitting on the car downstairs about quarter to eight. 'Cause he comes in at eight o'clock and I was going to talk to him.

"I told, 'I'm sitting on the car, I'm looking at your office, and I'm looking at my boy's classroom. And I'm deciding if I should go there before I go upstairs. And she's lucky I decided to go upstairs to talk to you first. 'Cause if I had to go there, I think I'd slap her on the face too.' "

Pua has touched several points. The first is when she refers to the teacher of her daughter, "if she don't like me to do that, then don't do that to my kids." This is taking the Hawaiian idea of retributive comeback literally into one's own hands. Pua does not wait for "divine providence" to provide retribution. Second, when she is talking to Mr. Nakano and says of her son, "I get hurt when anybody hurts him," she is articulating the direct, emotional child-parent link that they are one and the same. What you do and what happens to you has a direct impact on your kin, in particular the parent-child dyad.

Pua, who is very articulate about this Hawaiian system of reward and retribution and has had direct experiences with the dramatic effects of emotional curses, purposely does not teach her children about these spiritual elements of this system. In fact, she refers to it as "hocus-pocus."

She has had two particularly dramatic experiences with spiritual retribution: when her godmother became possessed (*noho*) and when her foster mother became paralyzed. In both cases, Pua was a witness to sudden and dramatic changes in each woman's life caused by the jealousy and spiritual curses of others.

She explained an incident with her foster mother in the context of frequent Hawaiian spiritual activities when she was growing up.

"Well, when I was small, man, we used to have these kind of *kahuna* jags, you know. *Kahuna*, you know what is that, huh? When they cast evil spirits on you.[11] My mother used to have that so much. And that

[11] Traditional *kahuna* were a category of specialists. Some were medical healers, *kahuna lapaʻau*, and others sorcerers, *kahuna ʻanāʻanā* (Kamakau 1964). Today most people do not make any distinctions and use the term to refer to spiritual specialists in both healing and sorcery.

was only through jealousy. You know, ladies was jealous of my mother. Curse her.

"My mother got—one time I remember, I was, I was seven, I think. Yeah, we were, I was just like in the second or, you know, third grade. We were going to school at that age, huh? My mother came home and she went sick. But not the kind sick doctors could cure. The doctors said nothing was wrong with her. And she got cripple. She couldn't walk. Yeah. She couldn't walk. Her legs was all paralyze. And we used to have to drag her. We couldn't carry her. We used to have to drag her.

"Like say, our house was long. Three times longer than this [gestures to include whole room] living room. Like, this was our bedroom and our living room about this big. And then the kitchen, the bathroom. So we would have to drag her from our, from her bedroom all the way to the— we couldn't carry her when we were little. You know."

A knowledgeable Hawaiian woman was called. "Yeah, my mother, we had to, you know, every time my mother feel pain, we had to run down and go call this old Hawaiian lady, who used to come and pray, and do the *ti* leaves and the Hawaiian salt[12] and—she really help my mother."

I ask, "Did she get, uh, was she able to walk?"

"Oh, yeah! My mother, yeah. After that she was better."

Then Pua describes an encounter with a *akua lele*, literally a "flying god" but thought to be a destructive spirit in the form of a flying ball of fire. The fireball could be returned to the sender by saying, "go back and destroy your keeper," or it could be destroyed by swearing at it (Pukui, Haertig, and Lee 1972:7, 25–26). In this case, the *akua lele* was the *lili*, or jealousy, one of the women who wanted Pua's mother's husband: a fireball of hostile emotion.

"And you know, they have those little red ball. That flies. Yeah, they have that. And that thing, uh, burst right above your house, it means somebody in the house going die. But, b—, like, you look out the window, you see it coming, yeah? They say if you yell or s-s-swear or something and it'll just vanish."

"Did you ever see it?"

"I saw it once."

"At your mother's house?"

"Yeah, was coming after my mother. You know, my grandmother stay. So they were able to stop it."

[12] *Ti* leaves (cordyline terminalis) and salt (usually Hawaiian salt [*pa'akai*], which can be purchased in any grocery store) are used for protection and purification. See Pukui, Haertig, and Lee 1972: 190–92 for a discussion of the current protective usages of *ti* leaves.

"They shouted?"

"Um hum. My mother came okay. My mother had a bad time. It all stem because this Hawaiian lady, you know, she ask question. And somehow—just like fortune teller, you know. But not really in the fortune, uh, future, they know what is happening and why. You know they find out why. It happened because this [other] lady was jealous of my mother. In other words, not jealous of my mother but she wanted my father. And you know, figure if this kinda stuff happen, then my father goin' come to her, yeah? But he won't come."

In the other incident, Pua was spending the weekend and playing records with her godmother's sister, who was Pua's age. Her godmother's brother, who was younger than the two girls, was sleeping in the living room.[13]

"And then I heard, 'Shadd-up! Shadd-up!' You know, and we came running out. And we heard, 'Bang! Bang! Bang!' and she, 'Ee-ee. Ee-ee,' laughing and screaming.

"And then I hear the husband say, 'Shadd-up! Shadd-up,' you know.

"So we run into the room. He tells me to go call somebody. Because, 'Your mother is getting crazy.' She was in the closet—all huddled like. 'Ee-hee-hee, hee hee. Eee-hee-hee.' She was going like *kahuna* [spiritually possessed],[14] eh? And somebody curse her. Her hand was like this [curled and bent up]—and stayed like this. And the Hawaiian lady come, bless her, prayer and *ti* leaf and all that—stuff—ritual—and anyway, couple hours . . . she, she came all right, uh, mentally. But her physical appearance was real—you see, they say because before, she used to—not curse but she used to condemn a lot of people. You know. She used to run down other people's kids, run down their place, run them down, you know.

"And that, uh, when she, you see—she just became a barber. You know and she was doing real good. Barbershop business and I don't know, whoever wen' *kahuna* her probably felt—okay, if you went to a barbershop, you wouldn't wanta go cut your hair by somebody who had a face looking like a half a dead person. And, and if your hand stay like this [curled up] you cannot very well do a good job, right? So that's what her husband was saying that somebody wen' *kahuna* her and I don't know—maybe she talk about the wrong person, eh?"

Pua's godmother washed her face and hand regularly in a local stream,

[13] Pua referred to the sister and brother as her godmother's "kids" even though she explained they were her younger siblings.
[14] *Kahuna* is used as both a noun and a verb.

and eventually her only symptom was a slight, unpredictable hand tremor. "Just like you gotta have one drink. Yeah? But she doesn't drink, you know."

After about a year her godmother recovered. Pua concludes: "It happens that way. I don't know but Hawaiians, there's some real spooky kind, boy."

"Doesn't happen too much anymore, does it?"

"No. Not that I remember anymore. This, all these things I remember, you know, I going when we was kids. I guess now days getting modern, you know. We don't do it too much."

When I ask Pua if she tells her children about her childhood experiences with Hawaiian spiritual things she replies simply "No."

"They wouldn't believe it?"

"Yeah. I guess they wouldn't—them. You see, my mother always told us that—if you believe in *kahuna*, you believe in Hawaiian—uh, Hawaiian legends and Hawaiian, you know, *kahuna* this and that. I mean, if, you know—you believe—'kay? But if you don't know and you do it—it don't harm you—'cause you don't know.

"Like say for an example—my grandmother always tell us not to sweep out of the house after dark. Bad luck.[15] So we don't. But my kids do. If they don't know, it won't hurt them right?"

Then Pua and I get into a long discussion of various Hawaiian superstitions, after which Pua concludes: "Be surprised all this things that we have to live through, so I try not to teach my kids. I mean it's good, to have them know because—like they said—the Hawaiians begin to becoming, you know, very few and then the legends and the Hawaiian ways are really getting less and less. We should pass it on to the kids but—that's why I feel, I feel if my kids don't know, you know, won't hurt them. Right? So if they don't know all this hocus-pocus, how can it hurt them. I don't even know how we got to hocus-pocus anyway."

Although Pua has purposely decided not to tell her children about her striking supernatural experiences or about Hawaiian superstitions, she does have firm beliefs that words and intent will return in kind, albeit sometimes with a little help from her own actions. As she stated earlier, "and we believe if you do anything to somebody, you know, anything bad, wish bad, it's gonna happen to you . . . if you do good to others. You know, good things come back to you." She is very clear and articulate as to how and why the comeback system works in a distinctly Hawaiian way.

---

[15] This was referred to by others as sweeping the good luck out of the house.

Not everyone has as clear an idea of retribution or reward from one's emotions, intent, or words. Iris Nakasone, married to Jack, a Japanese American, is a good example. When I ask her about retribution that affects the children rather than the adult who originated the negative emotions, intent, or words, she stumbles:

"It doesn't . . . well it depends on . . . I don't know. If you do something wrong, it might not fall on you but it might fall on, on your children. Some people, like if they do something really wrong against somebody, and it might not hit that person that do it . . . but it falls on their children."

"Why is that?" I ask.

"It's like punishment. If . . . like . . . say like God cannot punish you so put it on something else."

"Well, how come He doesn't do it directly to that person?"

"Well, like I don't know why. Sometimes . . . I don't know. It's a like saying: 'if it doesn't hit you and if it hits . . . and sometimes it hits your children and you wonder why or they're sick and you cannot find their own sickness . . . might be punishment.' That you did something wrong."

"Have you ever seen that happen?"

After a long pause, Iris says, "Not really."

Then she turned to her oldest daughter, who was in the same room, telling her to get ready for some extracurricular event. When I continued my questions, Iris interrupted me and asked when I was going back to the mainland, avoiding further discussion of the topic.

When I asked some months later about how Hawaiian she thought she was in her ways and beliefs, she said: "Somewhat. 'Cuz when I hear sometimes, sometimes I believe in those *kahuna* stories. Well, sometimes when you think about it . . . things . . . and then you remember, happen and then you believe it, you know." She would not elaborate.

Like Pua, Iris also incorporates the idea of comeback in a secular way by using personal retaliation. Iris talks a lot about work. During this particular visit with her, she had spent considerable time telling me of the hassles she had been having at work with some new, young workers who had been flagrantly goofing off by taking long breaks, smoking *pakalōlō* (marijuana), and talking on the telephone for hours. She says that they are the daughters of people in management so they get preferential treatment—unlike Iris. For example, when Iris stayed home sick with a fever, the boss sent over a nurse to check on her, not believing she was sick. The nurse came, took her temperature, confirmed that she had the flu, and urged her to stay home and in bed. This diagnosis irritated Iris even more as she noted that, of course, she had already consulted her own doctor who told her the same thing: she had the flu and should stay in bed. Then the boss disregarded the nurse's report and said that Iris was able to come to work. Iris was outraged, thinking the nurse had given her boss a false report. She called the nurse. The nurse denied telling the boss that Iris was not sick. So Iris then called her boss and confronted her with this falsehood, and her boss backed down, allowing Iris to stay home on sick leave. Iris then said to me, "It'll blow back on her," meaning this incident and the sickness would return to her boss in some way. The second thing was a bit more direct. Iris told her boss to "Kiss my Royal Hawaiian" and warned her not to walk in front of her car or she would run her over.

In spite of Iris's disavowals about understanding the comeback system, unlike Pua, she teaches her children about it as a specifically Hawaiian system. When I asked her what it meant when someone criticized another person's children and then that person said, "Look to your own kids, first," Iris explained that you should criticize yourself before criticizing others. Further, she tells her children never to tease or criticize Hawaiians because they could curse them. It might happen to them now or maybe not until they have children or they have grandchildren. She told me that the old Hawaiians could place a curse. She tells her children to be careful because they do not know if another child who they teased or criticized will go home and tell a parent. That parent may be able to put a curse on you by asking your name and saying it in "prayers"—to whom is unclear.

In this same conversation, Iris also agreed that one should not criticize others while one was pregnant: "Yeah, your kid will come like that," explaining that whatever trait you criticized would reappear in your offspring. Again, she echoes the reflective relationship between the consequences of negative maternal talk and the birth of a child. It is significant that Iris socializes her children to this Hawaiian system because it shows how this cultural system is passed on.

That this Hawaiian system is internalized as well as taught is illustrated by a discussion I had with Nohi and the interruptions made by her irrepressible 12-year-old granddaughter, Kalena, whom Nohi had adopted when 10. While discussing criticism and in the middle of a story of how she kept Kalena out of karate class because some of the other children were teasing her about her healing chicken pox scabs, Nohi explained:

"So yesterday, somebody tease her because she get little bit marks and she came tell me that, you know. Uh, who and who wen' tease her. I said,

'What Grandma say, what everybody tell—go right back to them. You know what you do? You go buy something and you stay with Grandpa. In the car.' And she went. 'At don't bother me. I don't talk about it. [The other children ask] 'Oh, how come Kalena don't come to practice?' [Nohi tells them] 'No. She not feeling too good today. She's going with her grandpa.' Because you know me. I not going make just like I proud. I feel, yeah? God give this kind, you know, sickness, you can't help it. The only way you can do—ask God to help cure. So I jus' wen' tell her, 'Go with Grandpa.' That's what they going tell me, 'Oh, how come Kalena no practice?' 'Oh, went with her grandpa.' "

Kalena, who had been listening, standing by the side of the table at which Nohi and I were sitting, interrupted her grandmother: "They know I get the chicken pox, then why they ask?"

"Never mind!" shouted Nohi angrily at Kalena. "You know what hurts is when you tease. That's no good, you know. Never, never tease." Nohi then gave several examples of how some elderly people walk funny and the children in the housing project tease them. Nohi described how she sternly admonished the children.

In the last example of several, she is scolding a laughing boy who is making fun of an elderly woman's walk, "She run-like, you know."

Nohi explains: "I say, 'Ey kid. Wise up, eh?' Tell, 'Wise up. Why, you like come like that? If you like come like that, you get, you know.'

"[The boy] Say, 'Shaddup!' Go inside karate." Nohi laughs.

"I scold him," she continues, "I no like tease anybody like that. Um, never."

I ask, "Is it—something can happen to you if you tease?"

Kalena pipes up: "Um hum! Just like me. That's how I got the chicken pox. I tease the boy down there," and she gives a little laugh, "Hee."

"Yeah?" I question her.

"Get the chicken pox on his back," says Kalena.

"And you teased him?" I inquire.

"Yeah, he say, he get chicken pox and the other day when I was over there, that was how I get the chicken pox."

Nohi, irritated by her granddaughter's interruption, tells her to go outside and play. Nevertheless, this discussion shows how a child understands the workings of this comeback system.

Nohi's firm convictions about the inevitability of retribution are evident in her warnings to her daughter Marissa about shoplifting. She includes an interesting cultural spin on an old American saying. She explains what she said to Marissa, " 'If you, you know, shoplift, that's one thing I no like.'

"That's what I went tell her. Tell her, 'You went just take care yourself and no think of shoplifting because you don't have to. Only for silly things. No, no, no, the kind.

" 'You can have lots of things but just that you, you no like make an effort. You know. Everything you go—go, go, go; partner [with her boyfriend, Russell]; go all around. Ah, shit. Forget it.

" 'But you. You never realize that. But the time going come for you. Time, yeah? Going be too late.' I tell her that.

"Just like, I always tell her this: 'Every dog get their day.' Same like the human being. If you no like listen now, fine."

I ask, "Just like you said? It always comes back to you?"

"Always come back," affirms Nohi.[16]

Earlier, Nohi referred to this explicitly as "revenge. Revenge-like." Or as termed in this chapter's title, there is "comeback" for those who transgress social and cultural mores.

---

[16] Evelyn used a similar transformation of the ironic American saying "Every dog has his day." Evelyn says, "Every dog get his dues," but she is also referring to the inescapable Hawaiian fact of retribution for transgressions.

[3]

"My Heart Is in My Friend":
The Ties That Define

In the previous chapter, Hawaiians spoke about how things will "come back." *Aloha*, goodwill, good intentions, and openness to others will strengthen and extend one's social relationships, making them the bountiful conduits of positive returns. Negative thoughts, behaviors, or words will tangle one's social relations, closing them to positive exchanges, capturing individuals and their associates in the escalating entanglements of hostile emotions and intent, negative meanings, and the retaliatory behavior called *hihia*. In this chapter, I discuss Hawaiian concepts of self, person, and individual, all of which have similar themes of openness and constraint, etiquette and breaches, and the importance of intent.[1] But first, self, person, and individual must be defined.

The three constructs of self, person, and individual are rarely investigated as discrete units within a single culture. The investigation of self and person has enjoyed a resurgence among anthropologists and cross-cultural psychologists (Becker 1995; Burridge 1979; Carrithers, Collins, and Lukes 1985; Heelas and Lock 1981; Kirkpatrick 1983; Kondo 1990; Lee 1982; MacCormick and Strathern 1980; Marsella, DeVos, and Hsu 1985; Ortner and Whitehead 1981; Rosaldo 1980, 1983; Shweder and LeVine 1984; White and Kirkpatrick 1985; Wierzbicka 1993; Wikan 1990, 1995). In contrast, little has been produced on the cross-cultural nature of individuality except for early classic theoretical works on the individual (Goodman 1967; Kardiner 1939; Lee 1959), although life history works in the culture and personality style on the individual still do

---

[1] Portions of this chapter appeared in different forms in Ito 1985b and 1987.

appear (Beck 1992; Behar 1993; Crapanzano 1980; Cruikshank 1990; Freeman 1984, 1989; Kennedy 1977; Nash 1992; Rodgers 1995; Shostak 1983). With the exception of that of Freeman (1989), these studies focus on the extraordinary rather than the representative individual—those who expose cultural boundaries by violating or expanding them.

A major problem with the use of the constructs of self, person, and individual is the lack of any standard definition. Further, these constructs often are confounded by differences between anthropologists trained in social or psychological theory. "Self," "person," and "individual" often are used interchangeably or without definition (see, for example, Geertz 1984; Lee 1982; Levy 1983; Rosaldo 1980). The conflating of self and person has been criticized by Melford E. Spiro (1993), Unni Wikan (1995), and Anna Wierzbicka (1993). Sometimes, as in Renato Rosaldo's works (1980, 1984), the terms "self" and "person" appear to be purposely interchanged in order to blur Western assumptions about non-Western concepts of self and individuality, perhaps to make "them" more like "us." Other scholars assume that their readers are familiar with Marcel Mauss's social evolutionary trajectory from the elementary "tribal" form of *personnage* (social and ritual roles) to the complex Western *personne* (person) which expresses an individual's juridical and moral rights in fulfilling those roles. In this schema, self encompasses the pan-human ideas of consciousness and reason ("self knowledge and psychological consciousness" [Mauss 1985:20]). The self is common to all, whereas the individual is a specialized development of being a Western person. According to Mauss, non-Western selves do not yet have notions of individual or person. While there are incipient tendencies, they are for the most part bound by clan membership, rank, and other social, collective roles.

Most recently, these terms, confounding Mauss's definitions, have been used to establish an opposition between broadly defined, non-Western sociocentric, interpersonal worldviews (self-as-person) and Western egocentric, individualistic ones (self-as-individual). "Self-as-person" is frequently contrasted to "self-as-individual" to distinguish between the collective, sociocentric "public" self-concepts of non-Western groups and the individualistic, egocentric "private" self-concepts of the Western tradition (Dumont 1970; Fortes 1973; Levy 1983; Middleton 1973; Read 1955; Rosaldo 1980:262, 1984; Shweder and Bourne 1982). This dichotomization results in the neglect of important non-Western dimensions of individuality as well as Western concepts of a sociocentric self as aptly pointed out by Spiro (1993). It obscures both the importance in non-Western groups of marking or characterizing other group members (as

[77]

well as oneself) with unique, individual, personal characteristics[2] and Western ideas of collective behavior and symbolic interaction which recognize the social embeddedness of Western individuals.[3] This distinction threatens to establish another implicit "primitive"-"civilized" dichotomy.

Obviously, two major problems with the use of the constructs self, person, and individual are the lack of any standard definitions and therefore the reduced possibility for uniform cross-cultural comparisons. The first problem suffers the added complexities of the historical developments of two different traditions in anthropology, the psychological and the social. The social anthropology tradition was strongly influenced by Emile Durkheim's ideas of undifferentiated society and members' related "collective consciousness" and complex society members becoming a "social person." "In other words, the self is a social product and reflects its social origins" (Ito 1987:48). Psychological anthropology, called "Culture and Personality" in its early days, immersed in personality studies and heavily influenced by Freudian theory, did not develop this concept beyond A. Irving Hallowell's work in the 1950s on the self and Paul Radin's earlier work on the ego (Fogelson 1982). It was not until the 1970s that anthropologists again began to focus on the self and person. Several early contributions were by social anthropologists (Fortes 1959, 1973; Dieterlen 1973). Interest in the reflexive nature of fieldwork has led to the discussion of the ethnographic creation of a cultural other (Crapanzano 1977; Dwyer 1977; Rabinow 1977; Reisman 1977) and concern about the other as self (Fogelson 1982; Kapferer 1979; Meyers 1979; Straus 1977, 1981; Wagner 1981). Thomas J. Csordas' 1994 work is an excellent, concise review of the developments of the constructs of self and person in psychological anthropology.

In the literature, there are implicit distinctions between the three constructs that can be made explicit. First, self has a reflexive quality, the ability to distinguish, evaluate, and objectify self and other, and a dynamic quality, the apperceptive ability to understand, interpret, manipu-

---

[2] For example, see Lienhart's 1985 discussion of the importance of the Yoruba (as well as other African cultures') "idea of a hidden, private self" that has been obscured by the preeminence of studies on the social self. Also Smith 1981 notes that while Maori believed that one had little control over one's destiny, there were plenty of outlets for individual accomplishments and identification. She insightfully notes a cultural prototype in the case of the Polynesian trickster god, Maui, "an impetuous, mischievous, daring, clever and generally successful rule-breaker." See also Fogelson 1982.

[3] Studies on ethnic identity do not directly address the constructs of self or person, but it is a specialized cultural form of both, e.g., DeVos and Romanucci-Ross 1995; Epstein 1979; Fischer 1986; and Keyes 1981. Thank you to A. L. Epstein for this insight.

late, and incorporate sensory judgments. Self is both the executor and object of evaluations, discriminations, creativity, and order. The classic Jamesian definition of the self is composed of the "me," which encompasses the material, social, and spiritual selves ("the self as known") and the "I" or ("the self as knower") (Spiro 1993). Shweder (1985:195) refers to the "I" as "the observing ego," "It is the 'I' that looks out at the work and out at the 'me' in the mirror . . . " Second, person is defined by a moral, legal status of maturity. Depending on the culture, it can be ontologically developed, learned, or achieved. As a person, one has certain culture-specific juridical rights and moral responsibilities. Finally, the individual is distinguished by unique traits such as various elements of personal identity, history and accomplishments, specialized attributes, talents, and descent, or a characteristic style or temperament that distinguishes one from other individuals. While traits such as these may or may not be central, or even important, in a particular culture, markers for individuality do exist in every culture.[4]

The second point, that studies on any one of these concepts should attempt to consider or to distinguish all three concepts, present a problem since rarely do these concepts exist as discretely separable in situ. To compartmentalize self, person, and individual may (more likely than not) violate their cultural integrity, but to investigate only one or two of them to the exclusion of the other(s) can lead to faulty conclusions or erroneous cross-cultural generalizations. Granted, cross-cultural generalizations are not at the forefront of the current ethnocultural examinations in a deconstructionist era but anthropologists must be committed to present not only a valid understanding of individual cultures but of the human culture as well. How is it that in spite of conceptual, linguistic, historical, and social differences, we can recognize each other's humanity and communicate with each other on some level? Anthropology is the one discipline that has both the scope and the specificity to answer the question of how we humans can be so very much the same yet remain so different.

Hawaiian Self

What is meant by "self" is not only the "me" element of self-identifiers but the reflexive component of consciousness, seeing one's self as both an

---

[4] For example, compare Levy 1983, Read 1955, and Geertz 1973: 360–61 for discussions of the nature of individuality in groups defined as primarily sociocentric.

object and a subject, both understanding the structural elements of who one is and the ability to see one's self as others do, as they might do, or as one imagines they do. It is a judgmental process of evaluation, change, and confrontation which occurs both internally in one's mind and externally in one's interactions with others and with one's physical environment. It is a reflexive process "of interaction between the I and me, and not merely a summation of the two aspects" (Meltzer, Petras, and Reynolds 1975:63). In this symbolic interactionist approach, the self is a processual product of an individual's internal psychological environment and external social and physical environment. The internal and the external environments, like the I and me of the self, however, are not dichotomized into two but thought to be part of a unitary "field" of "life space" as Kurt Lewin terms it.[5] The creative, impulsive "I" interacts constantly with the conventional, socialized "me" to function as an ever-evolving self, which in turn exists in and interacts within a social community of shared attitudes and meaning.

The Hawaiian concept of self is grounded in affective social relations.[6] The structure and dynamics of interpersonal relations are provided by the interpersonal network linking individuals and the emotional tenor of those relationships. Therefore, the Hawaiian self is tied to the quality and quantity of one's interpersonal relationships. Not only are the bonds of emotional affect the ties that support and protect each member, but they define one. One's affect with others illuminates both self and other.

[5] Wierzbicka 1993 and Wikan 1995 have challenged the study of "self" as "Anglo-centric" because it is a word peculiar to English. As Wierzbicka notes, however, "I" does exist cross-culturally, and Wikan struggles to present a well-defined vision of a more narrow "self" as represented by self-experience (the "I" of "private knowledge and assessment"), self-construction ("the work . . . to cultivate and defend . . . aspects of their own self"), self-representation ("the templates by which they conceptualize and know themselves and others"), and self-representation ("accounts of themselves they seek to communicate to . . . others") (1995: 266, 287). Their definitions still seem to support the self as classically defined by James's "me" or material, spiritual, and social self and the "I" of reflection and reflexivity.

[6] The consideration of Hawaiian ethnic identity would be appropriate under the concept of self, but it is developed in interaction with non-Hawaiian others. What is of concern here is how Hawaiians develop cultural constructs of self vis-à-vis each other, not with outsiders. The topic of ethnic identity in a multicultural place like Hawai'i, which resonates with postcolonial issues of nationalism, tourism, and commercially constructed images, and the American ethnic matrix itself would require another book. In addition, the acceptance and spread of the Hawaiian Cultural Renaissance and the current sovereignty movements have greatly altered Hawaiian ethnic identity since this research was initially conducted. See, for example, the discussion in the introduction of the change of the usage of the terms Hawaiian and part-Hawaiian.

The linking dynamic of these self-other social relations is the recipro-cal exchange of emotions. Anthropologists, of course, recognize reci-procity and exchange as important for the establishment and perpetua-tion of social relations, but they have focused on material and pragmatic exchanges and obligations. Exchanges of people, food, service, or cere-mony can establish an obligation that perpetuates a cycle of reciprocity. For Hawaiians, these bonds of reciprocity and exchange extend to emo-tional exchanges between the self and other (see also Howard 1974:207). Self and other are linked by the emotional nature of one's interpersonal relationships.

The quality of these relationships is denoted by four primary emo-tional complexes which I derived from participant observation and ethnographic interviews about emotions and self-other concepts. The first is a cultural self-ideal glossed by the word *aloha*. Someone with *aloha* is an expansive, giving person of generosity, love, sympathy, hospi-tality, a person with "heart," a person of *na'au*. The imagery is of one who reaches out to others. The second is a cultural failing exhibited by a small, retentive character, glossed here by the words for jealousy (*lili*) and stingy (*pī* or *manini*). Here the imagery is of one who is grasping and closed to others, one who holds back his or her affections and resources in a tight, miserly manner and who covets and envies the affection and material resources of others. The third is a shame-guilt complex one ex-periences when there is a cultural failing of one's *aloha* spirit. This failing is directed internally at one's self. The fourth is a hurt-anger complex, which is directed externally at the other. All are part of Hawaiian emo-tional exchanges that define self and other.

The themes of *aloha* gestures, *lili* or *manini* failures, the shame (*hi-lahila*) and guilt of these personal failures, and the expression of hurt and consequent anger as important elements of self-knowledge, self-repre-sentation, and reflection were constant and favorite topics of extensive talk story sessions with lady friends and their families although no one used such academic terms as "the self as known (me) and knower (I)," the importance of these emotional complexes to the Hawaiian self was eloquently expressed again and again, as will be evidenced in the ex-cerpted passages from these talk story sessions.

Aloha and Lili

The ideal Hawaiian self is characterized by *aloha*. While the word *aloha* has developed a trite familiarity in the minds of many tourists and would-be tourists to Hawai'i, for Hawaiians it still has rich connotations of grace, kindness, and love.

When Ellen said, "Like if I going to do a favor for you, . . . I going to do it because my heart is in my friend," she was expressing an important element of the Hawaiian cultural self—extending herself so fully to another that she placed her very being, her *na'au*, in that friend. This characteristic is an important element in the Hawaiian self: it indicates a freely giving person of generosity, empathy, love, and hospitalty.[7]

Someone of *aloha* reaches out to others, is expansive and inclusive, a giver of largess and empathy. He or she enjoys having others drop by for a visit just to talk story, "stay for eat," and sleep over. It is a form of interpersonal self-validation that others gravitate toward you and feel welcome and comfortable in your presence.

An often stated sign of someone who is "real Hawaiian-style" is one who immediately calls out to you as you approach the house saying, "Come! Come eat." (In Hawaiian, the words are *Mai! Mai e 'ai*. Another version is *He mai! Mai, mai*. [Welcome! Come, come.]) This welcoming call is traditionally known as a *heahea* (Handy and Pukui 1972:172). Junie describes her brothers as being "Hawaiian-style" in their musical preference (popular, modern Hawaiian music), lifestyle (defined in terms of food: "you know, raw fish and *poi* and stuffs like that"), and hospitality: "They make you feel at home, you know. If they see you, 'Come in,' you know, Hawaiian-style, 'Come eat, whatever we have.' Share food, like that." Ellen also defines someone as being Hawaiian in terms of the call "*Mai, mai!*" which she explains as meaning. "When they tell you, 'Come,' you know. They real that, uh, friendly people: 'Come inside!' Even though you don't know them, you know." This last sentence expresses the ultimate in hospitality, the transformation of a stranger into a friend through a sharing of one's self and one's goods (see also Kanahele 1985:477).

---

[7] Newton distinguishes altruistic *aloha* ("without egoism or . . . any thoughts for personal gain") from "non-altruistic *aloha*," which is "cooperation and good fellowship" and reciprocity is expected (1978: 88–89). Reciprocity is defined in terms of peer group friendships, sports, gambling, sharing, lending, and food distribution. He notes that nonaltruistic *aloha* brings as "much potential for social conflict as there is for social union" (1978: 92). In spite of this distinction, Newton's dissertation is concerned with the types and causes of hostility rather than *aloha*. While it appears that unfulfilled reciprocal expectations are the overall cause, he does not discuss hostility in specific terms of nonaltruistic *aloha* but with variables such as social hierarchy, economics, insults, and enmity. In my own research, nonaltruistic *aloha* is an oxymoron because *aloha* must be done without regard to what one can expect in the future. Still, recipients of *aloha* feel the need to reciprocate and if thwarted can become angry.

Evelyn gives an extended explanation of this *aloha* hospitality spirit and the modern laxity of its expression. She ends with the importance of sincerity of "heart."

"They going come to the door [and call a welcoming greeting to passersby]: 'Hoo-eee!' 'Cause Hawaiians before—when you travel—you not suppose to go sit on the side of the road 'till you half dead and somebody's suppose to call you for come in. When you see them—whether or not you know them—you're suppose to invite them in. That's the old Hawaiian style. They give you whatever they have. Now days you hardly find that. They don't invite you. 'Oh, you like eat?' " she states with a sarcastically disingenuous tone. "Sometimes, he's even eating and you sitting over there as one friend—they not going invite you eat. I don't know if you've ever run across families like that but I've seen families like that."

Then Evelyn goes on to use her mother as an example of the generous, sharing Hawaiian with an open house and a ready meal no matter how meager. As she had said earlier, their house was like the Grand Central Station, with her mother feeding all the friends of her children in shifts. The watchword was sharing.

"My [mother's] house, whenever my girlfriends came, my mother always make for everybody. I no can eat if my friend no eating and me, if I one candy, I gotta break one in ten million pieces for all of us. That's how my mother is. And if only get one doughnut—going cut 'em up or nobody going get it. You see? If no more for all—well, nobody get.

"But like in the old days, like I say—when they come and used to be some people, eh? Say, 'Come! Come eat.' Then, when you eat—let's say you was traveling for three days without eating and you going eat plenty. And then they complain after you leave: '*Wow*! You see how much he wen' eat! Now we going starve for two days!' You know the kind? And they no think.

"You open your house—that's for eat—no complain. If the person is taking advantage, that's another thing but if they're starvin' you not going tell, 'Oh. Come, Karen. Come eat.' And after you go: 'Wow. Man, next time I not going invite her eat.' But next time [they will say], 'Oh, hi, Karen. You like come . . . ?' You know, this kind stuff. You know, it's only the front that.

"So they tell you do it from your heart or don't do it at all."

Again, the proper behavior or words are not enough for an *aloha* self. Motivation and sincerity are central factors that are evaluated.

When Hawaiians interact with others they evaluate themselves and others in terms of the emotional quality of these social relationships

[83]

(which include both people and the physical and spiritual environments). The ideal is to express one's *aloha* self and be thought of as friendly, open, or warm rather than jealous, stingy, or cold. The expression of either of these dimensions of self requires the engagement of another. One cannot give or take, release or covet, grant or withhold without the involvement of others.

For example, Pua's discussion in the last chapter about a lady friend's coldness and jealousy combines many of these reciprocal, interactive, evaluative elements. Pua discussed in more detail this friend's retentive, competitive, and self-destructive jealousies, as well as Pua's and another friend's attempts to support and draw her out to accept their friendship.

This woman is part of a friendship among three couples. Pua describes the three women as being "like bread and jelly" and further demonstrates this closeness by taking her spread-apart three fingers and drawing them tightly together so there is no space in-between. The men also are close. But Pua detailed in a long discussion the nature of the friendship with the less than agreeable woman of the trio, in which Pua generally complained about her lady friend's inability to tell the other two friends when she does not have enough money to participate in some 'social gathering or, if she does participate, how she tries to bring too much or too costly food or drink. She comments:

" 'Kay. To me a friend is—when you in need—talk it over with us, you know. When you in want, tell us. But don't only tell us things like, oh, when you have plenty money. Or you know like, this one, she usually spends more than the other, the both, me and this other lady friend together . . . 'cause we know she needs—financial help but she still wants us to think that she has everything. I feel that, you know, you should share, you know, if you figure that you're real good friends and sharing means, uh, not being ashamed of telling your friends, ' 'Ey, I'm broke.' . . . If we have enough for everybody, that's it. If we don't have, we don't have . . .

"So me and this other friend of ours keep talking, 'Why she did things like that?' You know. I mean we don't have fabulous things. We don't have rip-roaring parties where, you know, you know where you just— whatever we have, we open a can of corned beef or a few cans of Vienna Sausages or whatever. Whatever you have but—it seems that whenever she comes she wants to buy a, a quart of Kahlua and you know. Or a half gallon of vodka, a case of beer. She wants to be so, you know. I say, 'Hey. If we have, we have, that's all.' But to me friends should be more open. They just—that's the one friend that we want her to spill out some things, you know. Don't try to act like, you know—sometimes we feel like she act like she better than us." Pua then discussed this woman's frequent trips to the hairdresser and excessive indulgences in pastries and soda for her children.

Pua has used the word "act" to describe actions that are viewed as putting on a show or display for public consumption despite the others' attempts to encourage her to be honest and open with them. There is a Hawaiian pidgin phrase, "No act!" which is an admonition to discourage or ridicule overdrawn, attention-getting behavior. The behavior is interpreted as overblown, insincere, or calculated.

I ask Pua about their desire for the woman friend to open up to them, to "spill out some things": "I know that some people feel that to keep things bottled up inside of them, more worse, eh?"

Pua explains: "To me I think it's worse. Because, even my husband has noticed. You know, she hides so much of this thing, she hold 'em in, eh? She getting so skinny, it's like, uh, her nerves and everything. Really." This is the same friend Pua described earlier as "something eating away at her, like cancer. Eating up her—heart. She really—cold."

Pua associates "holding things in" (retention) or a lack of openness and trust in others with becoming skinny, the physical, bodily evidence of an emotional state or self-presentation, an external confirmation of an internal state. Further, retention is associated with a coldness of personality.

Pua continues, "She's—"

"[It is] working on her?" I interrupt.

"Yeah, it's working so bad—honest truth—it's working so bad, she actually jealous of her husband coming here and talking to my other friend and I. Because he told us. Now he's friends with my husband, this other lady's husband, and he opens up to them and to them that's how they feel what friends are, you know."

The husband is contrasted with his wife as someone who "opens up." He is willing to expose his frailties and vulnerabilities to his friends. He extends himself, trusting in their empathetic support.

Now that Pua and her other lady friend are aware of their friend's jealousies, they are reluctant to joke with the husband or to sit by him.

"But as much as possible," explains Pua, "we try not to even sit by him. I mean, it don't make no difference if she sit by my husband. All to me, it's friends are friends, eh? But if we sit by him, she'll find a way to nibble her way in. Yeah. She'll find a way to nibble her way in-between."

The use of the word "nibble" gives a contrastive picture of small, furtive behavior in comparison to Pua's egalitarian, big-hearted depiction of "it don't make no difference . . . it's friends are friends, eh?"

Because of this lady friend's bad behavior, the other two men are thinking of ending the friendship with her husband. This example illustrates how family members bear the burdens of the transgressions of other members.

"We love her husband so much; he's so nice. And my husband hate to break his friendship. But it's getting to the point that our husbands realize that if it's going to have to be, it's going to have to be because they can't take much more of this lady. Already. And all she have to do is open up and say, you know: 'Yes, I don't have,' or 'Yes, I cannot go because—' But every week she's worse."

Again, there is the desire for a confessional trusting, a willingness to be open rather than closed. This dialogue is complex. First, jealousy is associated with competition and rivalry: the overbuying, the personal indulgences of herself and her children. "It's jealousy mixed with pride."

There is a familiar saying about Hawaiians' jealous, competitive nature as being like the behavior of crabs scrambling in a bucket. This behavior is explained by Evelyn and her cousin Bradley.

"Like many times, Hawaiians, you know, they used to be jealous. They're really a jealous people. And that's how come they have that expression, see Hawaiians never get ahead. 'Cause when one try get ahead, they make jealous. They may push down, whatever, fall down. So nobody get ahead. Everybody stay in the same pit—together."

Bradley interrupts, "Like the crab in the bucket."

Evelyn explains, "The example of the *'a'ama* crab: one it try to climb out of the bucket, but everybody pull 'em down. So never really—"

"The crab trying to get out of the bucket, grab 'em down," interjects Bradley.

"So it's like jealousy?" I ask.

"Through jealousy," confirms Evelyn. "Hawaiians have to move together, eh? But if you think you're better, they look at you like, 'Gee, who you think you are?' "

"So it's both a good thing and a bad thing," I state.

"It is," responds Evelyn.

I start to restate, "They all want everybody to benefit and they also—"

Evelyn interrupts me: "If it benefits everybody—the Hawaiians all work together but if it don't—forget it. Because the Hawaiian, they're very—the family, the *'ohana* is very tight. It's very close-knit. That's how come, you know, families, many families—like my girlfriend. The mother is pure Hawaiian, the father is Spanish. Now, when they get *ho'opono-pono* [a discussion format to resolve conflict], something wrong, if one cry—all cry. That's how close they are. It if effects one: a-a-l-l-l. Effects everybody—everybody gets involved.

"And not like some families, they only close to talk. This one, they really feel. They really care. You know this is the real feelings that come out. But some don't. See, but that expression, that you know, Hawaiians, eh? Many Hawaiians used to go against their own. Saying is: '*Kanaka 'ai kanaka e.*' "

"What is that?" I ask.

" 'Hawaiians eat Hawaiian.' That's why when 'alligator-head' you keep putting me down and all kinds stuff or you going make Hawaiian seed [*sic*] for me so I no can get ahead. 'Cause you no like see me get ahead."

Later, Evelyn is more explicit: "If I can't have, nobody will have."

With this last remark, Evelyn summarizes the destructive element of *lili*. This is comparable to Evelyn's earlier example of sharing a single doughnut even if it means cutting it into small pieces: "If no more for all—well nobody get." This statement illustrates the interrelationships, the reflexive qualities of *aloha* and *lili*. Both have elements of the generative and destructive because they represent the positive and negative aspects of the spirit of Hawaiian self.

Second, Pua associates her friend's emotional retention with bodily indicators. The woman's need to act superior, her holding back of herself from her friends, and her jealousies are tied by Pua to the conclusion that she is being eaten away by her agitated nerves, like a cancer, the price to pay for such withholding and competition. The evidence is her increasing thinness.

Physical size and bulk is a favored state for Hawaiians. It is symbolic of a good, open life, of someone of substance, of largess.[8] This is evidenced by hearty appetites. When Iris asks her Japanese American husband, Jack, to help give examples about her brothers' "Hawaiian ways," he jokes, "Hawaiian ways, only for eat." Iris roars agreement.

Physical bulk is seen as vital and sexually attractive. Ka'ahumanu, Kamehameha I's favorite wife, was six feet tall, politically powerful in her own right, ample in girth, and considered beautiful by Hawaiians and Westerners alike (see, for example, Vancouver 1798). Mary K. Pukui, E. W.

[8] This traditional Polynesian value of the large figure is well known. Shore 1989 and Sahlins 1981 note the association of *ali'i* (royal) *mana* with amplitude, "abundance," and "corpulence." This prized amplitude has led to serious modern health problems related to obesity such as high blood pressure and diabetes.

Haertig, and Catherine A. Lee cite various accounts about the attractiveness of amplitude: "An ideally beautiful women [*sic*] had 'a face as round and full as the moon.' An early description of a king's daughter read, 'she was not very big, *but* she had pretty features. Royalty might be as fat as Princess Ruth who was known to eat 13 *haupia* [coconut custard] pies at one sitting. Mothers worried when their daughters were thin and gave them medicine to fatten them up" (1972:7). Pua spoke disdainfully of her husband's earlier "skinny" state, approving of his current more rotund condition. At an evening gab fest with Evelyn and two other Hawaiian lady friends, we got on the subject of physical attractiveness. Two of the ladies were full-sized but confidently attractive. The third would be considered to have a striking figure on the mainland, being slender through the hips, tall, long-legged, and full-breasted with a very pretty face. Nevertheless, she bemoaned her "skinny" state, telling me that when the three of them were in high school she tried everything to gain weight including a then-popular diet supplement called "Weight-On." She was ridiculed and called "Stick." The other two nodded and agreed, adding some more teasing for good measure. The woman was still depressed about her slender "shape," slumping in her chair as she finished her tale of woe. Because I was thin, Hawaiians always thought I was ill and frail. Ellen would worry that I would blow away in a stiff wind, fussing over me whenever we were standing outside in blustery weather. One time, Evelyn gave me the "once-over" and said that men do not like women who are skinny; they like "something to get ahold of." She swayed her generous hips seductively, batted her eyelashes teasingly, and laughed a bawdy laugh. While I was doing research in the village of Miloli'i on the Big Island of Hawai'i, several ten-year-old Hawaiian girls sternly chided me for being skinny. They urged me to eat more: "How you going come like us?!" While all of these young Hawaiian girls were very thin, they nevertheless had a clear self-image that associated being full-bodied with being Hawaiian, "like us."

A robust body means a robust life: generous, strong, expansive, open, warm. A thin body means a thin life: stingy, weak, small, closed, cold. In contemporary slang, *manini* (stingy) also means small, undersized, inadequate, skinny.[9] Pua's lady friend's protracted *lili* and *manini* behavior is revealed in her increasing thinness.

---

[9] An explanatory cartoon appears in a local publication, *Pidgin to da Max*, in which a hefty woman with a small piece of cake is complaining to a slender woman, "Oooh! Dat Gerald so *rude!* Look da manini piece he wen geev me! Say he helping me *diet!*" (Simonson 1981). This cartoon wonderfully juxtaposes body types with the generosity (or lack thereof) of servings and hospitality.

Third, Pua constantly emphasizes the importance of openness. The key to restoration of the friendship is to be open, both a letting in and a letting go. This friend is afraid of being vulnerable, of opening up. She does not trust the others; she is closed to their attempts to *aloha* her.[10] Months before, Pua told me that sometimes she and her "good" lady friend talk about their "difficult" friend, qualifying, "We no talk stink," meaning they do not criticize or speak disparagingly about her; they just try to figure her out—and her motivation. Their theory is that her behavior stems from her terrible childhood. Pua explained that she was "like Cinderella," made to work hard while a child and given only scraps of food to eat. Now that she has found a husband who loves her, she is desperately afraid of losing him. Pua and her lady friend are confident that sooner or later this woman has to open up to them and tell them about her feelings: "She'll have to open up to us pretty soon." The consequences if she did not, which Pua outlined, were that she would lose their friendship, she would have a "nervous breakdown," she would lose her husband, and "other happenings" such as the poor health of her children. In other words, the self-destructive retribution for her antisocial behavior was clear and foreseeable. But the antidote was clear: "to open."

In Hawaiian pidgin, "to open" refers to the metaphoric release of things and is used in a variety of ways. It is important to keep one's emotional relationships "open," not to tangle them with distrust and thereby close options for emotional exchange. People say "the way is open" to indicate a condition in which one's plans will not meet any obstacles toward successful completion. This usually means that your emotional relationships are not blocked by negative social entanglements (*hihia*). There are historical Hawaiian examples of the importance of a clear emotional and spiritual path for any endeavor. Traditionally, "clearing the way prayers" were performed before any task was undertaken (Pukui, Haertig, and Lee 1979), and a "path-clearing ceremony" (*aha'aina māwaewae*) was held shortly after the arrival of a firstborn child to clear misfortune from life's way for this and subsequent children (Handy and Pukui 1972; Pukui, Haertig, and Lee 1979). This task-clearing procedure is still performed by Nohi, although less formally. She explained that before you embarked on a task or went to a meeting that you wanted to turn out well, you said a prayer. "You ask for the way to be open," gesturing with both her hands unfolding and opening wider and wider. You ask that no

---

[10] Rather than adding the infinitive prefix *ho-*to *aloha*, the colloquial or pidgin method is merely to place "to" in front of a word.

obstacles be put in your path; with that she placed her hands in a chopping vertical motion to indicate barriers in the previously cleared path.

These prayers and other activities such as *aha'aina māwaewae* and *ho'oponopono* were traditionally called *ho'okuakāhi*, to clear the way of obstacles or to free, as in "open" (Rocha n.d.; Pukui, Haertig, and Lee 1979:11–12, 130–31; Pukui and Elbert 1986).[11]

Nohi continues: "Once you leave, you never come back. Even if you forgot something; never come back. Just go."

I ask if turning and coming back would close the path.

"Yes! That's right. That's right."

Further, explains Nohi, "My mom always tell us, 'Never call in the back.'

"See, when you going out the door, right? And I say, 'Hey Karen! Come back, you forget the key!' My mother [said], 'Never [do that],' [she would] tell to us."

It is based on the belief that it is bad luck to call someone back once he or she has started to leave (Handy and Pukui 1972:186). It is not clear if the call back is considered a warning or omen that the "way" is not clear of obstacles, if the return entangles the good intentions and blocks success, or both.

In a second example, she explains the possible problems that could occur if you did return, either on your own or because of a call to do so.

"Where you going not going be good. Going be even worse for you. Uh, uh, you know, I mean the problems. Maybe the car not going start, no can start. Or maybe your thinking going be wrong. Can be that too. Can be lots of things."

Evelyn said earlier, "Okay, if you open up and he admit to me," referring to a confessional release of one's true intent. To "cut" or *'oki* the precognitive power of an unsettling dream, one "opens" or tells the dream to the first person one sees upon waking, releasing the negative emotions associated with the dream.[12] People say they "open" their clothes or slip-

---

[11] The "disentangling" sessions of A'ara of the Solomon Islands serve a similar function to "clear blocked" relations and emotions between people (White 1990), as does the Samoan *fono* (Duranti 1981, 1984, 1990), which uses the metaphoric image of "clearing or cutting the grass and weeds (bush)" for the words and acts of the *fono* "to put in order" or the "straightening up" of social relations entangled by conflicts or transgressions (Duranti 1990: 467, 468).

[12] Pukui, Haertig, and Lee (1979: 245) interpret this *'oki*-ing as a guilt-lessening act for unconscious hostilities toward others as expressed in a dream. See also Bathgate 1990 and Pukui, Haertig, and Lee 1979 for a discussion of the types and significance of Hawaiian dreams.

pers, meaning to release them or take them off. To turn on an electrical appliance such as the lights or the television is to "open" them, releasing the current or images.[13]

Clearly, Pua wants her lady friend to release her emotions and be free and honest with her other two friends in a similar cathartic confessional as Evelyn's example with her cousin. In the meantime, Pua and her sympathetic friend remain "open" in their relationship with their Cinderella friend—available to provide her with support, love, and understanding.

Expression of an *aloha* self is not only a letting in, a willingness to let others "touch" you, but a letting go of the urge to retain goods or negative emotions. Rather than being "open," people who are jealous or stingy are likely to "hold on" to a negative feeling, to have an inability to "let it go" or yield, tangling their social relationships and leaving them vulnerable to retribution.[14] (The details of the type and mechanisms of this retribution will be explored in the next chapter.)

The element of jealous rivalry is apparent in the stubborn holding on for victory in some dispute, usually involving angry and hurt feelings. A person refuses to "let it go," hanging onto the knotted emotional blockage in the relationship, thereby constantly renewing the emotional hurt and anger of the original offense. Hawaiians often speak of the need to "let it go" in a long-standing argument (*hukihuki*) when an impasse is reached. *Hukihuki* means to pull back and forth as to argue back and forth. It is felt that "one side gotta give," or an innocent third party, usually a child, will be hurt. This ability to "let it go" and yield is seen as a distinctive Hawaiian characteristic, as Evelyn does when talking about *hukihuki* between two different cultural sides of a mixed marriage, fighting over the raising of the child:

"I'll tell you something. Any example I've ever known—like Hawaiian and Portagee [Portuguese] or Hawaiian and one other nationality—the Hawaiians will always yield."

[13] Linnekin 1985 cites the similar use in the rural town of Keʻanae, Maui, of the Hawaiian word *hemo* which she states originally meant only to loosen or unfasten but now is used for any act of opening, pulling free, or cutting. Pukui and Elbert 1986 define the current meaning of *hemo* as encompassing all these elements plus discharge, separate, to take off as clothes, or to be open as a store. In *Pidgin to Da Max, hemo* is listed as a pidgin word ("Hemo yo' shoes when you eenside da house!") and adds the phrase "hemo skin" to refer to peeling, sunburned skin. In my own fieldwork on the Big Island and on Oʻahu, I did not hear the use of *hemo*, but "open" was freely used. But I did not systematically inquire about the knowledge of *hemo*.

[14] Pukui, Haertig, and Lee (1972: 71) define *hoʻomauhala* as "to hold fast the fault. To continue to think about the offense."

[91]

I ask: "Why is that? Because of the child?"

"Well, because they know what's going on—Hawaiians. Most of the time, Hawaiians will yield."

"To save the child?" I ask again.

"To save the child. So no be friction. That—with the child or even how much they love. They going let them. They going let the father, you know, take 'em on that side."

She adds a bit later, "Because you love them you let 'em go."

The connection is between release, giving, and yielding—again being someone of *aloha*, not holding on to things or affections, giving to others—even what you love—not being possessive. In contrast, one who is retentive and self-centered is jealous of others' accomplishments and affections, withholding him or herself through the retention of his or her emotions and hospitality, holding on to the most petty of things, a grudge, or being unable to open up and accept another's gift of *aloha*.

To demonstrate one's generous, hospitable *aloha* nature, one must not only be able to give but to accept—thereby allowing others to express their *aloha* selves. For example, Pua had a hysterectomy a few years ago. While she was in the hospital, one of her lady friends and her husband took care of Pua's husband, Emery, and the Kahana children, having them over for dinner every night. Recently, this lady friend had to go into the hospital so Pua wanted to repay her by having her children stay with Pua and Emery and by feeding the children and husband dinner each night. The woman declined, saying, "No, that's okay, he [the husband] promised me that he'd stay home." Pua insisted. The woman explained that while she appreciated it, her husband had promised her and he was going to keep his promise. But Pua would not take no for an answer and insisted again. The woman indicated her appreciation for the offer but again explained that her husband had promised her and it was an issue between her and her husband.

Pua was infuriated and asked the woman what was the matter with her. Was she too good for them? Pua said she hoped they would never see them again and to forget about calling them ever again. The woman started to cry, but Pua was angry and told her, no, forget it, and hung up. Then later, Pua felt bad that she had said such things to her friend and called her. The woman was crying, and Pua said she was sorry that she had spoken to her so angrily. The woman again explained that it was all right but it was an issue between her and her husband and he had promised to stay home with the kids. Pua said yeah but she still should let them come over. In fact, the children did come over after the first day of the woman's stay in the hospital. Pua explained that the woman was jealous and did not like her husband to go anywhere she did not know about, which is why she had made him promise her he would stay home while she was confined in the hospital. Although Pua understood the woman's motive, she was outraged for other reasons. The first was that she wanted to repay this woman for her previous generosity in a like manner. Her friend was blocking Pua's attempts to *aloha* her and to express her *aloha* self. As Howard observed, "Ideally, in fact, all transactions are viewed as metaphoric displays of relationship affirmation. . . . In more abstract terms, it is social rather than material capital that is the center of attention and in which individuals are expected to invest. . . . Commodities are perceived as being primarily in the service of affirming old relationships and consolidating new ones." (1974:207). Second, by refusing her offer, the friend was rejecting Pua. Third, by denying the gift, she was placing herself above Pua, holding her forever in her debt. She was saying that Pua "was not good enough" or not in a position to reciprocate adequately. The friend was revealing her superior, competitive attitude. By her refusal of Pua's *aloha* hospitality, she was being *ho'okano*, or taking a haughty, superior attitude. Retentive, jealous individuals are seen as ones who cannot let others do anything for them. One who is unable to accept is thought to be unable to give (Pukui, Haertig, and Lee 1972:9; also see Mauss 1967).

Further, when the friend denied Pua the opportunity to reciprocate emotionally, the woman was left in a dangerously vulnerable state because emotional exchange links are not only of altruistic indebtedness but hostile, hurtful indebtedness as well. This dual quality of reciprocity is inherent in the Hawaiian word *pāna'i*, which means both to reward and to avenge, to "reciprocate, whether good or bad" (Pukui and Elbert 1986). Pua's anger and hurt left the woman open to possible misfortune, her social relationships no longer protective but endangering. (This concept will be detailed in the following chapter.)

Shame and Guilt

In spite of the ideal of an *aloha* self, it is not always something easy to be. One can succumb to the petty jealousies of envy and greed, generating feelings of shameful exposure and guilty transgression.

"Well," Junie sighs as she explains: "That's another problem too. I, myself get jealous. And when I find myself like that I gotta *really*, you know, ask God to get that feeling away. Jealous because, um, you know. I wanna

[93]

home so badly and I try to live an honest life and try to do things that's honest and yet—some people aren't that honest, you know. They do all kinds of things so they got so many beautiful things and, and I'm sitting over here thinking, 'What the hell am I doing? I don't have nothing. I can't get nothing.'

"And then you know, quick I catch myself and ask, 'Oh forgive me—'

"You know, 'Don't, don't let me think that way.' Then I get back on the right track again.

"So I think that jealousy is in everybody."

"I think they call it *lili*, huh?" I ask.

"Yeah. And I think everybody gets that little streak in them now and then."

"Um hum," I respond. "Sometimes it's the cause of a lot of trouble between people."

"Um hum," agrees Junie, "But—I'm not jealous whereas, um, you know some people get jealous and then like for instance, okay. Like for instance, okay. You. I'm jealous of you. There's some people, you know, call up your husband and say lie. You know. People tell all kinda lies. And that's, that's what happen to me. You know.

"People get *so* jealous of me and I have *nothing*. I've nothing. I've, you know, I only have *anything* that people should be jealous about. Yet they call over to my husband, tell my husband that I'm in the bar and I'm, I was seen with this guy, and that guy. And when we come home, we get big trouble! And he says, 'What the hell you doing down Kaneohe?[15] You know you was—'

" 'Kaneohe? I was down the church.'

" 'Don't lie. Somebody called.'

"But he don't tell me who called. And another time, I was s-s-someplace, I don't know where the heck I went. His auntie called. And told him that she seen me down this restaurant. And when I came home, my husband gave me a black eye. And then, I knew that they were so jealous that they just couldn't see us being happy. They can't, they can't see my husband doing all kinds of things to me, yet—I still—take good care of him, you know, I treat him good, you know. People can't see that. So they make trouble. And I'm glad that I don't have that kind of jealous [*sic*], you know. Where I'm gonna call somebody and tell them lies. I got the

---

[15] Although this Oʻahu city is properly spelled Kāneʻohe, June pronounced it without the stressed *a* or the glottal stop so I have transcribed it as she said it.

kind jealousy that, I wanna house and I wanna be like s-s-somebody else. I want this, I want that. But not the kind jealousy where I'd make trouble with anybody. So I do. I do get jealous sometimes. Some people having *so* much, you know. And other people don't have anything. But other than that—I've never had any trouble, you know, with myself, I mean being jealous with anybody."

Junie movingly, if plaintively, is explaining not only the desirous element of *lili* but her embarrassed feelings of exposure of her failure to be someone of *aloha*. She has committed a transgression, violating Hawaiian proper behavior (*hana pono*). Junie's discussion of her jealousy and covetousness indicates that she is both ashamed of her less than ideal behavior and guilty about her transgression of *aloha*. Therefore, she asks forgiveness, in this case, from God.

Shame and guilt are extreme forms of self-consciousness (Epstein 1984). In addition, shame involves identifying with the other as a spectator viewing one's exposure of a failure to attain or maintain an ego ideal (Epstein 1984, Lebra 1983). As Thomas J. Scheff vividly explains: "According to [the psychoanalyst Helen] Lewis's view, intense shame not only is a matter of ridicule or scorn coming from others, but also involves one's own inadvertent and vicarious participation in the scorn, since we spontaneously and almost automatically continuously orient ourselves by taking the role of the other. If the real and/or imagined other is an admiring or accepting other, we glow with pride. But if he or she is a scornful other, we writhe in the hell of uncontrollable shame" (1984:158). Shame is a shortcoming, a failure. But it is also the empathetic taking of the role of the other and his or her judgment of such failure of self.

The complexities of shame for Hawaiians cannot be adequately explored here. For example, the phrase "I shame" is used to refer both to an almost incapacitating sense of humiliation and to a less intense feeling of shyness or bashfulness. The Hawaiian term *hilahila* can be used for both the feelings of shame and shyness.[16] (See Carr 1972: 147 for a short discussion of the possible sociolinguistic origins of the phrase, "I shame.") Children will say, "I shame," in both positive and negative situ-

[16] Parish 1991 explains a similar merging of the feelings of shyness and shame in the Newar word *lajyā*, as does Carr 1972: 147 for the Korean word *bukkurupta* and the Japanese word *hazukashi*, which she states both mean shyness and shame. However, *bukkurupta* and *hazukashi* refer much more properly to shyness than to shame (Kunae Kim, personal communication).

ations where they may be singled out from the group (Newton citing an elementary school teacher 1973:1/288;[17] Jill E. Korbin, personal communication). According to Ronald Gallimore and Alan Howard, "Being singled out for evaluation is always a matter of great apprehension," which is feared primarily because the prospect of a positive evaluation is perceived as "a personal gain [which] increases the risk of public failure, shame or ridicule" (1968: 13). (See also Ritchie and Ritchie [1989: 116–17] for the Polynesia-wide occurrence of this feeling.) Pukui, Haertig, and Lee (1979: 239–65) discuss shame and guilt in both traditional and contemporary Hawaiian life in which they mix Pukui's Hawaiian knowledge with modern psychotherapeutic definitions.

Of concern here is the feeling of shame when one fails to maintain an *aloha* ideal and the strong Hawaiian identification with the judgments of others.[18] For Hawaiians, demonstrations or thoughts of petty jealousy, stinginess, or self-centeredness shamefully expose one's failure to be the ideal generous Hawaiian of *aloha* and largess. And Hawaiian empathy with the other is a painful reminder of one's failure as viewed by the other. It compounds the original shameful failure because Hawaiians feel not only the hurt that they directly cause but the pain they cause others who have to view such an embarrassing failure.

Guilt focuses less on generalized self-exposure than on a specific error or transgression. In this case, one suffers guilt by transgressing the etiquette or proper behavior of *aloha*. Rather than creating empathy for the other's pain or embarrassment at having to see one's shameful failure, guilt makes one empathizes with the other as a victim of one's error (Epstein 1984; Lebra 1983). For example, by not offering food to a guest who one later finds out was hungry or thirsty, a host would feel both guilt for the transgression of hospitality and empathy for the discomfort and neglect the guest felt. This transgression of hospitality is of particular concern for Hawaiians. The proper treatment of any guest is not to ask if he or she is hungry or thirsty but to serve something to drink and eat as soon as a guest, even an unexpected one, arrives. To ask implies one does

---

[17] The number and a slash indicate the volume and page numbers of Newton's fieldnotes.

[18] *Hilahila* and "shame" are also used as admonition or judgment: "What you no more *hilahila* (or shame)?" might be said to a child who misbehaves without thinking or conscience or "Sheee, she no *hilahila* (shame), or what?" for someone who flagrantly violates social mores. This concept demonstrates Parish's observation that "moral emotions are moral judgments" because "feelings of shame, *embody* moral evaluations: to *feel* moral judgments of self in this way alters the way people know moral values and know themselves" (1991: 333).

not want to give. Once one becomes a friend and thus no longer a guest but a kinsperson, one is not served but expected to help oneself, as Ellen pointed out. The first few times I visited, she made me a cup of instant coffee. After a while, when I arrived, she would stay plopped on her battered sofa and say teasingly, "You know where the coffee is. The first time you're a guest. After that, you make your own," which meant, of course, that she was extending a familial or inclusive right to help myself. If a daughter were present, however, she might be immediately directed by Ellen to "get Auntie juice." And any older, esteemed person, be they kin or friend, would automatically be served something out of respect.

Transgressions are not isolated to social or emotional errors and oversights with other people but include the natural and spiritual environments as well. For example, Nohi explained that one should not carelessly throw stones when clearing the ground but carefully pile them because "you might hit some spirit you couldn't look [see].[19] Then you may come sick—night time, get fever night time," because you were careless. This means that even unintentionally, you could hurt someone and would have to suffer the consequences.

Further, one must extend hospitality to potential natural and spiritual beings. If you are eating under a tree, according to Nohi, you should share your food with the people who live in the tree: "You cannot see them but they there. Maybe they can see you. You never know that?"

When I asked what kinds of people live in the tree, Nohi replied, "Oh, maybe giant, maybe dwarf. You cannot see them but they there." Just as one must care for those one can see, one must anticipate those one cannot.

Similarly, you must be careful to treat with hospitality and respect those who previously lived and died in a place where you are now living. When you move into a new house, you should make an offering to what Nohi calls the "spirits of the land." Nohi kills a chicken and cooks the heart, stomach, and food bag along with some of its blood and puts it on a sill or rooftop "so they can come in. Because it's a strange place you going, yeah? You don't know nothing about this place. And you have to make sacrifice with prayer for you going live in, and you know, bring better luck for the future and gotta give thanks, yeah? To people we don't know." Then Nohi takes a bowl of water, places some Hawaiian salt in it,

[19] Stones also have spiritual properties. One must ask a stone permission or apologize to it if one wants to move it. Otherwise, *pilikia*, particularly in the form of illness, will result for the mover. For example, one should never take a stone home from the beach (some extend that to shells as well) without asking its permission.

and, taking a *ti* leaf, walks through the house sprinkling the saltwater with the *ti* leaf. She called this a blessing, the other a sacrifice.[20] Then she opens the front and back doors "so all the spirits from up, down [stairs]— go out." She leaves the food out overnight. Nohi tells me that one can tell that the food has been eaten because "all come small already. Funny though? Come small." It is important to treat even spiritual strangers with respect and hospitality, a hospitality they appreciate as evidenced in their eating of Nohi's offering. Handy has described traditional Polynesian methods and beliefs in offerings: "Unquestionably the dominant belief with regards to most gifts of food was that the gods were sustained or strengthened by the offerings" ([1927] 1971: 183).

In reference to her current house, which is part of a large public housing complex along the slope of a valley wall, Nohi said she heard that people used to live on this land when it was covered with keawe trees. When she moved in, she gave her food offering to those who lived and died on the land before she arrived. Nohi has strong views about the abuse of the land and the spirits of those who lived on it. She is particularly angry about a controversial subdivision in Kailua/Kāneʻohe on Oʻahu called Enchanted Lakes.

"The Kailua people, they bad. They only like money. More worse, Enchanted Lakes. They going give the name, ay! You know what the meaning enchanted, eh? Mostly the singing kind. Mostly they beat the drums. And they dance. All day, all night. You know they can go days and days for that kind."

"The spirit[s]?"

"The spirit[s] can do that, you know. The spirit can go day and night, day and night—nobody know. How can they know? You know they [people] cannot see [the spirits], you know."

I ask, "But can they hear—"

Nohi interrupts, "But can hear! People can hear but they cannot see."

"Because of the people who used to live there?"

"Yeah. Sure! Lots of people, old people, uh, the dead knew there many, many years ago when people never get [modern] homes over there. So gradually, they [the developers] don't even know—they only like the money. The people today, they only like the money. So they just

[20] Nohi clearly retains the traditional Polynesian distinction between a blessing and a sacrifice. Handy ([1927] 1971) reports that the sacrifice and offering of food are important ways of establishing a bond between the human giver and the spiritual dead or deity. Traditional methods of purification or *tapu* removal involved water, "both salt and fresh," to wash away polluting conditions.

plow, dump, plow, dump, plow. And they put the place [subdivision] on top. Then something [bad] happen, yeah? '[And they say] Oh, how come? How come?' " Nohi barks a laugh at their foolish ignorance and bewilderment about the source of the *pilikia* (troubles) that come their way after they have shown such disregard and disrespect for the land and those who came before.

She was disgusted that I never made such offerings, especially when she said, "You! You, Japanee! Aahh!" she spat out. I pleaded ignorance, but Nohi turned her head away in disgust. Ignorance (even by outsiders) of proper behavior is no protection against a transgression (*hala*).

Since both a transgression of proper behavior and an ego failure to be a generous Hawaiian of *aloha* involve another as the victim of this transgression and failure, shame and guilt are intertwined.[21] In fact, the meaning of the Hawaiian word for transgression, *hala*, embodies both a personal shortcoming and a violation of social rules, incorporating in one word both guilt and shame generating actions.[22] Handy ([1927] 1971: 234) defines *hala* as an error or wrongdoing ("broken tapu") as well as a shortcoming "to miss the mark aimed at."

Evidence suggests that the portion of this system that holds that a *hala* leaves a person vulnerable to retribution has historical links throughout the Polynesian culture area. According to Handy, when an error or violation of *tapu* occurred in Polynesia it was called a variety of related terms: *hara* in Maori, *sala* in Samoan, *hala* in Tongan and Hawaiian, and *ara* in Mangarevan. "When a person through his own fault brought about a condition of *hara*, he was subject to all the evil influences in nature, and these conditions in one way or another would bring about his death through sickness, war, accident, or in some other way" (Handy [1927] 1971: 234).[23]

In addition to possible spiritual retribution in the form of illness or misfortune, the shameful exposure of a failure of the *aloha* ideal leaves one vulnerable to retributive attacks of anger by the object, the victim of such *lili* or *manini* acts or thoughts: the other. (Spiritual retaliation is discussed in the following chapter.)

The emotions of shame and guilt focus on the internal state of one's

[21] See also Parish 1991 for a discussion of the interconnections of shame and guilt as expressed among the Newar of Nepal.

[22] Valeri 1985 and Heighton 1971 use the term *hewa*, but Pukui, Haertig, and Lee 1972 use *hala* in relationship to *hihia*.

[23] See also Levy's discussion of the historical Tahitian changes in *hara* and the meanings of *hapa* (1973: 344–45).

self, just as *aloha* and *lili* focus on the interrelationships between self and other. The self and the expression (and feeling) of these emotions of shame (*hilahila*), guilt, *aloha*, and *lili* cannot exist without the other.

Hurt and Anger

In the final emotional complex of hurt and anger, the focus is more on the feelings of the other. Traditionally, *hala* acts were *kapu* (*tabu*) violations that offended *'aumākua* (family gods or ancestors), *akua* (spirits), or the spiritual *mana* of a god or someone of a higher rank. People still talk about offending *'aumākua* and *akua*, but the most common *hala* offense is behavior that is abusive, disrespectful, or impolite to other people and, to a lesser degree, the general spiritual nature of the natural environment. In place of *mana*, people speak of God as the important specific force of concern but do recognize an unnamed, spiritual source as well.

Although a *hala* precipitates interpersonal and spiritual troubles (*pilikia*), Hawaiians are most concerned with the social context and emotional effect of transgressions. Ethnographers have noted that it is the consequences of behavior rather than the rule violated that is important for Polynesians (Firth 1963; Gallimore and Howard 1968; Howard 1971, 1974). Hawaiians tend to interpret behaviors in the context of whether they are indicators of retentive affect or hurtful to others.

Culpability is less the issue in resolution than the unraveling of the hurt and pain inflicted. As Pua explains: "Well, to me, it doesn't make a difference whether who's right or who's wrong. It's a matter who's hurt and who's not. You know. Like if, uh, I felt hurt, because of, you know, something. I just like to know why. You know that person said that or did that knowing that it would hurt another person. I wouldn't, I wouldn't go too much on who's right or who's wrong but mostly, you know, who's hurt and who's not."

Pua is concerned with motivation: why would that person want to hurt her? Transgressions hurt and anger people because they are affective messages. Even if the person did not intend to inflict pain, the disregard for another embodied in a hurtful transgression means the transgressor did not think about the other or care enough to avoid the hurt. It is this disregard, like forgetting to share food with unseen spirits, that brings doubt into the affective value of the relationship. The transgressor's future altruistic intentions become open to question. The victim becomes suspicious of the other's goodwill, viewing the transgressor as a retentive, selfish person, unconcerned about the feelings of friends and relatives. Out of hurt and anger for such disregard, the victim will retaliate in a vengeful, defensive manner. Recall Evelyn's words about her cousin lying to her: "And for him to hurt me like that. It's going cause me great hurt. Hawaiians, when they get hurt—they get hurt. And can be something really minor sometime but it's just the principle of the thing *or what it represented*. And it going to hurt me and . . . the feeling just going grow. . . . Somebody going to have to pay for that mistake" (emphasis was added, although Evelyn's entire tone was emphatic).

The emotional nature, the trust in the relationship, is changed. As both Pua and Evelyn note, it is the hurt feelings that are salient. The vulnerable extension of an *aloha* self leaves Hawaiians sensitive to being hurt by rejection or disregard. They have exposed themselves in an open posture and, when rebuffed, or worse, ignored, they are deeply hurt—and then very angry. They become angry because they feel they have been taken advantage of or made to look foolish.

A good example is in an incident related by Evelyn. One afternoon, she was meeting her *haole* (Caucasian) boyfriend at his apartment. On the way over, she decided to bring a pizza. When she got to the courtyard, her boyfriend was lying by the pool conversing with another resident, a *haole* female, who also was sunbathing. Evelyn offered the woman some pizza. The woman refused it. Evelyn said she was haughty and dismissive. Evelyn was first hurt and then angry about the refusal. Later she talked to her boyfriend about it and was further angered when he thought Evelyn had no reason to be upset. This is a complex example because Evelyn most likely felt some jealousy and competitiveness (*lili*) when she saw her boyfriend talking with another woman. She also may have felt some threat because of their common bonds as members of the same mainland dominant white American group. Both feelings were amplified by the boyfriend's dismissal of her complaint about the woman's refusal. But it also appears that Evelyn extended herself in a gesture of giving and possible exculpation for thinking jealous thoughts. When the woman rejected Evelyn's apologetic, supplicating gesture, she indicated that both the offer and Evelyn were neither appropriate nor adequate. The woman withheld herself from social interaction, thereby indicating superiority. Evelyn was humiliated by this rejection; a hurt reaction very rapidly turned into an angry one. And as Evelyn said, "Somebody going have to pay for that mistake" beginning a *hihia* cycle of hurt and anger.

Anger is a much more important emotion in defining Hawaiian personhood than self. But in self-other relationships it is important as the secondary reaction to hurt. And hurt is the result of the other's abuse of one's *aloha* giving and extension of self.

The relationship and dynamic of definitions of self are based on the four emotion complexes of *aloha, lili*, shame (*hilahila*) and guilt, and hurt-anger. The quality of these relationships and hence definers of self are characterized by the ability to give, take, and feel *aloha, lili*, shame and guilt, hurt and anger (*huhū*). The Hawaiian self is intricately linked to the other as recipient, victim, audience, evaluator, retaliator. The other can be another human, the emotional tenor of one's social relationships, the physical and spiritual environment, an unseen or unknown force, or even one's imagined self. And the key component in these exchanges with an other is empathy, the ability to define one's self in relation to what the other is feeling, when "my heart is in my friend."

Hawaiian Person

The construct "person" reflects early Durkheimian and Maussian ideas of the Western "social person" that emerges from the "collective consciousness" of undifferentiated non-Western societies. With increasing labor specialization and population density the collective consciousness is lost and the creative, moral specialist appears. This construct, however, is no longer used as the distinguishing characteristic of only specialized, Western societies but as represented in all cultures.

Personhood is an achieved status or a developmental, maturational condition of a fully socialized, moral being (Burridge 1979; Read 1955; Poole 1982; Strathern 1981). In some cultures, it is both a moral and a legal status that can be lost when certain heinous, antisocial acts are committed (Straus 1977; Hiroshi Wagatsuma, personal communication). Persons are defined by the social and moral order and by their status in that order (Burridge 1979; Poole 1982, 1985; Read 1955). In addition, personhood is closely tied to responsible, proper action and self-control: "Personhood refers to those critical attributes, capacities, and signs of 'proper' social persons that mark a moral career (and its jural entitlements) in a particular society. . . . The concept of the person involves some attribution of culturally delimited powers to the person which are linked to notions of control and intentional agency in a sociomoral order and to related ideas of responsibility for choice and action" (Poole 1985:184–85).

The Hawaiian conceptualization of person seems at first glance to be defined in the label *kanaka makua*, meaning someone who is responsible, hospitable, warm, thoughtful, with a "cool head." According to Pukui, Haertig, and Lee, a *kanaka makua* is a "mentally and emotionally mature person; a person even a child, who demonstrates mature behavior. The term can apply to both sexes" (1972:118).

In spite of this characterization of a mature person as being even-tempered, likable, and rational, there is an additional element of Hawaiian personhood that incorporates the legitimate use of anger (*huhū*) in both verbal and behavioral violence. Verbal violence can range from abusive gossip ("talk stink," "*pilau* [garbage] mouth"), to placing a curse on someone, to direct confrontational language. Behavioral violence runs the gamut from dirty looks ("stink eye"), to physical attack ("time for t'row blows", "bus' up"), to hostile thoughts.

Legitimate violence is viewed as appropriate, mature behavior because it is defensive and is based on justifiable anger. This anger reaction is similar to Lutz's explanation of the Ifaluk reaction of justifiable anger (*song*) as a proper response to something immoral or socially inappropriate. She further notes, "To become justifiably angry is to advance the possibilities for peace and well-being on the island, for it is to identify instances of behavior that threaten the moral order" (1988:156–57). It is the only type of anger (one of several) that "is morally approved" in Ifaluk.

For Hawaiians, justifiable anger is generated by an outsider's threat or abuse to oneself, one's child, relatives, or close affiliates. A person who will fight without hesitation to protect oneself or another is a person who is respected.

In a study of an O'ahu Hawaiian Homestead settlement with the pseudonym of 'Aina Pumehana, it was reported: "Physical aggression is presumed by many to be a high probability behavior of Pumehana youth. Most of those we interviewed denied being aggressive but there was nevertheless an acceptance of violence as inevitable, and as a social tool, for self defense, protection of honor, and in some cases, an expression of outgroup hostility" (Gallimore, Boggs, and Jordan 1974:207).

Long suffering of abuse is also seen as a basis for justifiable anger. The mature reaction is initially to ignore the provocations. Eventually, however, one must defend oneself. Pua gave me an example of her teenaged daughter Emmalene. Emmalene is very quiet, almost shy. Pua said that because she is quiet, "She's not loud," the boys like her. Two other girls at school were jealous of Emmalene's popularity. They began to wait after school for Emmalene to taunt her and challenge her to fight. She

[103]

would ignore them even though they followed her home, harassing her all the way. Emmalene finally told her mother, who offered to pick her up from school, but Emmalene demurred. This situation lasted for about six weeks. One day, Emmalene was two hours late coming home from school. Pua was furious. When Emma entered the house, Pua noted that she seemed to be in the same physical condition as when she left in the morning. She asked her daughter, "Where have you been?" Emma looked angrily and defensively at Pua. So Pua firmly repeated herself, and "then the tears came," said Pua. Emma explained through her tears that today she had had enough of the abuse and beat up both the girls. But then she was afraid that her mother would be angry with her so she stayed away from home until 4:30 P.M. Pua could barely suppress her grin of pride, not only because Emma had beaten up both the girls but she did not look any worse for wear—no torn clothes, bruises, or cuts. Pua also was pleased that Emma was afraid to come home because she respected her mother's rule that she should not fight and the need to "act like a lady." Pua, still trying not to smile, told Emma that while it was wrong to fight, sometimes one just has to.

Pua followed this story with another about Emmalene punching out the front teeth of a young man who challenged her after she told him to "Watch it" after he almost hit her while tossing at some decorations over her head. He wanted to know if she wanted to go outside and "tangle," to which Emma replied, "Any time." He said how about now, so they went outside and he threw a punch and she ducked. Then she took a swing, "but he never duck so I punched him." He was knocked over and began to cry. Just then his older, much larger brother appeared on the scene, where a large crowd had gathered. His eyes sweeping angrily over the group, he demanded, "Who did this?!" Emma, terrified, said in a small, squeaky voice, "Me." "*You?*" said the shocked older brother. She nodded meekly, and the now bemused older brother repeated, "You? You the one did this?" Emma explained what happened, and he threw his younger brother into the car and drove off. The young man she punched was twenty-one years old while Emma was fifteen. Pua did not know that this fight had happened because Emma was again worried that her mother would be angry and did not tell her. But Pua heard about it through a friend and then by questioning Emma. Again, Pua was conflicted with pride and caution, finally said to Emma, well he did challenge you. Again, the violence was justified by the need to defend oneself after provocation. This is further emphasized by the deferent respect the young man now pays Emma. Pua is tickled by this development because the young man is the son of the manager of Pua's favorite bowling alley and, because of his father's position, could have made trouble for Pua or Emma if he thought his son was wronged.

For Hawaiians *aloha* and hostility, gentleness and violence are intertwined. As Bruce Knauft (1984) noted, "violent behavior need not negate or impugn norms of gentleness or harmony."[24] Gentleness and violence, *aloha* and hostility do not have to contradict each other, as is provocatively expressed in the remark made by Ellen's husband, Richard: "No fight, no love."[25] He was responding to a woman visitor who noted, somewhat quizzically, that after years of continual brawling, mainly on weekends, she and her husband had not fought for three years. Richard's eyes took on an impish gleam and he stated: "No fight, no love." Although Richard was teasing the woman, Ellen nodded solemnly in agreement, looking directly at their woman friend. Indeed, Richard and Ellen engage in physical fights that they openly and jointly discussed with me. Ellen once explained how she lost her two front teeth when she stood up from the bed to confront Richard in an argument and he punched her in the mouth. She was not embarrassed and in fact said it was her fault for getting so angry and physically approaching him. There was an element of pride in her telling the story of how tough Richard was.[26] They engaged in playful, if determined, "roughhousing" with each other: punch-

[24] Newton, following Simmel and Coser, refers to hostility (conflict) and *aloha* as "two components of a single phenomenon" (1978:312). He is not concerned about the affective nature of these two emotions but rather their social functions in the dynamics of group solidarity.

[25] An advice column in a Moloka'i newspaper used this same phrase as the headline for an advice column in 1984.

[26] Domestic violence as a social problem has been only recently recognized in Hawai'i. A recent survey of 311 women from domestic violence shelters and counseling services across the state showed that Hawaiians and whites were disproportionately represented in comparison to their population percentage in the state. In the survey, 19.5% reporting domestic violence were Hawaiian women as compared to the state's total Hawaiian population of 12.2%, and 39.4% reporting domestic violence were white women as compared to the total white population of 33.4% (Hawai'i, Commission on the Status of Women 1993). These figures are only estimates of the true incidence because these are women who have sought help or refuge. OHA's *Native Hawaiian Data Book* (1994) did not report domestic violence figures in the "Crime" chapter, although it did report figures for child abuse in the "Human Services" chapter. By 1996 OHA included a list of the victims of domestic violence–related homicides by ethnicity from 1985 to 1994 (OHA 1996: 452). The top three groups of victims, representing over 70% of the homicides, were: Caucasian, 33.1% (49); Filipino, 23.0% (34); and Hawaiian, 16.9% (25). Similar figures were reported for the offenders: Caucasian, 38.3% (54); Filipino, 19.1% (27); and Hawaiian, 18.4% (26) (OHA 1996: 454).

ing in the arm, pinching, pushing. These are demonstrations of their emotional engagement, their involvement with and affection for each other.[27] It is not merely the quality or nature of the emotional relationship that defines its fulfillment but the intensity, which can include hostility and violence, sadness and tears along with love and affection, sharing and kindness (see also Gallimore and Howard 1968:13).

While one can express anger with explosive force and violence, one should not be irrational (*pupule* or *pupule*-head). Anger is protective but it is still considered dangerous and must be controlled. It has the dual potential to protect and endanger. When retaliatory anger entangles the protective affective bonds, it rends the social network, and members (particularly children) are left exposed and vulnerable to the retribution of curses, illness, and misfortune (Ito 1982, 1985b). If not properly managed, anger can cause the very end one wishes to avoid: the endangerment of self and others.

Mothers show concern for offspring who are trusting or too passive, that is, who cannot or will not defend themselves, who are vulnerable to others. One mother told of her concern for one of her quieter, docile sons whom she described as "soft."

Mothers will fight to protect their children, demonstrating the most intimate emotional engagement of mother and child. Pua described her attack on Emma's kindergarten teacher: "So, when she comes home and tells me that the teacher wen' pull her hair, I went there and I yanked that teacher's hair right back. And I told—and then you know then they start calling the principal and the vice principal and everybody came running. I say, 'Well, if she don't like me to do that, then don't do that to my kids.' " Pua responded immediately without inquiry and felt justified in being angry over an attack on her child. Evelyn said her mother and her best friend's mother were considered the toughest mothers in their housing project when they were growing up. If someone hassled them, one of their mothers would go to the culprit's house and either beat up the culprit or the culprit's mother. Once, Evelyn was being chased by a former boyfriend who was angry with her after she severely provoked him. She ran toward her mother's house screaming, "*Mom!*" Her mother, sitting outside the door, did not wait for an explanation but jumped up, swore strongly at the teenager, and shouted, "You leave my daughter alone," chasing him away from the house. Evelyn said that her mother often

---

[27] Evelyn and a lady friend refer to fighting between couples as "Hawaiian kine love." See also Newton 1974: 5/367, 1975: 4/27, 28, 29.

saved her and her sisters from boys intent on beating them up. This un-questioning loyalty and willingness physically to defend one's own is more impressive in light of Mrs. Rosario's comment to me about Evelyn. Mrs. Rosario shook her *'ehu* (red) hair, took a drag on her cigarette, and said, "That girl is spoiled." She felt that Evelyn often tended to exagger-ate or even bend the truth to suit her convenience. But even so, she would immediately rise to her defense, as did Pua for Emma and for her son.

A protective skepticism, a scowling demeanor, a flashing anger are en-couraged and admired: parents attempt to socialize an attitude of exter-nal toughness. Ronald Gallimore, Joan W. Boggs, and Cathie Jordan dis-cuss two oppositional personality types and social groupings identified by adolescent Hawaiians as "nice" and "tough": "There is a major distinction that adolescents make among themselves to sort out people into poten-tial friends and enemies: those who are more and less aggressive. Put it simply, 'some kids are tough and some kids are nice' " (1974:175). They then discuss, in spite of this dichotomy, how tough adolescents "can be very polite and thoughtful" and "some tough people objected to fighting" when it involved harassment, bullying, or picking on "someone who can't take it" (1974:177). Both nice and tough adolescents valued friendship and "openness."

It seems more likely that nice and tough, rather than a dichotomy, are combined with a core niceness and external toughness. The core *kanaka makua* is the pleasant, rational, patient, "cool head," and the external protective shell is the quality that "don't take no shits," as Evelyn said of herself. She, the bountiful earth mother, opening her home, taking in all "my strays." Or Iris who cries over a sentimental moment yet threatens to run over her errant boss for not believing she was ill.

Tough and nice represent two emotional dimensions of Hawaiian per-sonhood: a passionate, intense engagement and a hesitant reserve or shy-ness (*hilahila*). Neither negates the other, but both are important com-ponents of being Hawaiian. This emotional tough commitment and diffident nice reserve mirror the emotional engagement of *aloha* warmth and the disengagement of the stingy coolness of the Hawaiian self. Therefore, the issue may be less one of *aloha* in opposition to *manini/lili* or nice as opposed to tough but a thematic representation of social en-gagement and disengagement. In this manner, *aloha* is aligned not with niceness or gentleness but with the emotional intensity and social en-gagement of violence and toughness while the cooler, socially distancing

[107]

emotions of stinginess, jealousy, niceness, and shyness are more closely affiliated.[28]

The ability to maintain rational coolness and a fierce defense, to be neither too much one or the other, is a demonstration of one's mature status. One who is too dispassionate is distrusted as aloof,[29] and one who is too violent is avoided as too troublesome. In both extreme expressions, one is removed from proper society and loses moral and juridical standing as a person in Hawaiian culture.

Hawaiian Individual

The rules of proper behavior apply most particularly to notions of self and person. In this way, these two constructs are culturally normative. It is within the construct of the individual that one finds latitude for aberrant, idiosyncratic, and variable identifiers, behaviors, and emotions.

The Hawaiian individual is characterized in several ways, but there appear to be two primary designations. One is encapsulated in the temperament descriptor "ways" or "style." "I get my ways," said Evelyn cheerily in reference to her extravagantly gregarious, if forceful, maternal sociability. "Ways" or "style" also describe an individual in a negative manner, such as dominant (bossy), combative ("short guts"), aloof (*hoʻokano* [haughty, conceited], "high nose," high *maka maka* [no doubt an alteration of "high muka-muka," because *makamaka* in Hawaiian means a close friend]), a bitter, unpleasant personality (*ʻawaʻawa*), or *lōlō* (stupid, stupidity; also a derogatory term for mental retardation). Nick Higginbotham (1985) also notes *hewahewa* (odd, eccentric, wicked, incorrect), *ʻaʻaka* (surly, cranky, complaining), *ʻaʻalaioa* (wild, demented,

[28] In Newton's field notes, his informants discuss instances of fright as a positive rather than a negative experience. In one case, a young woman complimented Newton for a good time because she had a scare while he happened to be with her. Again, the element of a strong emotional response, even a negative one, is seen as a positive, enjoyable event. Gallimore and Howard note, "Whereas some groups of people tend to distinguish between personal and impersonal relationships, Hawaiians seem only to make distinctions of intensity" (1968: 13).

[29] This may be one of the reasons Hawaiians are often distrustful of Japanese Americans, whose cultural affect is much more reserved and formal. Although it is usually with a "nice" presentation, it is nevertheless too disengaged for proper Hawaiian behavior and easily interpreted as aloof dismissal and disdainful rejection. And Hawaiians must seem too emotionally volatile and intense to meet local Japanese Americans' ideas of proper behavior.

uncivilized), *huhū* (angry, offended), and *kūlola* (which he defines in colloquial use as "to act as an idiot" and Pukui and Elbert 1986 define as sluggish or lazy). Once an individual's ways are publicly or commonly known, Hawaiians usually are tolerant of these individual expressions of personality, although they are not above complaining about those with disagreeable ones. Nohi explained that one elderly man is disliked for speaking up at housing meetings because he has an abrasive way of expressing himself, but that it was acceptable because he always speaks from the heart—and was often right in his complaints. Frank N. Newton (1978) observed that once someone's negative style is publicly known, no sympathy is given to victims of that individual's temperament. In an example from Newton's fieldnotes in South Kona, a mother is reprimanding her son for getting into an argument with his uncle: "You know how Uncle acts when he drinks, don't you? You know his ways, eh? Well, you should know better than to talk to him like that when he drinks. It's good that now you can sit around with the men and talk intelligently and maturely, but you gotta use your head and not get [him] going when [he] drinks, 'cause you know how he is when he drinks" (1975:6/209). This is an interesting example because the mother also is giving a lesson in *kanaka makua* behavior, telling her son to "use your head" and to be rational in his assessment of a social situation instead of immaturely egging his uncle on when he had been drinking.

Jill E. Korbin (1990) notes that children also are known as having their "ways" and that this trait is a factor in adult-child interactions. Evelyn, while pregnant with her second child, attributed very specific "ways" to the fetus which remarkably were evident in the newborn baby and retained as the girl grew older. She was tough, tomboyish, feisty, and very stubborn. Her sweetness was also apparent but interestingly not considered as part of her "ways." That characteristic belonged to her older sister, Millicent, whose primary "ways" were an incredible sweetness, grace, and obedience, but she too was able to be tough and curt when threatened.

Victims are chided that they "should have known better" and in a sense held more responsible than perpetrators. This seems to indicate that an individual's ways or style are not motivated by negative or personally directed intent so she or he is not held accountable for her or his actions. A mature person can tolerate an individual's temperament, but it is generally assumed that eventually individuals' negative, or, more specifically, hurtful ways will "come back" in form of some personal misfortune to themselves or their offspring. "Ways" and "style" encompass the behavior and affect that are unchangeable elements of individual temperament.

A second important individual marker is more a social identifier in that it involves personal names (*inoa*).[30] Most Hawaiians have both an English and a Hawaiian given name. Children often have unusual, creative English names that have familial meanings and associations. Ellen gave several of her daughters names that ended in -dine, such as Coradine, Geraldine, Donaldine. Ellen was proud of these names, and one was for a favorite brother, Donald. Their similarity also marked the girls as siblings. Ellen, however, did not continue this tradition with her other daughters. (Coradine and Geraldine were the two oldest children, and Donaldine was her fifth child.) Her first son (their third child) was named after Richard, but, like many young boys, he was called Richie-boy. Commonly, the first son will be given the same name as the father, but not always. Iris named her first daughter Jacky, after her husband, bypassing three older sons. Therefore, not only is there a uniqueness of names, such as Ellen's creations, but also a familial tie that links the child to the family, such as a name developed from that of a parent or other relative. This practice appears to have traditional roots as familial names were important connections of *ali'i* children to their genealogy and for commoner children to indicate a relational association with their extended family (*'ohana*) (Handy and Pukui 1972:98–101).

Sometimes a single Hawaiian name, such as Kalani or Noelani, is given instead of an English name. But usually these Hawaiian names are portions of a long, prose Hawaiian name chosen in consultation with a grandparent or other older kin. The yearly State of Hawai'i *Data Book*, provided a table of the most common names by sex, which includes the shortest and longest names. The longest name for a girl in 1986 was Kauanoeokalaniulumahiehi and for a boy, Kananiomaunalokukiekiema.[31]

"Night names," or *inoa pō*, are names a mother (or other close relative such as the mother's mother) dreams for an unborn child or infant.[32] If the child is not given this name, it is believed that the child will become sick and perhaps die. Names have *mana*, and an improper choice can

[30] See Feinberg 1982, Goodenough 1965, Kuschel 1988, and Reinecke 1940 for Oceanic usage of personal names.

[31] The *Hawai'i Data Book* for the years 1993–94 no longer lists the longest Hawaiian names for boys and girls born during that period.

[32] These dreams are often thought to be sent by one's *'aumākua* (ancestors). See also Handy and Pukui 1972: 99–101 and Pukui, Haertig, and Lee 1972: 95–96.

bring the child bad luck, illness, misfortune, or a wandering spirit called *'uhane hele*, which can be interpreted as a loss of self. For example, in South Kona, a young girl's spirit was seen by relatives wandering in a town that was a forty-five-minute drive away and again in another town in the opposite direction about ninety minutes away although both times she was playing at home. On several subsequent occasions, her spirit was again seen wandering in places away from her physical body. She was also suffering from a chronic fever and severe headaches. When the mother and a friend heard a "whistle" while driving through a forest, they interpreted it as meaning that there was something spiritually wrong with the girl. So the girl's maternal grandmother, maternal aunts, and mother took her to the local Hawaiian spiritual specialist (*kahuna*). He diagnosed two things. One was a *huli* stomach or "turned" stomach which requires massage to right it. The second involved the girl's Hawaiian middle name, her *inoa pō*. Her maternal grandmother had a dream shortly after the girl's birth in which she thought she heard the name for a heavenly wind from the mountain. Pukui refers to such a name as a "voice name," or *inoa 'ūlāleo*, which is thought to be said by an *'aumākua* as "both a gift and a command" and "must be given to the child" (Pukui, Haertig, and Lee 1972:95). According to the *kahuna*, the whistle that the girl's mother and her friend heard came from the *mauka* (mountain) side of the road. The whistle was a warning that the name was incorrect. The *kahuna* said it was both *kāpulu* (sloppy or untidy) and an *ali'i* name. Since the girl was not of *ali'i* blood, she was being punished.[33] The girl was given a new name by the *kahuna*, which contained the word for sea, *kai*, combined with *noa*, which means common or free from *kapu*. The spirits of the mountains seemed to be placated by the redirection toward the sea and the removal of both the *kapu mana* of sanctity and pollution with the use of the neutral word *noa*. Additionally in Hawai'i, directions are oriented toward the center of the island where the mountains are, *mauka*, or toward the sea, *makai*. This further contextualizes the name change by removing it from the possible *kapu* mountains for this girl and toward the neutral sea. Also, seawater was used as a purifying agent. Another important point about the timing of this incident is that the girl might have reached menarche during this period, signaling a dangerous, transitional

[33] The Hawaiian woman who reported to me that the *kahuna* said the name was *kāpulu* explained that the word meant sacred, identifying it with *ali'i*. But most likely, if the *kahuna* did use the word *kāpulu*, he was referring to the careless, improper use of a sacred name.

stage. The mother said that she changed the name "to cut with the name," fasted for two weeks from 6 P.M. to 11 A.M. as directed by the *kahuna* (who was also a Mormon), and her daughter recovered and her spirit no longer wandered, nor did she continue to suffer from a fever and headaches.[34]

Specialized Hawaiian names, like unique English names, fulfill an individualized function because they are idiosyncratic, and yet because many are given by a mother or grandmother after a traditional dream or vision, they are also a relational link not only to one's ancestors but to one's cultural heritage.

Pukui notes that Hawaiian names often are the source of anxiety and *pilikia* because people are concerned that they do not have permission from the original owner of the name or from *'aumākua* who control the name. The name also can have an unknown *kapu*. Further complications can arise when one has permission to use the name from the living relative but there is a like-named ancestor whose permission cannot be obtained. Various contemporary ceremonies to *'oki* the name or the *kapu* include prayer, fasting, purification rites (*pī kai*, which is the sprinkling of seawater or saltwater made from Hawaiian salt combined with prayer), or any combination of these.

Fasting is done as an atonement or perhaps sacrifice of self to obtain a successful response to prayers. Pukui traces fasting to Christian, specifically Pentecostal and Mormon, influences but expresses confusion about the reasons for its widespread acceptance and pervasiveness (Pukui, Haertig, and Lee 1972:3–6). She feels it contradicts basic Hawaiian practices and beliefs "that chose pleasure rather than pain, self-gratification rather than self-denial. The early Hawaiian made his contact with the supernatural through satisfying, rather than depriving himself of food," but Pukui speculates that it may have been used as "dramatic proof of conversion. For, in refusing food, they cast off the old gods so closely associated with food" (1972:5). If one considers the extension of self as a cultural ideal and fasting as an act of self-sacrifice, such refusal is a form of selfless giving. Aside from death or mutilation, it is the extreme offering of self. In most cases I knew of, often the parent fasted as part of a prayerful request or *'oki*-ing ritual for the sake of her child. This would

---

[34] This incident is compiled from the fieldnotes of Newton (1975: 6/369–72), a personal communication from Jill E. Korbin, who worked in the same village, and a personal account given to me by a good friend of the mother of the girl. I also worked in this village during 1973 and have returned over the years. I have not included personal names in this incident because Korbin and Newton used different pseudonyms for the same individuals.

be akin to offering one's self in place of one's offspring in a paramount devotion of *aloha*.

Other individualization by naming is the use of nicknames, although this may be a marker of social context because nicknames are normally reserved for use by family or other intimates such as agemates or community members. For example, in South Kona, the grammar school children used their given English names at school but used nicknames or Hawaiian names at home and in the village where they lived. One boy used one English name at school and a completely different one at home, unbeknown to his parents. Children's nicknames changed with age and were often dropped by the time they were out of school (Newton 1975:4/281). Adults have nicknames used by family and close friends. They can be nonsense names, terms of affection (Honey-girl, Sweetheart, Ipo [Hawaiian for "sweetheart"]), trait descriptors (Stick for someone thin, Ah-Ahn for a stammerer), or sometimes an arbitrarily given first name. Pua's name ("blossom" in Hawaiian) is a nickname of endearment that has become so familiar that she no longer responds to her given name of Jane. She showed me her bowling shirt with "Pua" embroidered over the pocket to indicate further legitimacy. Her husband, Emery, has the nickname Pelo as a play on the word for both mackerel, *'ōpelo*, and the teller of tall tales, as fishermen's stories. Nohi changed her first name from Elizabeth after she began working on her genealogy, taking her mother's name. She becomes angry when people still call her Elizabeth. June is called both June and the diminutive Junie. Evelyn adopted a nickname and, later, a long Hawaiian name, both of her own choosing.

These two types of markers of individuality are the most common to all, but there are others such as mythical ancestors, other genealogical relationships, and personal talents or "gifts" of a spiritual nature such as the ability to heal, have or interpret visions, or send curses.

Conclusion

Theoretically it is possible to discriminate self, person, and individual, but methodologically it is more problematic. But for any advances in comparative analysis, each of these concepts must be discussed uniformly. The terms cannot be applied interchangeably to the same phenomenon or variously applied to different phenomena. As more research is done in this area, the urgency for terminological standardization increases.

There is a great deal of overlap between Hawaiian concepts of self, person, and individual. They do not exist as mutually exclusive units. For example, the *aloha* ideal of self has relevance for the *kanaka makua* person. The *pī/manini* (stingy) or *lili* (jealous) emotional faults or shortcomings of the *aloha* self could be tolerated or justified as an individual's "style" or "ways." The individuality of one's "ways" could represent the rule breaking "I" while the *kanaka makua* person could represent the socially correct "me," both interacting to make up the processual self. They are all part of an interactive dynamic process of personal and cultural creativity as well as control. Social control and standards for proper behavior are most applicable to the constructs of self and person, whereas for the construct of the individual, there are less normative constraints and more allowances for variability and eccentricities which defy the rules of proper behavior *(hana pono).*[35] Nevertheless, it is clear that the onus of proper behavior toward possibly hurtful or rude, if characteristic individual behavior, lies with the other, who must display the *aloha* of forgiveness or the maturity to accept. Self and person also are more closely associated, not only because of their more normative link but because of their relationship to the social dynamic of emotions; both incorporate elements of emotional engagement and disengagement, the involvement of passions and the withdrawal from them. The individual construct incorporates the allowance for idiosyncratic, unique, even rule violating, behavior and affect. But all three constructs are interactional because they require social or spiritual others for definition: the self with a reflexive other, personhood with social and cultural definitions of maturity and responsibility, and the individual with those who interpret and label.

While these issues of self, person, and individual are of theoretical and methodological relevance, the cultural system that binds these constructs together is one of *hana pono*, or correct behavior as described in the previous chapter. *Hana pono* is a system of both etiquette and morality (Pukui, Haertig, and Lee 1979:54–55). Etiquette refers to the proper social behavior of members of specific social categories, such as class or gender, in a society, while a moral system defines universally correct behaviors for all members (Norbeck 1977) and often carries sacred sanctions. Etiquette requires that one introduce a spouse to a boss in a dif-

[35] Studies of deviance (or what Edgerton aptly refers to as "trouble" [1976]) in Hawaiian society would be particularly useful. Unfortunately, they are few in number. For example, see Lemert's brief discussion of stuttering (1962), Korbin's cultural analysis of child abuse, which she labels *hana 'ino* (1990), and Dubanoski's comparison of Hawaiian and European-American patterns of child abuse (1982).

ferent way than to a friend, whereas friend, spouse, and boss equally violate the moral system if they torture a child.

Norbert Elias (1978) discusses the development of etiquette as part of the "civilizing" process of western Europe, used to protect one's own purity, decency, and sensibilities from the threatening and contaminating emerging classes in the post–Middle Ages era of the sixteenth and seventeenth centuries. Traditional Hawaiian society, with its hierarchy of classes, used *hana pono* in a like fashion, particularly to protect the sanctity (*mana*) of the ruling *ali'i* class from the commoners (*maka'āinana*), whose lack of *mana* rendered them *noa*, common or free from *kapu* (*tabu*), and to protect both classes from the contaminated *mana* of the despised *kauwā* or outcast, *kapu*, slave class.[36] But the Hawaiian system included both etiquette and morality because breaches of one were often breaches of the other (Ii 1959:22, 23, 35, 59–61), particularly when class barriers were violated, and were punishable by death (Malo 1971:56–57). Etiquette and morality are not always as clearly distinguishable as the difference between eating with the improper utensil and a son marrying his mother in American society. (In contrast, in traditional Hawaiian society, it was immoral for men and women to eat together and yet entirely appropriate for a brother to marry a sister in the *ali'i* class.) Systems of morality and etiquette are codes of proper behavior and often are difficult to distinguish as distinctive categories.[37] Thus the Hawaiian term *hana pono* is particularly appropriate because it encompasses both systems under the rubric of "proper behavior."

In this chapter, contemporary Hawaiian etiquette was presented as proper behavior that defines self, person, and individual. Violations of *hana pono* are violations of the other: rude, self-centered acts that assault the altruistic *aloha* spirit. Unlike the traditional Hawaiian rules of etiquette and morality which defined order and separateness in an indigenous class system, the contemporary Hawaiian system is used not to protect one's own purity, decency, or sensibilities from threatening, contaminating others, but rather to protect *others* from the negative affect of a faulty or improper self, person, or individual. It is not an etiquette for self-protection but for protection of others; the danger lies in one's self and not in others.[38] As Junie said, "I, myself get jealous. . . . And then you know, quick I catch myself and ask, 'Oh forgive me—' "

---

[36] See Valeri 1985 for a discussion of how *mana* has "different degrees of purity" as one moves from the *ali'i* class to the *kauwā*.

[37] See, for example, Edgerton 1985 on the overlap of sanctions and emotional responses to violations of rules of etiquette and morality.

[38] See also Lévi-Strauss 1978.

[4]

Ho'oponopono and Conflict Resolution

Ho'oponopono literally means "to make right, to correct." It refers to a Hawaiian form of conflict resolution and discussion that "opens" the "closed" relations between people which have been entangled by hurt feelings and consequent painful retaliations. As discussed, the two themes of "open" and "closed" link Hawaiian ideas of relationships and people. To understand the cultural meanings and interpretations of *ho'oponopono* requires some knowledge of the Hawaiian and Polynesian origins of "open," "closed," and the protective entanglements of inter-personal relations. The importance of open, protective relationships is mirrored in ideals of expansive, loving people while their negative coun-terparts are seen in the constricted, tangled relationships of closed, re-tentive people. Pua expressed the need for her lady friend to "open" her life and emotions to her friends. People "open" their clothes or the lights, signifying a release of confinement.

Nohi spoke about how paths to the successful completion of a task or appointment must be kept free from barriers by prayer. When troubles (*pilikia*) entangle (*hihia*) relationships and lives, things are said to "come all jam up," depicting those very barriers described by Nohi's blocking hand gestures. The negative affect of bad dreams must be *'oki*-ed (cut) by "opening" them or telling them to someone upon awakening, imply-ing that an entanglement of negative affect closes off future positive af-fect and events. These conceptualizations of and metaphors for openness and entanglements are characteristic of Polynesia ideas of *noa* (a state of freedom, without restrictions) and *tabu* (the ritual binding and control of *mana*) (Shore 1989, Steiner 1967). *Kapu* and *noa* are best represented by "the simile of tying and untying" (Steiner 1967:41) or restricted and free. In a reference to current Samoan life, Bradd Shore explicates a situation that is applicable for contemporary Hawaiians as well: "Although these modern Samoan notions have largely lost their explicit traditional religious grounding in *tapu* and *noa*, these notions are deeply implicated in modern Samoan life" (1989: 151–52).[1]

Mana, kapu, and *noa* were difficult, esoteric concepts for the urban, working-class Hawaiians I interviewed. People knew that *kapu* meant forbidden and *mana* referred to some type of power or had something to do with the old Hawaiian gods. But presenting a word list of relatively routine Hawaiian terms (such as *kanaka, kapu,* and *mana*) made most people extremely uncomfortable and their answers were brief, awkward, and, even when they responded with enthusiasm, many of the definitions were thin in explanation or garbled. For example, Iris did not like me asking her the list of words. She was wary, perceiving it as some sort of test and public demonstration of competence—or possible incompetence. She responded curtly to *kanaka*: "Hawaiian." She added, "And *wahine* is girl. And *kāne* is boy." I then asked, "What about *kanaka makua?*" Her response was very unsure: "*Kanaka makua* is—some kind a king. *Makua* is king." When asked about *maha'oi* (offensively nosy), she explained, "Like *maha'oi*, we knew about all those simple words. But not the kind long word, man! Chee!!" Or as she stated more explicitly, "We weren't raised in Hawaiian. Us was only English." Nevertheless, the elaborate use of the open and entangled metaphors in everyday life points to Hawaiian "continuities with classic Polynesian notions of *tapu* as well as changes in the application of such concepts when deprived of their traditional cosmological underpinnings" (Shore 1989:167).

The changes in application appear to indicate that while the metaphors for openness and for binding entanglements show a strong relationship to the traditional Polynesian metaphors of *noa* and *tapu* as elaborated by Shore (1989) and Franz Steiner (1967), the contemporary significance has taken the underlying, oppositional meaning of these tra-

---

[1] Keesing discusses *abu* as the cognate for the Polynesian *tabu* for Melanesians among the Kwaio speakers of Malaita in the Solomon Islands. He describes it as a polarization between two "off-limits" areas between female and male, blood of menstruation and war, flesh and bone, uterus and skull, female locus of power and ancestral locus of power. These polar oppositions are mediated by a middle ground of *mola*, "which corresponds to though not a cognate with the Polynesian *noa*" and is glossed by Keesing as ordinary, profane or non-*abu* (1982:64–74). There are Polynesian similarities, but they and their differences, particularly with the concept *mana* (Keesing 1982: 46–49; 1984), would require yet another book.

ditional concepts. Shore's reexamination and interpretation of *tapu*, *mana*, and *noa* compares the primarily desirable ritual acts of *tapu* to contain, bind, and control *mana* with the more feared *noa* states of free-dom, lack of *mana*, lack of constraint, and possibly chaotic disorder. *Tapu* affiliated people with the gods and their power but it constrained them as well. And though the condition of *noa* could bring people into contact with unrestrained polluting elements, it also freed them from restric-tions. These secondary interpretations have taken primacy among con-temporary Hawaiians: *noa*-like states of unrestrained openness are pre-ferred to the *kapu* restrictions of entangling, binding *hihia*. As is true of many Polynesian meanings, however, there is an oppositional unity of positive and negative (Smith 1974 as cited in Shore 1989: 155–56) even in contemporary life. Too much openness could lead to chaotic disorder. The lack of constraints could lead to the dangerous, uncontrolled state of *pupule* or crazy, insane behavior. The *hihia* (entanglements) that bind and endanger are based on the social ties that secure and protect.

The use of the metaphors "open," *hihia*, *hukihuki* (arguing back and forth), "jam up," "the way," and "cut" suggest Hawaiian conceptualiza-tions of social relationships and their dynamics. Social relationships are the protective net linking people and forming a shielding structure. The dynamic of the relationships is the affective nature of those ties. The phrase "the way" and the terms *hukihuki* and *hihia* imply the structure, while "jam up," "to open," and "to cut" imply the emotional dynamics that flow along the relational paths among people. The emotional valence of the network determines its protective or endangering nature.[2]

The symbolic frame of the net has possible origins in line and net fish-ing because tangled or cut lines create difficulties for fishermen but also release fish from their entanglements or confinements.[3] Furthermore, while line and net fishing can be solitary or collective efforts, the coop-eration necessary for certain kinds of net fishing enhances the richness of this metaphor since missed or misread communications, lack of deftness or perceptual acuity, or individual deviations can result in an unsuccess-ful venture.

The imagery of emotional ties as forming a net is further strengthened when one considers a type of net fishing (which can also be done alone or

[2] This analysis is modified from the one presented in Ito 1985a.

[3] Niko Besnier (personal communication) reports that on the Tuvalu atoll of Nukulae-lae, the use of the fishing basis for metaphors for negative emotional exchanges and the release of apologetic forgiveness is overt.

in a group) called *hukilau*, which literally means to "pull ropes." The term *hukihuki* refers to a continuing disagreement between parties but actually means to pull back and forth. A coordinated pulling back and forth is involved in a group *hukilau* to encircle and net the fish. This image of pulling back and forth is retained in a *hukihuki*, especially between parents, which can entrap one of their children entangling him or her in their negative affect and leaving the child vulnerable to *pilikia* (trouble).

A traditional nonfishing use of nets with symbolic implications for Hawaiian relationships is the *'upena 'alihi*, a net spread over a patient by a *kahuna la'au lapa'au* (medical plant specialist) to entrap evil spirits who might block a cure. *'Upena* means "net" but has the figurative meaning of "trap." *'Alihi* refers to fine cords strung through the tops and bottoms of nets and used to attach floats and weights and has an additional meaning of "deceit, trickery." Again, there is the traditional overlay of figurative meanings onto literal ones. Hawaiian oral traditions of oratory, riddles, puns, and songs are rich in *kaona*, or hidden, inner, multiple symbolic meanings for literal phrases. The *'upena 'alihi* further suggests the cultural roots of the binding, netlike structures of social relationships (both spiritual and human) which can protect or entrap.

A further addition to the net metaphor is Adrienne L. Kaeppler's discussion of the making of a feather cloak. The cloak's base is a net (*nae*) that may have had protective powers "if the netting was fabricated while chanting prayers, it could *ho'oheihei* 'entangle' and capture them" (Kaeppler 1985: 119 cited in Shore 1989:154), making a cloak of continuous prayer for the wearer. Again, there is the imagery of a net(work) that both protects and entraps.

The greater number of positive affective exchanges one has, the more secure and protected one will be. Negative affect or exchanges cause emotional entanglements (*hihia*) that leave one's protective netting bunched up, exposing one to attack and resulting in illness, misfortune, or death. Most commonly, a resistant, intractable illness is the retribution or sign that a *hala* (transgression) has been committed. Usually the illness is characterized by the multiple, fruitless visits to a physician that Junie encountered with Lisa's life-threatening illness. As Nohi describes this situation, "When we feel sick, you know, [and] cannot be cured, *gotta* be some da kine [the kind]. Especially when the doctor tell you come back tomorrow, and come back tomorrow, and come back tomorrow, and still the same you feel. 'At's you know already, the *kahuna*. Doctor no can cure you. Cannot."

Nohi means that until the *hihia* is cleared away, a medical cure will not be effective. Hawaiians fully recognize that germs, viruses, and contagion cause disease, but, as in many cultures, they believe the moral or social cause must be identified and rectified before a permanent medical cure can be secured.

Such cases of trouble, *pilikia*, are the actual and feared consequences of *hihia*. If such cases of *hihia* are left unresolved, not only the individual but other members in the conflict, most particularly the "weak link" of a child, will suffer. Further, children are the tangible exemplification of the love and intimacy between a man and a woman and the affiliation between consanguines and affines. Children are the connections between generations and lineages. Therefore, they are the primary points at which discord between spouses or families is manifest.

For example, the death of a child is the most severe sign (*hōʻailona*) of a recalcitrant individual involved in a *hihia* or persistent *hala* acts. Evelyn told of a man who was a petty criminal. His long-suffering wife endured his extramarital affairs and acquiesced in his demands that she support him through prostitution. She remained with him and tried to get him to change his "ways," but he ignored her pleas. Shortly after his return from a stint in prison, while he continued his characteristic behaviors, their son was suddenly and, according to Evelyn, inexplicably run over and killed by the school bus he had just left, with his horrified mother a helpless witness. Family members and friends lectured the father that it was his fault and it was "God's way" of punishing him and getting him to change his behavior. They were attempting to socialize him and persuade him to reenter the Hawaiian moral and social system. Their actions were also taken as a public announcement, a public *hōʻailona* of his antisocial, unmanageable attitudes. He changed for a while but was soon back to his old "ways." Evelyn did not suggest what might further happen to this man. The point of the story was the death of the child and the father's implication. No doubt he represented an unruly element in the social and moral system of retribution. Nevertheless, the fact that his child was killed in an incomprehensible way was proof to those who do believe in this system that the forces of retribution for *hala* acts and parental *hihia* are active and constant and children are the most vulnerable.

Metaphors for social relationships or social problems have certain associated, "natural" solutions, actions, and goals, consistent with the metaphor (Ortner 1973; Schön 1979; Wagner 1981). For example, root metaphors, "by establishing a certain view of the world, implicitly suggest certain valid and effective ways of acting upon it" (Ortner 1973; 1342). For Hawaiians, negative emotional exchanges draw others into the entanglements of *hihia*, causing the pathways of social relationships "to come all jam up." To resolve these entanglements and the subsequent "jam-up" requires some method of untangling the negative exchanges and opening the paths for the flow of positive exchanges of emotions. The method used for this untangling is called *hoʻoponopono*.

Hoʻoponopono is a form of conflict resolution to untangle the *hihia* and incorporates discussion, apology, and forgiveness to reveal, release, and cut the knotted emotions, opening the relationships once again to positive protective exchanges.

Traditionally, *hoʻoponopono* sessions were held before any illness was treated to prevent "obstruction of the *kahuna*'s work from within" (Handy and Pukui 1972:143) and, as noted by Jane and James Ritchie, "it is likely that in earlier times the gods were thought to play an important role" (1989: 120). Indeed, contemporary Hawaiian *hoʻoponopono* practitioners in family therapy (Ito 1985a:208) and certain churches still hold that spiritual forces are central to effecting cures. It was used regularly to clear away small hurts and hostilities before they developed into convoluted *hihia* (Pukui, Haertig, and Lee 1979). Currently it is used in various forms ranging from the formal to informal and settings such as institutions or homes, but all retain the key elements in the unraveling of interpersonal troubles involving hurt and angry feelings.[4]

Hoʻoponopono is used in a formal, secular way as family therapy based on traditional Hawaiian procedures conducted by professional family therapists and developed by the Queen Liliuokalani Children's Center; the formal rituals of the Church of the Living God to solve personal problems (spiritual, physical, marital, familial, business, social) of church members conducted by church specialists; and the informal, everyday application by families to discuss and settle arguments, heal hurt feelings, rectify angry words, or alleviate disturbing thoughts or dreams. All three forms have similarities of purpose, procedure, and metaphoric understandings.

---

[4] Duranti 1990 discusses similar functions for conflict resolution in the Samoan *fono*, where social order is restored or reorganized through "the process of 'straightening up'" relationships through formal discussion and oratory. White's extensive work on the *gruarutha* or "disentangling" sessions among the Santa Isabel A'ara speakers in the Solomon Islands (1985, 1990) covers a Melanesian conflict resolution method that has remarkable similarities to *hoʻoponopono*, including the understanding that arguing between adults will cause an offspring to become ill.

The formal versions of *ho'oponopono* have the most explicit structures and procedures that contextualize the informal, less structured use in everyday life. The most formal form of *ho'oponopono* as practiced by family therapists is perhaps the least widespread because it requires the intervention of some public or private agency and a trained family therapist. *Ho'oponopono* as practiced by religious specialists of the various branches of the Church of the Living God is mainly for church members, although nonchurch individuals or families can solicit a session or church members can offer it to outsiders, often as a means of proselytizing but it varies by branch. The informal form is probably the most widespread because it does not have to be conducted by specialists. While people may not refer to it as *ho'oponopono*, the methods and forms of conflict resolution bear the hallmarks of the two formal versions: the opening of blocked social relations by discussion and the cutting of negative emotions entangling relationships to deflect retribution by the use of apology and forgiveness.

Ho'oponopono as Family Therapy

The family therapy method has been described by many authors (Ito 1985a, 1985b; Paglinawan 1972; Pukui, Haertig, and Lee 1972; Shook 1985). It contains the basic structure, dynamics, and metaphors of all versions of *ho'oponopono*. Trained Hawaiian family therapists attempt to get families to learn and independently use the techniques as the need arises. *Ho'oponopono* in its ideal form can be called by any member of a family and is led by the senior member. An outside expert known to the family or a respected individual from the community also can be a leader. In such cases it is assumed that the leader is of Hawaiian ancestry and preferably is close to the family.[5] All members of the family, even infants, are included. Everything must be revealed in the session. The key to its success is that nothing be concealed and everyone participate sincerely, actively, and openly.

The family therapy form encompasses four stages. The first is two-part opening prayer (*pule wehe*). The first part of the prayer is a request for spiritual help to give an atmosphere of conciliation, openness, and sincerity. The spiritual forces addressed depend on the beliefs of the family

[5] Shook 1985 has described the use of non-Hawaiian leaders and as a general group therapy method for unrelated and non-Hawaiian individuals.

but usually combine both the Christian God and family *'aumākua* (ancestors, gods). Sometimes a generic "powers that be" is used. In the second portion of the *pule wehe* the problem is stated. This is called *kūkulu kumuhana*.

The second stage involves discussion, or *mahiki*, which has two lexical definitions of note, "To cast out spirits, exorcize" and "To pry; peel off, as a scab; to appear" (Pukui and Elbert 1986). The connotation is of a discussion that "pries" and scrapes off the crust of old emotional wounds to reveal the underlying problem with a subsequent draining and clearing away of festering bad feelings.

Through the *mahiki* discussion, the family members develop an understanding of how an original *hala* (transgression) became a *hihia* (entanglement) of hostile emotions of anger, hurt, revenge, and miscommunication. When all members reach understanding and contrition, the leader moves to the third stage of forgiveness (*mihi*). The key element of this stage is that both the original wrongdoer and the offended person must apologize and ask each other for forgiveness. Both must be open and willing to ask and to offer forgiveness. The premise underlying this double forgiveness is that once a transgression is made, in the resulting exchange of escalating negative emotions and hurtful acts, the difference between offender and offended is blurred; both become offenders and, in turn, both are victims. In addition to the double forgiveness and apologies, there is a request for the interpersonal release of the other person and the personal release of oneself from the emotional transgressions and entanglements. This is first done by a double request to *kala*, or loosen, the negative affect that binds those involved. Then a request to *'oki*, or cut, is made to release the guilt and anger that one may feel for wrongs committed or received. In this way, *aloha* is extended by both parties in the request for forgiveness, releasing their retentive "holding on" to negative, entangling emotions. Here again are evident the important cultural dynamics and metaphors of emotional entanglements; loosening, cutting, and releasing of knotted, negative affect; and the need for openness, sincerity (heart), *aloha*, and the extension of self to remedy conflict.

The relationship between *mihi*, *kala*, and *'oki* is explained by Lynette Paglinawan, one of the original Hawaiian therapists involved in the Liliuokalani Trust's development of a clinical version of *ho'oponopono*. She elaborates on the emotional nature of release involved in the processes of forgiveness and apology, focusing particularly on *kala* and *'oki*: "*Mihi* is the step where you request forgiveness from the power that

[123]

is greater than yourself, the power that you believe in. Uh, *kala* is the step where you psychologically tell yourself, I have to let it go. Let go in the sense that 'I never more have the need to bring it up.' And emotionally, what it means is—your, your, your mind is working with your feelings so that you, your heart become lighter. You see? It's not just an intellectual thing. You've gotta feel it—letting go. Like a burden's being lifted. You know sometimes when you're very depressed and you talk with people and you—ventilate. Sometimes it helps you. But it's temporary. Because you're still heavy. But if you're talking then they add something that you never quite saw before in that light, and then it makes sense to you and you begin to say, 'Oh, I never knew that! Oh, I *really* feel so much better!' You're psychologically and emotionally, you're letting go. Because your reason now shows you a way out. And as your reason begins to show you the way out, it affects your emotional being too."

I asked Lynette, "That's the feeling of *kala*, of letting go?" and she confirmed: "Letting go. Yeah. Then the next step is to *'oki. 'Oki* means to sever. To completely cut. And that is the feeling where, uh, let's see, how can I explain it. I just makes you feel *so* good!! Like you've *done* something. You've accomplished a *big* task, you never thought you could overcome and it just makes you feel *so* good inside. And so light. You know. And when you get to that feeling of elation, you know in your mind, it is all *pau*. It's never more, anymore gonna be brought up."

"Does the *'oki* come during or after the *mihi*?" I ask. Lynette explains, "Yeah, *Mihi:* you forgiveness [*sic*]. You *kala*, and then you *'oki.* Okay? When you have forgiveness, you can intellectually, you can emotionally ask forgiveness. It's the form. But you also see, with *kala* and *'oki*, you asking for their emotional feel [*sic*] of actually *being* forgiven. Of actually forgiving *yourself*. Because many times you know, you ask the person to forgive you and you feel so good that they don't hold it. But your own conscience won't allow you—to forgive yourself. And these rituals are set up so that *you* go through it internally to let it go."

Later she sums it up: "Okay. For example, I've done something very uh, wrong. Okay, it's hurt you. So I ask you to forgive me. And I'm so glad that you still come to my house, okay? And that's good; I accept it. But— in the way, I'm not comfortable yet to go to you. Because *I* haven't forgiven myself. You see? To ask your forgiveness is one step. But in order for it to be complete—I have, my conscience has to be able to say, 'I forgive *myself*.' Sometimes your worst enemy can be yourself."

Two interesting aspects of Lynette's discussion are the use of the phrases "hold it" and "to let it go," reaffirming the Hawaiian ideas of holding a grudge as less a metaphoric idea and more a literal description, and her idea of forgiveness as expressed in the acceptance of extended *aloha* hospitality and, by association, acceptance of oneself: "I'm so glad that you still come to my house."

Finally, there is a closing ritual called a *pani* in which a prayer is offered and food or other refreshments are shared. The shared food or drink represents the reestablishment of trust, exchange, and hospitality. It does not have to be elaborate and can be simple and makeshift but no doubt recalls for participants the communal, festive feelings of work and feasting associated with *lūʻaus*.[6]

The therapy combines the themes of openness, entanglements, and the need to clear emotional ties through acts of revelation, release, and cutting.

Ho'oponopono in the Church of the Living God

These themes are maintained but in an entirely different setting and for an entirely different purpose of *ho'oponopono* by members of the Church of the Living God. The founding body of the Church of the Living God (*Hoomana O Ke Akua Ola*) was established in 1904 by John Matthews[7] and John Wise (Aiona 1959; Peterson 1975) with origins in the early Congregational Church in Hawai'i but now is a mix of elements of traditional Hawaiian religion and a fundamentalist Christian approach. Darrow L. Aiona notes, "Members have clung tenaciously to certain customs and beliefs from ancient Hawaiian religion. They have revised others to fit into a Christian context and have added Christian principles, forming a new theological system of Christian and Hawaiian elements" (1959:62–63). Church members, however, deny the Hawaiian influences and adamantly insist on the purity of the Christian form. A member of the original church (Mother Church), in the Honolulu neighborhood of Kalihi, stated, "But like the Hawaiian language, it's—you're talking backwards. You know the Hawaiian language is backwards. When you're talk-

---

[6] There was a traditional Hawaiian "feast of forgiving," or "feast to forgive sins," called *'aha'aina kala hala*, which was held to ask forgiveness of *akua* or *'aumākua* and was done independently of *ho'oponopono*. But the use of the terms *kala* (to loosen or untie) and *hala* (sin, offense, error) echo two key elements in *ho'oponopono*. Pukui sees elements of the festive *lūʻau* originating in this earlier solemn rite (Pukui, Haertig, and Lee 1979:2–3).

[7] Peterson 1975 spells Matthews as Mathews.

ing in Hawaiian, it's going backwards."[8] Nevertheless, until relatively recently, services at the Mother Church were conducted entirely in Hawaiian. And Aiona, in his classic, detailed study of one branch, emphasizes the importance of the church for Hawaiian social and self-identity: "They seek refuge in their Hawaiian organizations such as this one, to which they can go with their problems, where the strain of living according to the imposed *haole* [Caucasian] values can be reduced, . . . where they can feel at ease among people of their own kind" (1959:84–85).

Several branches of the Church of the Living God exist and vary in certain practices, but the basic tenets are the same in all. They are that God controls one's life entirely; God's being is spiritual and therefore defiled by worship through any "graven images" or symbolic representations such as crosses, candles, pictures, or Christmas trees; the sins of the father are visited upon the son; and the devil (*kepalō*) exists as tempter and punisher.

This third tenet holds that punishment for earlier "pagan" beliefs of ancestors is visited upon present-day descendants. Punishment is given in the forms of a problematic life, spiritual harassment by both the devil (*kepalō*) and Hawaiian spirits, or illness. An individual who joins the church must accept God as the only true spirit. The acceptance of God to the exclusion of other forces violates earlier generations' pledges to honor *'aumākua* and angers those spirits. "The spirits are jealous and bring sickness and misfortunes to the individual. Thus every illness, abnormality, accident, and problem has a spiritual cause" (Aiona 1959:65).

According to the church, to divest members of these burdens from a heathen past, Hawaiians must *'oki* their genealogical ties in a ritual called *ho'ola'a mahiki*. Members refer to this ritual as a form of *ho'oponopono*. The ceremony also is referred to as "cutting (with) your genealogy." *Ho'ola'a* means to consecrate, but the root *la'a* means both sacred and cursed, recalling the similar dualities of *kapu*. *Mahiki* is used here to refer to the exorcism of spirits. Many of these spirits are the remnants of obligations and covenants which earlier generations made with Hawaiian gods and spirits. *Ho'ola'a mahiki* was defined by a church member to mean "to *'oki*, to cut, and close the door" on the non-Christian beliefs and consecrations of past generations. The use of *'oki* implies ties that bind people to past beliefs that hold them in spiritual bondage unless ritually severed. Previous generations' commitments to *'aumākua* bind future individuals through their genealogical descent lines. The basis for the

---

[8] I have not identified members of the church in any way, even with pseudonyms, because some expressed trepidation that by talking to me about church affairs, they were being seduced by the devil and drawing attention away from God and to themselves.

obligations is that the spirits act as protectors for future generations as these generations are pledged to the devotion and care of the spirits. On the negative side, descendants must also carry the burdens of sins committed by their progenitors. A present-day individual may have to suffer the punishment for a sin of an ancestor; in this way, the sins of the "father" are visited upon the "son." The punishment usually takes the form of severe or recurring illness or misfortune.

A member of a Waimānalo branch of the church, who eventually developed her own ministry which included *ho'oponopono*, explained: "See what my ancestors on my mom-them side—they believed, they worshiped gods, worshiped idols. They worshiped [the Goddess] Pele. Believed in that. Believed in the Mo'o, the lizard [spirit]. They believed in the [spirits of the] sharks. And maybe in the olden days, they kept those things—even my great-grandmother—the one [my youngest child is] named after.

"I heard people were deathly afraid—they would not steal nothing out her [grandmother's] yard. They would not steal nothing. Nobody would go near her house. It was said that if they went, took something out of her yard—they no like their hand get crippled. That's how my great-grandmother was. Her mother on my grandfather's [*sic*] side—and, uh, we don't know what they believed in. You see—if we're going to be Christians or whatever we're going believe today—let's say I want to be a Christian, I want to believe in the Lord. My grandmother-them believed in these other gods. So that conflicts [*sic*] of interest, so the Lord, He punish them but in order to make me a better Christian, He's going to punish me to make me realize what my family did. You see? To make me more aware. And this way—if He makes me realize that—my kids will never carry the burden. For what they [the ancestors] did. It'll stop at me and it'd be [done]. Understand?"

Not all that confident, I reply, "Yeah—sorta."

She continues, "Because that—what I went through as far as my, with my kids—that the sickness and everything that my kids went through—my oldest girl—you think I would sacrifice going back to that thing? Knowing what my daughter went through? I would have to turn more towards a single, Christian type, Christian faith—where there was only one God. Because in all these—you could offend one god that you never knew was a god."

"Because there were so many [gods]?" I ask.

"There were so many. Because there [was] nature worship—you couldn't go in a certain place—when you have your period, you could go here you couldn't—really. They had lots of *kapus* that you couldn't do then. A lot of things that was unknown to you."

[127]

I try to clarify. "So you could get into trouble for not—"

She interrupts, "Oh, for something you wouldn't even be aware. But you see you get punish whether you're aware or not. You see? With the Lord, He doesn't like—they believe the kids are without sin till they come to a certain age. Then they carry their mistakes, their burdens, their mistakes."

"How old is that?"

"I guess eight. I've heard."

"Eight? That's when they sort of—they get—" I stumble.

"They can function as to right and wrong." She returns to her previous subject: "But uh, like an example is when I went into the faith, I went into—my church. And they look, made *ho'oponopono* for me, and they had their Visioners too. Men who vision things and they have the Prophesier and the Rebuker.[9] Now as they pray for you they, and he make you open the *'ōlelo* [randomly chosen biblical passage].[10] The Bible. And the passage that is shown to them. Now when they do this—they believe in the Lord and His Word is ultimately, ultimately truth. They don't go by nothing else. They go by the Word. Now if and when it's open [the *'ōlelo*]—to them—whatever it is—then they 'prophesize.' Now when they open the passage, the Prophesier has a vision, what that passage is— but that's shown from the Lord.

"Yeah, [the Visioner and Prophesier] both have visions. Then they open their Bibles to verify [that] what they have in their head is from the Lord Himself and not from the devil. 'Cause while they feel the devil can come in—well, the devil—they say the devil can represent Christ in his own way. He can change himself into anybody. He's so cunning, he can come as Christ himself. Only if you were Christ, you would know who he is.

[9] There are four basic participants in the Waimānalo *ho'oponopono* sessions: a Visioner, a Prophesier, a Rebuker, and the person with the problem. The Visioner, as the name implies, has visions at the beginning of the session. The Prophesier interprets these visions. Throughout the entire session, the role of the Rebuker is to admonish the devil and other evil spirits lurking about. It is said that the devil and other evil beings try to interfere with the sessions by giving false visions and interpretations to the Visioner and the Prophesier. The Rebuker also gives strength to the person with the problem so it can be corrected.

[10] The Bible is opened randomly to a page and an index finger is dropped anywhere on the open page. Some practitioners say that the index finger can be dropped on either the left or the right side, while others feel only the right side should be used. The finger is drawn down the page until an applicable or appropriate passage is discerned. One of my lady friends confessed that if she gets a passage she does not like or understand, she will do it again. This practice is not confined to the Church of the Living God but is also used by other Christian denominations.

"But the point I'm saying is that when they, I—they have visions—they open to verify what their—their vision is from the Lord and not from the devil—putting thoughts into their heads to throw them off the track—so that the ministers cannot help you, you see.

"So anyway, when they have this, then the minister will ask questions. Then the Visioner would give the visions. And I mean when they were cutting off my genealogy, 'cause this is one aspect that they work on is cutting off the genealogies. Ask for us not to carry the burdens that we had in our family. To carry only what we, ourselves—we stand by our own mistakes. Right?

"So, found out that they had claimed my daughter and myself—my oldest daughter."

I ask, "The ancestors did?"

"Yeah."

To clarify, I ask, "Are these the '*aumakuas*?"[11]

"Yeah, that's what they call 'em—the guardians. The '*aumakuas*, the guardians. They claim that I belong to them and my daughter [too]. Now this Visioner, he kept seeing this old, old *kahuna* man in my daughter. And he would [not] come out. And how many wen' come out of her. But this one wouldn't come out."

I inquire, "So there were a lot—" but am cut off.

"There were a lot. See like, they choose you, see. These spirits or '*aumakuas* or whatever—they choose which ones special to them. That's how come a child is gifted. It because through them—if the [*sic*] don't even believe through them—she could be whatever she wanted. You see. Like before [my daughter] has the ability to see things. When she had all these guardians come in and visit her—these *menehunes* [legendary helpful, small people] used to come up and visit her. I used to tell people things, they used to think I was crazy. I'm not kidding."

"You used to see them too?" I ask.

"I could never see them. Only [my daughter] could see them. They used to come in my room and she's sleeping with me and she sit up on the bed and she see 'em and talking to them and I don't even see 'em. Yeah, they coming to see her. They always came whenever she was in trouble. When she was sick, they came to help her. They never made her sick—they never harmed her. The point is—"

[11] It is common colloquial practice to form the plural of a Hawaiian singular noun by adding an *s* at the end, as in English. The proper way to form the plural of '*aumakua* is to make the second *a* stressed: '*aumākua*. The Glossary gives other examples of properly pluralized Hawaiian words.

I interrupt but do not get a chance to finish, "So they came to protect her—"

"Yeah, to protect her. But the point is that, that was good—but we never knew the Bible [then]. But let's say [my daughter] would be doing something and not even knowing that was bad—she'd get punished for it. See?

"Oh the good parts. Oh, yeah. I was happy to know but when I found out about it—when I found out what it really represented—I couldn't keep it. Even if it was good or not. You see?

"So you see when they finally was praying, trying to cut off the genealogy—it showed our family came from Pele, from the volcano; from the sharks, from the lizards.

"All of them because my grandmother, she had her own and my grandfather had his own. See? So my grandmother always used to tell my grandfather, 'I don't care what your *'aumakuas* were. Mine is stronger. Mine come from the mountain to the sea,' she'd tell my grandfather. She'd say, 'Mine is Pele and the shark.' "

Then she discusses her previous spiritual ability when angered to call upon sharks to attack the father of her youngest daughter whenever he went skin diving. She also describes dreams that indicate her affiliation with sharks.

Finally, she concludes: "They were good in their own way."

I ask, "So they did try to protect you?"

"Yeah," she responds, "yeah, but many times—if I made a mistake—I never knew I would be punished for it."

"And you would be punished for whatever went before?"

"I used to carry the burdens for our family."

Even after one joins the church and "cuts" with one's non-Christian spiritual entanglements, one is not free from the possibility of illness or misfortune as punishment. The devil also punishes people with illness and misfortune when they break any of God's commandments. "Once the individual has professed 'the truth' that was given by God only to the Hawaiians to free themselves from evil, he must live by God's law. Any infraction of the law of God makes the person vulnerable to the *Kepalō* who then has the right to inflict harm" (Aiona 1959:66). This church member also saw humans as pawns between God and the devil. Once loyalty to God had been declared, the devil might challenge God as to that person's faith. God then might invite the devil to try to tempt that individual's faith. An exemplary case of this use of humans as the playing pieces between two larger forces is that of Job, which she recounted in dramatic detail. As they were for Job, these illnesses and misfortunes may be trials to test an individual's faith and strength to remain a Christian.

Hoʻoponopono is used by the church not only to break the spiritual entanglements of a pagan past but also to solve unusual or troublesome problems members face. The branch of the church that Aiona studied used *hoʻoponopono* specifically to find the source of a person's illness. He called *hoʻoponopono* a "method of healing" and a "mental cleansing; the old Hawaiian method of clearing the mind of a sick person by family discussion, examination and prayer" (1959:68). The two *hoʻoponopono* methods for finding the source of a person's problems were Bible readings and interpretations called *"wehe I ka Paipala"* and the interpretation of dreams, *"ku I ka kumuhana"* ("presents a problem"). Both interpretations were done by church leaders called prophets or *kaulas* who were given by God the gift to interpret dreams and *ʻōlelo* and the ability to heal the sick (Aiona 1959).

In a study of a branch of the church on the island of Molokaʻi, called *Ierusalama Pomaikai*, John Peterson (1975) reported two forms of *hoʻoponopono*, an informal discussion (*hoʻoponopono*) and a formal problem-solving, illness-curing ritual (*hoʻoponopono kumuhana*). The informal church *hoʻoponopono* discussion format was conducted without any formal leaders or religious specialists and centered around spiritual or interpersonal problems. It used *ʻōlelo* to guide discussion. One person might initiate the *hoʻoponopono*, but there was no real leader and everyone participated actively. No specific prayers were required although prayers may be given during this form of *hoʻoponopono*. The end of the discussion might be a prayer, an agreed-upon plan of action, or just a drifting off of the discussion. Forgiveness or apology did not seem to play a part in these sessions. *Kumuhana* had two uses in this branch. The first played off the word *hana* in *kumuhana*, which means work and was used to refer to fund-raising work.[12] The second meaning was to find the source of a problem: "The ritual of *kumuhana* not only gets at the cause of a problem or illness, but also by getting to the cause offers a solution" (Peterson 1975:204). Here, *kumuhana* refers to a three-day fasting and prayer ritual which was part of their formal *hoʻoponopono* version called *hoʻoponopono nawaliwali*. *Nawaliwali* refers to a weakness in an individual caused by an illness, the precipitating, improper behavior, and the

---

[12] This is not the usual definition of *kumuhana*, which Pukui and Elbert 1986 define as "topic, subject."

weak, fallible individual church member. The formal *hoʻoponopono* version was held with an experienced *hoʻōla*, or leader. After a session of prayer and perhaps an opening *ʻōlelo*, the patient or sufferer (*nawaliwali*) might be asked to fast and pray for three days. This was the *kumuhana*, during which dreams and *ʻōlelo* were used to find the source of the problem. As few as two people could be involved: the person with the problem (*nawaliwali*) and the leader (referred to as *hoʻōla*, which means to heal or save; healer) of the *kumuhana*. A third witness usually attended as well and, more often than not, relatives and others involved in the problem were present. The fasting and prayer of *kumuhana* could occur as a form of repentance without the formal *hoʻoponopono nawaliwali*. Peterson does not specifically note apology or forgiveness as part of the *kumuhana* or in the formal and informal *hoʻoponopono* sessions.

Members of one of the two branches on Oʻahu that I was familiar with said *hoʻoponopono* was used "to find the reason for the problem." The problem could range from an obscure Bible reading (*ʻōlelo*), a bothersome dream, a persistent illness, or generalized *pilikia* (trouble). According to a member of the Mother Church, the problem could be "anything. With your job, it can be anything. Doesn't only have to be children. Now maybe somebody else wants your job, and that becomes a burden to you because you don't know where to go. You don't know how to face it. You can't accept that there's, you know, there's somebody who's going to take your place, and you can't understand why this other person wants your job. And then you try to seek spiritual help. . . . Then you turn to the Lord. You seek His help wondering why this came about. [To ask help] to understand myself more and give myself a lift." In this way, she uses *hoʻoponopono* to clear away an unsettling obscurity in her future, to clarify meaning.

The branch located in the Hawaiian community of Waimānalo stressed that *hoʻoponopono* was not the solution to the problem. It was up to the individual to resolve it with God by "humbling oneself to God," repenting, and asking his forgiveness. *Hoʻoponopono* was used only to identify the source of the problem. The church workers who conducted the *hoʻoponopono* did not help the person recognize, work out, or even admit the problem uncovered at the session. They said it was not their duty to help the person resolve the problem. This form is similar to the therapeutic version in which resolution is not externally imposed on the participants but must be internally generated within individuals as a reflection of their personal motivations to resolve the conflict. But the secular solutions of the family therapy or informal, everyday versions primarily involve interpersonal resolutions rather than spiritual ones.

Church workers who conduct *hoʻoponopono* emphasize that God is the source of their ability to understand the problem or find the solution. They view themselves as mere vessels transmitting the word of God. To resolve the problem, the person must accept the workers' interpretations, correct the problem as they determine, and repent to God. The repentance is termed *mihi* and is considered an apology-forgiveness offering, although one does not ask the wronged person's forgiveness. This notion derives from the church's tenet that one does not humble oneself before anyone but God. Only God is worthy of such an act.[13] When a person repents and asks God's forgiveness, he or she clears the emotional and spiritual pathway between the self and God.

The Waimānalo church member who had her genealogy cut spoke briefly about how this *mihi* was done. "So I could believe in the Lord and understand all what we had in the past. But you see, it could hurt me. Like I could go walk on one grave and let's say I never know was and I could get punished for that. I could go to my ministers and they'd show me, through *hoʻoponopono*, they'd show me why—why I'm like that [i.e., having troubles], 'cause the Visioners will show why. That I went there and did something so the Lord is showing them through the Visioners and through the Word why I'm like that."

"Then you could correct it?" I ask.

"Then they make me repent my sins. And through prayers—*pau*, corrected. You see?"

Referring to the Hawaiian belief that someone who cures another "takes on the burdens" or the illness of the cured person, I ask, "So they're able to take on some of the problems for you?"

"Like—that's the difference between ours. They don't take on the burdens of people. They cast it out in the name of Jesus. So when they help you—it's all done. Everything is *pau*. They don't carry it. They rebuke 'em so there is nothing left. Which is good."

Of note in this example is how, in spite of one's belief in God, one could be punished by unknowingly offending Hawaiian spirits by step-

---

[13] Some branches of the church are stricter about this idea than others. For example, one member of the Mother Church regularly mentioned the need for the person to request forgiveness of a wronged party whereas a member of a Waimānalo branch insisted it was incorrect and never done. See also Aiona 1959 for details of a WaiKāne, Oʻahu branch.

[133]

ping on and thereby desecrating an unmarked grave. In that way, the Hawaiian spiritual world, though repudiated, is still a real force for members. This contradictory feeling was illustrated in an earlier conversation with the Waimānalo church member about the need to be careful when walking on trails that might have belonged to *menehunes*.

"But you know like the trails before—people cannot even go on the trails. Yeah, that's the crossing for the *menehunes*. You cannot. 'Cause at that time that you're there—whether you believe in them or not—they can make themselves known to you. Your faith gotta be stronger than what you believing in right then and there. And you know—they will help you."

"You mean," I ask, "like you were walking on [those] trails and if you didn't ask permission you'd get in trouble?"

"Well, let's say—even *I* could [get in trouble]. Like even our church, we don't believe in that stuffs no more. But we're not going out defying everything just because we don't believe in it and because we believe in God. We're not gonna trespass on someplace—'cause many times now—you have spirits even [in] your own family would come back and hurt you. If you did wrong. You know, you go to the grave and you consecrate or dedicate the grave right?"

"Um hum," I mumble without confidence of understanding.

"They would come back and they would harm you," she adds in finality.

As is apparent, this church member both believes and denies belief in the potency of Hawaiian spirits. She feels both that "they will help you" and that they "would come back and hurt you." When I asked earlier if it was necessary to ask permission of the local spirits, which is a common courtesy for those who believe in the Hawaiian spiritual world, I assumed that she believed in them, which she denied, saying, "we don't believe in that stuffs" but added some equivocation, "But we're not going out defying everything just because we don't believe in it. . . . [These Hawaiian spirits] would come back and would harm you."

Asking God's forgiveness is the solution, although God many "tell" a person to ask forgiveness of the wrong person through the Visioner's *hō'ailona* (vision) or the Prophesier's *'ōlelo* (Bible reading). Or should the Prophesier and the Visioner find that the source of the problem is not with the sufferer but with another person, the victim must pray to God to show that other person their error so he or she will come to the victim and ask forgiveness. God's affect is used to change human relations. He is asked "for to put love in that person's heart" to "soften" his or her "hard heart." "Hard heart" means that a person's angry and hurt feelings make him or her obstinate and unwilling to forgo the need for emotional revenge. Thus the way is blocked for resolution because the person is unwilling to yield or "let it go." God is used as a supraintermediary to send positive emotions over rather than through tangled interpersonal relations. If the request to God to put love in the other person's heart is successful, he or she will gain compassion for the other party, will "soften" their stance, realize the suffering they have caused, and apologize.

Unlike the therapeutic version, this religious version emphasizes the individual's relationship to God over the interactive relationship with other people. The important relationship to keep open or free from entangling, negative affect is that between an individual and God. Nevertheless, entangled relations with other people can displease God, thereby affecting one's relationship with the Deity, just as doing good deeds and extending *aloha* to others (assumedly in his name) keeps a person's relationship with God open and flowing with *aloha* and godly blessings. Therefore, one may be directed through the *'ōlelo* to apologize to the offender as well as to God.

Ho‘oponopono in Everyday Life

Rarely does one find urban Hawaiians who have the detailed knowledge of *ho‘oponopono* used by family therapists or religious specialists. *Ho‘oponopono* in daily Hawaiian life usually refers to any discussion initiated between individuals or families to settle a conflict or to uncover a dispute that may be causing sickness or other *pilikia*. Junie felt that even our talk story discussions were a form of *ho‘oponopono* because we were searching for answers to problems. Yet even informal, secular settings bear similarities to the two types of formal sessions. As in the formal sessions, key elements in the informal discussions are openness, honesty, and the ability to "let it go," referring to the release of hostilities, hard feelings, and the desire for revenge. There is the need to reestablish an *aloha* extension of selves and to clear social relationships of the negative entanglements of hostile and jealous exchanges. The cultural resiliency of Hawaiian urban life is demonstrated by the metaphoric richness and thematic constants in this everyday use of *ho‘oponopono*.

These everyday sessions are usually called or initiated by a concerned older person, most often the senior female in a family. She sometimes will take the role of mediator and discussion leader or as the interpreter of *hōʻailona* or *ʻōlelo,* but often she merely gets the conflicting groups or individuals together. Nohi's two-year-old grandson, Roman, had been sick with what she said was whooping cough. She explained that his parents took him to a local clinic but were turned away and told that they had to go to their "own doctor," meaning a private physician. When her daughter Donna and her boyfriend came over with Roman and told Nohi what had happened, she told them they must be arguing. Nohi said that she "knew" that because Roman was sick and could not get medical aid, the parents must be arguing: "I never know they was fighting but I knew!" She told me that children sometimes get sick when two people are struggling with each other, making a gesture as if she were in a tug-of-war (*hukihuki*). Therefore, the parents needed to "open," making a gesture with her two hands as if they were a closed book opening. I asked if this was *hoʻoponopono* and Nohi replied, "Yes!" Nohi did not stay with them to mediate but went upstairs leaving them alone. When she came back down, they said they had worked things out. Nohi then took Roman to the clinic. The attending physician immediately looked at the boy, prescribed cough medicine, and he recovered. Nohi noted that the availability of medical attention and a cure after the *hoʻoponopono* confirmed the need for the parents to talk things over before their child could get help and return to health. This case represents one of the simplest versions of *hoʻoponopono* but nevertheless uses basic cultural components. A *hukihuki* between parents causes their innocent child to become ill because he is caught in the web of *hihia* (emotional entanglements). *Hoʻoponopono* is used to "open," to clear away the entangling *hihia* through discussion and resolution, usually through apology and forgiveness. It is a necessary step before the child can receive efficacious medical treatment, as in the traditional use of *hoʻoponopono.* According to Lynette Paglinawan, "No matter how many pills the doctor gives you, if you're still under that pressure, you're living in a household where there's a lot of tension, things gonna erupt. And no amount of medicine is gonna work. Well, Hawaiian doctors *knew* this! So you go through this mental cleansing process which is the *hoʻoponopono.* And the feeling behind it is, once you take care of your emotional and mental stresses, then you release all that energy—to go into the soma—to your body, so that your body can then heal. But if your energies are being used to ward off emotional and psychological stresses, how much less of an energy for your body to heal itself. So. This is why even the doctors of old had to know this process. Because they would ask, 'Have you folks done the *ho'oponopono*?' And if they hadn't, that would be the first thing they would do."

The apology-forgiveness exchange remains a central, if not always overtly expressed, part of *ho'oponopono*, even if no session is called. The social and psychological goal is to remove the negative feelings that entangle individuals. Double apologies and mutual forgiveness are important but do not need to be expressed in a formal way. The extension of a friendly gesture can be sufficient, as explained by June: "Like if you and me had an argument, you know. And you accused me of something. And, um, I'll tell you that I didn't do it. And you keep telling me, 'Oh yes, you did do it.' And then we get into a hassle, you know. I'll say, 'Okay then. If you think I did it, then you think that way. But just, you know, get outta here—you know. Go home!' Or I'll leave. And then I'll think it over: 'I should call her and I should say I'm sorry.' But I won't, you know, I won't call you and apologize. And then, in my heart, I'll pray—that someday, that you'll, *you'll* be the one to call. And I'm very grateful because that's how it turned out to be. It turned out to be that the people that had made trouble with me were the ones to call and realize that. They were wrong. And then we were friends again. And that's how it always is.

"You know how I told you how certain persons, one of my neighbors? You know, she accused me of turning her in [for welfare abuses]. And I did—I didn't even turn her in. I didn't know what she was doing, you know. And we stayed bad friends for two years. But I never forgot her. I, I've always asked God to touch her heart. 'Cuz she'll realize that one day—and one day I was washing the dishes. She came and knocked at the back door, said, 'This is New Year's, June. I'm having a party. Could you come over?' And the way, my auntie [a Christian pastor] always taught to us, they're washing your feet. In other words, she's asking forgiveness in her own way. She doesn't have the understanding that we have. Like if I would say, 'Forgive me, Karen. 'Cuz what I did to you was wrong.' That's how I would say it. But because *they* lack understanding, the kind of understanding that *I* have, they invite me to their house. And if I refused her. And if I didn't go to her party, that meant I didn't give it to her. I didn't forgive her."

Junie viewed the change in the relationship to one of hostility as making them "bad friends," not enemies. The friendship was still intact; it was the affect that had changed. Further, she did not talk directly to her friend because she felt the friend's heart was hardened by contentious feelings, as well as her own feelings that she had been the one wronged.[14] She asked God to intervene to soften her friend's hard feelings. Since the relationship was entangled by the *hihia* of negative feelings, a third party, in this case a spiritual force, was required to circumscribe the human "jam-up."

Finally, June, like Lynette, used hospitality in the form of an open house as a metaphoric offering of self as an example of apology and for-giveness. In this way, apology is a tendering of one's self, forgiveness is acceptance of that vulnerable, open offering, and neither always requires words. Nohi expands: "But then, you know—suppose to be forgiving in the right way. You know. Suppose forgive and, uh, forgive in a nice way and forget in a nice way. See, person come to you, tell you, 'Sorry what I did. I like you forgive me.' If you can say, 'Yes,' good. And what if he say no? Well. Then you can, then you can—they, you can—you can [do] something else. That you be forgiven. So, well.

"You know already, you know already, we get one high Man above us.[15] So that Guy, you can ask forgiveness. Now He can do the impossible for you. So maybe He can put some thoughts in the one, uh, the one who you forgive. Can put some thinking or some thoughts in this, uh, lady heart, like that. That you can be forgiven. And then He do that for you. 'Cause you know already He just like one judge already. He know that you wen' go forgive and you want answer and then she no say and then you feel maybe she still hate you. So, well, you forgive to the Big Man that's the One and He can help you out. In some miracle way, which you don't know. But then, yeah? Maybe you might get surprised," and Nohi cocks her head and gives me a smile.

She continues, "Maybe the next day, she going tell you, 'Oh, yeah. I suppose to forgive you, yeah? You wen' forgive me and then I never say nothing. Maybe you think I still hate you. Yeah?' See? Like that. So then you going know that, 'Oh yeah, something was done,' by somebody which you don't know—maybe you know.

[14] Earlier in this conversation, June explained that she previously asked forgiveness from the other party even if she were not at fault, but "I've learned that when you apol-ogize to somebody else—they'll, you know, they'll ridicule you and they'll make fun of you so I always ask God to forgive me for the wrong that I've done to the other person." I asked her, "Even though it might be their fault entirely?" "Yeah," confirmed June.
[15] Nohi was a convert to Catholicism late in her life; her husband, Roberto has been a lifelong Catholic.

"See? I think you change. Change toward you. You laughing, she's laughing at you. You folks laughing, smiling. So 'at's right there, right off the bat, forgive already."

I ask, "But it won't work if she won't forgive you?"

"Yeah. Because you know why? If she won't forgive you, her conscience going be the one bothering. But—if the Big Man can do something—then, [she will say], 'Oh, yeah. I gotta forgive her. I go talk to her. Talk nice.' She going talk like that. 'Hey,' [she will say in a moment of understanding].

"And when she see you tomorrow, [she will say to you], 'Hey, howzit? How you?' All that kind, yeah?

"And, 'Oh, we all right,' you going tell like that. Um hum. 'What you going do today?' Tell, 'Oh, I going school,' and, and then you just drive the car. You just go. You used up plenty words already."

This affective change in the relationship ("You laughing, she's laughing at you. You folks laughing, smiling.") illustrates not only the extension, acceptance, and exchange of apologies and forgiveness but a reinstitution of the relationship and the opening of emotional pathways for positive communication. As in Junie's example, God was used to circumvent hostile, angry *hihia*. Formal words, "in the right way," are not necessary once the affect has been softened. A friendly gesture, a reaching out, and an extension of self are acceptable: "You used up plenty words already."

Nohi also uses apology and forgiveness interchangeably, almost as synonyms, again illustrating their intertwined associations. Of course, this restorative apology-forgiveness exchange does not always go so smoothly. An offered apology-forgiveness request may be refused, as noted by Nohi and experienced by June. There appear to be two interpretations of the refusal and who bears the onus for it. First, if a party in a conflict makes genuine efforts to correct the entanglements and to act with heart toward the other party but is rebuffed, that rejecting person, by holding on to the hostile feelings, is vulnerable to the *pilikia* sanctions for grudge-holding: illness, misfortune, or even death.

A second interpretation puts the blame on the person reaching out. If one party asks forgiveness too quickly, it is felt that the other person has not been given enough time for a chance to soften his or her resentment and be open to reconciliation. The asking party is being selfish in not considering the affective condition of the other. The requester is believed to have made an error in judgment. Patience and the use of prayer are counseled. In this case, no *hala* is committed by the refuser. In fact, the

[139]

requester may be thought to be contributing to the *hihia* because now more hurt feelings and hostilities are enjoined.

Junie recounted an experience that illustrates these elements. She was at a church meeting where members gave testimonials about their troubles and how they faced them. Other members with similar problems listened carefully, using the testimony as *hō'ailona*, or signs of what to do or say in their own situations. The testimony is taken as God's method of "opening the way" to show the solution to one's problems. Junie gave testimony about how she had to learn to love her philandering husband "all over again" after discovering his infidelities. She said she is now "more mature" and that even though she and her husband are divorced, she hoped, "someday, try to make a go [of the marriage again]." Unbeknownst to Junie, a woman was listening who had left her husband and come "seeking help" or a solution to her husband's unfaithfulness. She thought that Junie's testimony was her answer. She left the meeting and returned to her husband.

Shortly thereafter, Junie saw the woman in the doctor's office. She had a broken leg, and Junie asked how it happened. The woman explained that she had heard Junie's testimony, left the meeting, and went straight back to her husband. But he beat her and broke her leg. Instead of being sympathetic, Junie was disgusted. She scolded the woman, telling her it was her own fault: " 'You didn't understand what I was trying to say. But see, when you hurt a leg, when you break a leg, that's stepping on the truth. Your leg, when you hurt your leg, that's stepping on the truth of God.' " I ask Junie, "What was the truth she was stepping on?" and Junie snaps back, "The truth she wouldn't accept. She didn't go back the right way. She went home with her husband still having that hate in his heart for her. She, she didn't go with her self-defense first. And asking God to heal her husband, plant love in his heart . . . she just went right home." The woman should have waited, using prayer and God to soften his anger so he would be able to see his own errors, accept her forgiveness, and ask hers in return. To Junie, the woman's attempt at reconciliation was a self-centered act. "You know, you ain't going get everything you want here," Junie growled. One cannot initiate a reconciliation only on the basis of one's own affective condition but must bear the responsibility for discerning the emotional disposition of the other party. In this way, one must demonstrate *aloha* empathy in being able to take the position of the other and evaluate his or her ability or readiness to accept and request forgiveness.

In addition, this example illustrates the need to take into consideration another's "ways," as discussed in the previous chapter. People who are known to be bitter, contentious, and irreconcilable are thought to be unable to act in an appropriate, forgiving way. Therefore, it is the duty of those around to be cognizant of these "ways" and to tolerate them as graciously as possible. For those who ignore these known "ways," there is no sympathy for the rebuff or the pain suffered, as Junie demonstrated with her fellow church member.

In both the informal everyday use and the formal religious use of *ho'oponopono*, the prominent mention of God "to put love" in another's heart to change a negative, closed emotional state to a positive, open state may have originated in the traditional Polynesian belief in "influence through psychic rapport" through the use of various techniques of emotional intensification which "the old Polynesians believed . . . generated or stimulated psychic impulses, which impinging upon their goal would produce the desired effect" (Handy [1927] 1971: 26).

In spite of a *ho'oponopono* session and a positive change in affect between parties, the conflict and hostilities can still remain. When Pua was still living at her parents' home, her brother married a "Puerto Rican" woman who lived next door. In both houses were sisters who did not get along, and physical fights, "rumbles," between the two households continued after the marriage. Naturally, whenever a fight would ensue, the brother's wife wanted to join her sisters against his sisters. Pua's brother wanted to stay out of it but found it difficult to convince his wife not to fight. Finally, Pua's aunt said that both sides had better sit down together and talk it over because they were pulling their brother back and forth every time they fought. "I can see that's what we were doing," Pua conceded.

They did sit down but without the aunt. In fact, the brother acted as a somewhat overly involved mediator, alternately pleading and threatening. He would get angry, saying he could not be held responsible for what happened, intimating that it would cause a divorce or the couple would have to move away. Then he would be in despair, bemoaning that he did not know what he would do if they did not stop fighting. The two households of sisters listened, "still looking daggers at each other," which Pua demonstrated with a fierce "stink eye." Pua and her sisters acknowledged that they were "tearing him apart" so agreed to stop fighting. Everyone agreed to cease the hostilities, "But still looking daggers at each other."

That same day, Pua said, "A cute thing happened." She and one of her sisters were walking down the road and passed one of the women from next door. The parties walked by each other, looking straight ahead. Pua demonstrated by sitting upright in her armchair with her arms over the sides of the chair swinging them stiffly as if she were marching. But just as she passed her neighbor, she looked over her shoulder to throw her the "stink eye," only to catch the other woman in the same act. Startled, both whipped back around to look straight ahead again. Nevertheless, they were so shocked and embarrassed that they began to giggle. Pua demonstrated, placing her hand over her mouth and giving her girlish twitter. Pua's sisters had been watching from their house and were convulsed with laughter at the incident. Nevertheless, hostilities continued. A clear omission in this *ho'oponopono* session was that the two conflicting parties did not talk with each nor did they apologize or forgive, so in spite of their agreement and a momentary change of affect, neither side relented. The women continued to fight and "look daggers at each other."

It is in these everyday attempts, successful or not, to resolve conflicts that not only are the basic elements of *ho'oponopono* evident, but they are intertwined with the cultural ideas of "open," *aloha* extension, and the *lili*, stingy retention of self. In the following episode recounted by Nohi, all of the emotional and symbolic elements of *ho'oponopono* are evident without the formal structure.

Nohi's mother was an attractive woman who had many boyfriends and three husbands. Her popularity aroused her two sisters' jealousy (*lili*). One sister went so far as to have an affair with Nohi's mother's husband. When Nohi's mother discovered the adultery, she was hurt and angered by this malicious theft of the affection and loyalty of her spouse. She told that sister and her other sister, " 'You guys all going pay back (*ho'opāna'i*)' " for this and other spiteful, jealous acts. And indeed, the *lili* of the seducing sister was returned when sometime later, she fell out of, ironically, a *hala* (pandanus) tree and broke her leg.

"You know, my mother said that that sister and one more sister, hate my mom. They were enemies. They never talk to one another. You know— Hawaiians get that. *Lili* they call it—jealous. *Lili* mean jealous. See, my mother was a beautiful lady, you know. And she attract men, you know— that's why. Anyway, my mother was, you know, the kind what she talk, or how her movements—the men like, you know. Anyway, that's why—that's my aunt, right? That's why my aunties, they don't like my mother. So they were enemies—until that day, [my aunt] went fell down and got hurt."

The aunt had climbed the *hala* tree to collect the *lauhala* (pandanus) leaves for her weaving. The tree was in an isolated spot, and after she fell, breaking her leg, she despaired of being rescued. She called faintly for help. Coincidentally, Nohi's mother was in the area collecting seafood along the shore when she heard a distant, soft cry for help in Hawaiian. Nohi said that it was odd that her mother heard the call because of the distance and the placement of the trees. Also the voice sounded like an echo, but the area where her aunt was lying was flat.

When Nohi's mother went to investigate, she was surprised to see her jealous sister, who was equally stunned to see who her rescuer was. After their initial shock, they began to cry, fell into each other's arms, and forgave each other. Nohi's mother went to get help and her sister was taken to a hospital. "My mom save her life," succinctly noted Nohi. In spite of the emotional forgiveness, however, they did not become close: "they were not the kind—maybe they just wen' forgive that minute and all *pau*. They wasn't, uh, very good friends, good terms."

This incident is rich with cultural meanings of social relationships, emotions, and metaphors. It exemplifies the escalating *hihia* of hurt and anger resulting from the affective transgression of the retentive, self-serving *lili* and the resultant "holding fast the fault" through a curse by Nohi's offended mother, locking the sisters in negative exchanges. The process of emotional release (*kala*) and mutual forgiveness (*mihi*) apparently began before the embraces at the tree. The first step was heralded when the sister fell from the *hala* tree and perhaps metaphorically fell out of her transgressing (*hala*) emotions of *lili*. *Hala* also means to pass, miss or die. Her accident could have been a *hō'ailona* warning of impending death as punishment for her *lili* and adultery. As Nohi interpreted it, "My mom save her life." Or it could have symbolized the passing away of her retentive *lili*, opening the way for reconciliation. Her breaking of a leg could be significant if Junie's interpretation of breaking a leg as meaning stepping on the truth is applicable. Junie was talking about the truth of God, but in this case it could refer to stepping on the truth by ignoring of her own adulterous and *lili* wrongdoings, or it simply could have been a punishment for her transgressions.

The second step was initiated when the injured sister had to extend herself through her cries for help. At this point she changed her behavior and thoughts from retentive ones to an extensive one, acknowledging her need for others, thereby providing an opening for her sister to respond and reaffirm the bond by rescuing her. Nohi's mother, in her extension of self in aid (*kōkua*) and comfort, offered an accepting gesture of *aloha*. This gesture was also an emotional release of her cursing constraints. Both sisters acted openly, unself-consciously, and without hesitation, clearing the relational link so the "way was open" for forgiveness and the restoration of their relationship, albeit an uneasy truce at best.

[143]

Conclusion

The cultural consistency of these three forms of conflict resolution points to the profound durability of Hawaiian culture, even under the adverse conditions of urban anomie and dispersal. It is understandable that *hoʻoponopono* could be revived and retained in a standardized form with the erudition and resources of specialists in family therapy and religion. But the persistence, consistency, and abundance of cultural metaphors and themes in everyday use, particularly those based on ideas of entanglements and openness, forgiveness and apology, *aloha* extension and *lili* retention, illustrate the strength and vigor of contemporary Hawaiian culture. There is a malleability and creativity in everyday informal usage that both pays homage to the past and vitalizes the culture for the future.

Conclusion

The literature contains a great deal about the historical changes in Hawaiian identity and society after the encounter with Europeans, particularly Captain James Cook in 1778 (Friedman 1993; Obeyesekere 1992; Sahlins 1981, 1985, 1989).[1] Most of these discussions are fascinating displays of academic analysis and interpretation, but they—once again—usurp and strip Hawaiians of control over their histories and identities. It is as if Hawaiians are of interest (and scholarly usefulness) only as models for theoretical arguments. Ironically, this literature was produced during a period of struggle in the Hawaiian community to regain control over their history, identity, and culture—their lives. The passion of Hawaiian political and academic leaders about this struggle for control is exemplified in the biting response by Haunani-Kay Trask to Roger Keesing's (1989) and Linnekin's (1983; Handler and Linnekin 1984) discussions of the "invention of culture" in the Pacific and Hawai'i. Trask responds to Keesing's article "Creating the Past: Custom and Identity in the Contemporary Pacific," which discusses the gulf between "the authentic past . . . and the representation of the past in contemporary

---

[1] Although Obeyesekere challenges the European myth that naive indigenous people viewed white explorers as gods (which formed the basis for justifications for dominance and colonialization), he attempts to reconstruct the cultural and psychological context of the Cook encounter in Hawai'i. See Valeri 1985 for a structural analysis of Hawaiian ritual sacrifice, religion, and related sociocultural features. Also see Buck 1993 for a Marxist and poststructuralist reinterpretation of Hawaiian history and a discussion of the use of Hawaiian music, chants, and *hula* in the symbolic structuring and restructuring of Hawaiian cultural identity.

[145]

ideologies of cultural identity" (1989:35), as "a gem of academic colonialism" and Keesing as "clinging to his sense of white superiority" (1991:159). Linnekin takes exception to Keesing's argument that an "authentic" past has been appropriated and manipulated in the service of contemporary goals and explains that Keesing misreads her and Wagner (1981). In using the term "the invention of culture" she does not mean it is "made up" but that the making of culture is a continuous process of creation and change. Linnekin argues "that tradition is a conscious model of lifeways that people use in the construction of identity" (1983:241). She asserts that the Hawaiian political and cultural movement is urban based:

> Seeking to rediscover their culture, the nationalists modeled their notions of tradition partly on their ideas about the rural community and partly on early accounts of Hawaiian society—most of these written by foreigners. . . . In their search for an authentic tradition, Hawaiian nationalists look to the rural lifestyle, use it, and idealize it to create a new version of Hawaiian culture. But in their self-conscious adherence to a model of Hawaiianness, the nationalists tend to circumscribe and delimit the range of behavior that conforms to that model. . . . The Hawaiian definition of "acting Hawaiian" takes on a new rigidity; [certain behaviors] become obligatory, rather than customary. . . . The Hawaiian identity is thus objectified, made into an emblematic icon to be sculpted and consciously emulated. (1983:245, 248)

She further notes that the rural people she worked with in Keʻanae on Maui have become self-consciously aware of their "Hawaiianness." Some villagers have joined Hawaiian political movements as representatives of their traditional lifestyle. For example, one Keʻanae man, after his son's tragic death in the cause of an early political movement called Protect Kahoʻolawe ʻOhana, joined the group "as a living symbol and taproot to tradition. As an 'uncle' to the ʻOhana, his presence at meetings lends credibility to the movement's link with the past" (Linnekin 1983:248). She also refers to a Keʻanae woman who "cultivates her Hawaiian identity" as one who "exemplifies the imitation of a tradition; a deliberate self-definition according to a model of Hawaiianness" (1983:244).

Trask is outraged by the terms "invention" and "creation" of culture because they imply, "Alas, poor, bedeviled Natives 'invent' their culture in reaction to colonialism, and all in the service of grimy politics!" (1991:159). Her anger and argument are specifically about the control of self-definition. She clearly states, "For Hawaiians, anthropologists in general (and Keesing in particular) are part of the colonizing horde because they seek to take away from us the power to define who and what we are, and how we should behave politically and culturally" (1991:162). In her footnote to that remark, she notes the inequities of "voice" when she states, "What Linnekin or Keesing or any other anthropologist writes about Hawaiians has more potential power than what Hawaiians write about themselves" (1991:166). And in fact, Trask's long-standing published disagreements with Linnekin stem from Trask's point that Linnekin misunderstands and therefore misrepresents "the contemporary struggle by native Hawaiians for their land and the practice of their culture" (Trask 1986:233).[2] Thus Linnekin gives non-Hawaiians a misperception of the cultural basis of the Hawaiian movement.

Trask's position is that "the [Hawaiian] movement is rurally based, arising in Hawaiian communities threatened with commercial development and focused on indigenous Hawaiian claims to the land" (1986:234) and that relationship to the land is signified by a traditional concept of *mālama 'āina* or *aloha 'āina*, which means to be responsible, loving, and caring for the land:

> To Linnekin, this value has been invented by modern Hawaiians to protest degradation of the land by developers, the military, and others. What Linnekin has missed here . . . is simply this: the Hawaiian relationship to land has persisted into the present. What has changed is ownership and use of the land. . . . Asserting the Hawaiian relationship in this changed context results in politicization. Thus, Hawaiians assert a "traditional" relationship to the land *not* for political ends as Linnekin (and Keesing) argue, but because they continue to believe in the cultural value of caring for the land. . . . The Hawaiian cultural motivation reveals the persistence of traditional values, the very thing Linnekin (and Keesing) allege modern Hawaiians to have "invented" (1991: 165).

Linnekin and Trask agree, however, that culture is constantly changing and being redefined. They agree that some elements of Hawaiian culture have been transformed and some persist into the present. A major point of contention is over the public control and definitions of Hawaiian identity and culture. Furthermore, for Trask, the importance of the persistence of a cultural valuation of the land and the land-sourced origins of Hawaiian culture is the basis for the political arguments for land repara-

---

[2] Tobin, as a self-described "student of both Linnekin and Trask," attempts to mediate their long-standing arguments while he critiques the "cultural construction discourse" (1994).

tions. The culture is in the land, and the Hawaiian people are the care-takers of both.

In the introduction to this book, I asked what happens to those Hawaiians who do not have a personal relationship to the land; who do not participate in the political struggles for a cultural renaissance, land reparations, or sovereignty; who cannot consciously articulate elements of Hawaiian culture if directly asked; and have only a fleeting knowledge of Hawaiian words, let alone language. Have they lost their culture or the right to claim access to it?

Although I am yet another outsider, I have attempted to demonstrate that such individuals, although they are alienated from their land, are not disfranchised from their culture. This book is about the unconscious living of Hawaiian culture and the everyday expression of Hawaiian self, person, and individuality through acts of *aloha* (love), *lili* (jealousy), *manini* (stinginess), *huhū* (anger), *na'au* (heart, sincerity), and the need for a balanced combination of emotional intensity and a rational "cool head." I have attempted to give light to the eloquent voices of so-called disfranchised Hawaiians who can well speak for themselves and their culture but have no means to make their words heard beyond their own social networks.

Through talk story and daily activities, urban Hawaiians with no connection to the land or any conscious phenomenological understanding of Hawaiian culture expressed a shared and negotiated organization of patterned ideas. They conveyed in their everyday lives through interpretation, actions, and words a Hawaiian culture with links to the past and transformations into the present. For example, *ho'oponopono* has been revitalized and transformed into a contemporary method of family therapy while retaining the form and substance of its traditional form. Yet its continuous, if unlabeled, presence in everyday conflict resolution practices, using the key elements of escalating emotional entanglements (*hihia*), the need to "open" oneself, the cutting (*'oki*) of bad feelings, and mutual forgiveness, has continued without artificial stimulation or formal instruction. That as a twelve-year-old, Kalena can interrupt her grandmother Nohi's explanation to an outsider of illness as retribution to confirm her own understanding of why she contracted the chicken pox demonstrates a cultural transmission from one generation to another. That Ellen Kam can speak so movingly about the necessity of doing things with sincerity, with "heart" (*na'au*); Pua Kahana can explain the deep need for trust and *aloha* in friendships; and Nohi Nacimiento can give detailed discussions of *lili*, retribution, and forgiveness attests to the persistence of cultural values.

These are not random acts of disparate cultural artifacts but are coherently organized into a cultural system of interpretation of motive, rich metaphoric language, definitions of transgression and retribution, the obligations, intensity, and entanglements of social relationships, methods for correction and resolution, and the bonds of emotions: the cultural ties that bind and define Hawaiians.

Since this is a book about the maintenance and transformations of Hawaiian culture, its end combines the words of my oldest lady friend, Nohi, "You used up plenty words," and those of the baby girl of my youngest lady friend, Ellen: "Nuff. *Pau*."

Glossary

akua	God, goddess, spirit
akua lele	Literally, "flying god"; usually used to refer to a destructive spirit in the form of a "fireball" sent by a jealous or vindictive person
aliʻi	Chief, ruler, royalty, person of royal class
aloha	Love, compassion, grace
aloha ʻāina	Love of the land or one's country
ʻaumakua, ʻaumākua (pl.)	Family or personal god(s); can assume animal or natural form; see *kino lau*
haʻi ʻōlelo	Speech, oration
hala	Transgression, error, wrongdoing; shortcoming, failure; pandanus tree
hana pono	Etiquette, proper behavior
hānai	Fosterage; foster child, parent; adopt, adoption
haole	White or Caucasian person; originally anything foreign
heahea	Greeting, welcoming call
hemo	Open, untie, loosen; remove or take off, as clothes
hewa	Mistake, error
hihia	Entanglement, snarled; difficulty, trouble

[150]

hilahila	Shy, bashful; embarrassed; shame
hō'ailona	Sign; symbol
ho'okano	Haughty, conceited, snobbish
ho'ōla	To save, heal; healer, savior
ho'ola'a mahiki	A ceremony to sever genealogical ties with family gods (*'aumākua*) and non-Christian beliefs of previous generations
ho'omauhala	To hold or bear a grudge; to hold fast a fault (*hala*)
ho'opāna'i	To seek revenge; to pay back, reciprocate
ho'oponopono	A conflict resolution method; literally, to make right, correct
hua 'ōlelo	Literally, fruit of word or speech; a rash or malicious statement whose affect will be returned to the speaker; a broken promise
huhū	Anger, angry
hukihuki	To pull back and forth; to argue, disagree
hukilau	A form of net fishing; literally, to pull ropes
hula	Traditional form of Hawaiian dance
inoa	Personal name
inoa pō	Literally, night name; a name a family member dreams for an unborn child, sent by family gods (*'aumākua*)
kahuna, kāhuna (pl.)	Sorcerer; can be used as a verb, to ensorcell; originally referred to an expert in a profession
kahuna 'anā'anā	A sorcerer of black magic
kahuna lapa'au	A medical healer
kahuna lā'au lapa'au	A medical healer who specializes in herbal cures
kai	Ocean, sea
kala	To loosen, untie; to forgive, excuse, pardon

kama'āina	Native born; literally, child of the land
kanaka, kānaka (pl.)	Human, person; Hawaiian (colloquial use is either derogatory or an affectionate in-group term)
kanaka makua	Mature person, adult
kānaka maoli	Native Hawaiians
kāne	Man, male; husband
kaona	Hidden, multiple meaning; usually as used in literary forms
kapu	*Tabu*, forbidden; sacred; restricted
kāpulu	Untidy, careless, sloppy
kauwā	Slave, outcast, pariah
kepalō	The devil
kino lau	Multiple forms of supernatural beings such as gods, goddesses; can be animal or natural forms, events
kōkua	Aid, assistance
kolohe	Mischievous, devilish; a rascal or rogue
konohiki	A headman of the chief
kūkulu kumuhana	In *ho'oponopono*, the statement of the problem; a pooling of thoughts and prayers by a group to solve a common problem
lānai	Balcony, porch
lauhala	Pandanus leaves used in weaving mats, screens, hats
lili	Jealousy
lū'au	Hawaiian feast, banquet, celebratory meal; colloquially spelled *luau*
maha'oi	Rude; presumptuous; brazen
mahele	Portion, division, section
mahiki	To pry, peel off; to exorcise, cast out spirits; the discussion portion of *ho'oponopono*
maka'āinana	Commoners

makai	On the oceanside, toward the ocean
mana	Supernatural force or power
manini	Stingy, skinny
mauka	Toward the mountains, inland
mele	Song, chant, poem
menehune	Legendary small people
mihi	Forgiveness; apology
minamina	Regret; sorrow for what is lost
moʻo	Lizard
moʻolelo	Story, legend
muʻumuʻu	Loose, full dress; usually long
naʻau	Heart, feeling, sincerity; literally bowels
nane	Riddle, puzzle
nīele	To keep asking questions; inquisitive, curious
noa	Without *kapu* or *mana*; free from restrictions
noho	Possessed by a spirit
ʻohana	Family, kin group
ʻoki	To cut
ʻōlelo	Speech, word; a Bible reading
ʻōpelo	Mackerel
paʻakai	Salt; usually refers to Hawaiian salt, a coarse-grained sea salt
pakalōlō	Marijuana
pānaʻi	Revenge; to pay back
pani	To close
pau	Finished, ended
Pele	Volcano goddess
pī	Stingy
pilau	Rotten, spoiled; garbage
pilikia	Trouble
pohō	Loss; out of luck
pule wehe	The opening prayer for *hoʻoponopono*
pumehana	Warmth; affection
punahele	A favorite child, "pet"

Glossary

pupule	Crazy, insane; reckless, wild
'ūhā kapu	Sacred lap
'uhane	Soul, spirit; ghost
'uhane hele	A wandering spirit; usually of someone living
wahine	Woman; wife

[154]

References

Aiona, D. L.
    1959   The Hawaiian Church of the Living God: An Episode in the Hawaiian's Quest for Social Identity. Master's thesis. University of Hawaii.

Akana, R.
    1996   Making OHA *Pono. Ka Wai Ola O OHA* 13(9): 15.

Alvarez, R. R.
    1995   The Mexico-U.S. Border: The Making of an Anthropology of Borderlands. *Annual Review of Anthropology* 24:447–470.

Andrade, K.
    1988   Loss of Identity Called Tourist Threat. *Honolulu Star-Bulletin*. August 26.

Blaisdell, K., and N. Mokuau
    1991   *Kānaka Maoli*: Indigenous Hawaiians. In *Handbook of Social Services for Asian and Pacific Islanders*, ed. N. Mokuau, pp. 131–154. New York: Greenwood.

Bathgate, J.
    1990   *Moe 'Uhane*—The Dream: An Account of the Dream in Traditional Hawaiian Culture. *Pacific Studies* 13(2):55–75.

Beaglehole, E.
    1937   *Some Modern Hawaiians*. Honolulu: University of Hawaii Research Publication.

Beamer, B.
    1996   What Kind of Trustee Do You Want? *Ka Wai Ola O OHA* 13(9):14.

Beck, L.
    1992   *Nomad: A Year in the Life of a Qashqu'i Tribesman in Iran*. Berkeley: University of California Press.

Becker, A. E.
    1995   *Body, Self, and Society: The View from Fiji*. Philadelphia: University of Pennsylvania Press.

References

Beckwith, M, and L. Green
1924   Hawaii Customs and Beliefs Relating to Birth and Infancy. *American Anthropologist* 26:230–244.
Behar, R.
1993   *Translated Woman: Crossing the Border with Esperanza's Story*. Boston: Beacon.
Birth, K. K.
1990   Review Article: Reading and the Righting of Writing Ethnographies. *American Ethnologist* 17(3):549–557.
Black, F. L.
1990   Review of *Before the Horror: The Population of Hawai'i on the Eve of Western Contact*, by D. E. Stannard. *Pacific Studies* 13(3): 269–279.
Boggs, S. T., and K. A. Watson-Gegeo
1979   Interweaving Routines: Strategies for Encompassing a Social Situation. *Language and Society* 7:375–392.
Briggs, J. L.
1970   *Never in Anger: Portrait of an Eskimo Family*. Cambridge: Harvard University Press.
Buck, E.
1993   *Paradise Remade: The Politics of Culture and History in Hawai'i*. Philadelphia: Temple University Press.
Burridge, K.
1979   *Someone, No One: An Essay on Individuality*. Princeton: Princeton University Press.
Carr, E. B.
1972   *Da Kine Talk: From Pidgin to Standard English in Hawaii*. Honolulu: University Press of Hawaii.
Carrithers, M., S. Collins, and S. Lukes, eds.
1985   *The Category of the Person*. Cambridge: Cambridge University Press.
Carroll, V., ed.
1970   *Adoption in Eastern Polynesia*. ASAO Monograph no. 1. Honolulu: University of Hawaii Press.
Chow, W. T.
1980   The Resurgence of Nonmetropolitan Hawaii. *Amerasia Journal* 7(2): 75–90.
Ciborowski, T., and D. Price-Williams
1982   Animistic Cognition: Some Cultural, Conceptual, and Methodological Questions for Piagetian Research. In *Cultural Perspectives on Child Development*, ed. D. A. Wagner and H. W. Stevenson, pp. 166–180. San Francisco: W. H. Freeman.
Crapanzano, V.
1977   On the Writing of Ethnography. *Dialectical Anthropology* 2(1):69–73.
1980   *Tuhami: Portrait of a Moroccan*. Chicago: University of Chicago Press.
Cruikshank, J.
1990   *Life Lived Like a Story: Life Stories of Three Yukon Native Elders*. Lincoln: University of Nebraska Press.

Cruz, L., and J. K. English
    1990   Review of *Before the Horror: The Population of Hawai'i on the Eve of Western Contact*, by D. E. Stannard. *Pacific Studies* 13(3):279–284.

Csordas, T. J.
    1994   Self and Person. In *Handbook of Psychological Anthropology*, ed. P. K. Bock, pp. 321–350. Westport, Conn.: Greenwood Press.

Daws, G.
    1968   *Shoal of Time: A History of the Hawaiian Islands*. Honolulu: University Press of Hawaii.

Deihl, J.
    1932   The Position of Women in Samoan Culture. *Primitive Man* 5:21–26.

DeVos, G., and L. Romanucci-Ross, eds.
    1995   *Ethnic Identity*. 3d ed. Walnut Creek, Calif.: Alta Mira Press.

Dieterlen, G., ed.
    1973   *La Notion de personne en Afrique noire*. Paris: Centre National de la Recherche Scientifique.

Dubanoski, R. A.
    1982   Child Maltreatment in European- and Hawaiian-Americans. *Child Abuse and Neglect* 5:457–465.

Dumont, L.
    1970   *Homo Hierarchicus*. Trans. M. Sainsbury. Chicago: University of Chicago Press.

Duranti, A.
    1981   The Samoan *Fono*: A Sociolinguistic Study. *Pacific Linguistics* (Canberra) ser. B 80.
    1984   *Intentions, Self, and Local Theories of Meaning: Words and Social Action in a Samoan Context*. Center for Human Information Processing 122. La Jolla: University of California, San Diego.
    1990   Doing Things with Words: Conflict, Understanding, and Change in a Samoan *Fono*. In *Disentangling: Conflict Discourse in Pacific Societies*, ed. K. A. Watson-Gegeo and G. M. White, pp. 459–489. Stanford: Stanford University Press.

Dwyer, K.
    1977   On the Dialogic of Fieldwork. *Dialectical Anthropology* 2(2):143–151.

Edgerton, R. B.
    1976   *Deviance: A Cross-Cultural Perspective*. Menlo Park, Calif.: Cummings.
    1985   *Rules, Exceptions, and Social Order*. Berkeley: University of California Press.
    1986   Review of *Culture Theory*, ed. R. A. Shweder and R. A. LeVine. *American Ethnologist* 13(4):807–809.

Elias, N.
    1978   *The History of Manners*. Vol. 1: *The Civilizing Process*. Trans. Edmund Jephcott. New York: Pantheon.

Epstein, A. L.
    1979   *Ethos and Identity: Three Essays on Ethnicity*. London: Tavistock.

1984   *The Experience of Shame in Melanesia: An Essay on the Anthropology of Affect*. Occasional Paper no. 40. London: Royal Anthropological Institute of Great Britain and Ireland.

Farrell, B. H.
1982   *Hawaii, the Legend That Sells*. Honolulu: University Press of Hawaii.

Fineberg, R.
1982   Some Observations on a Polynesian Naming System: Personal Names and Naming on Anuta. *Journal of the Polynesian Society* 92(4): 581–588.

Finney, B. R.
1979   *Hokule'a: The Way to Tahiti*. New York: Dodd, Mead.
1991   Myth, Experiment, and the Reinvention of Polynesian Voyaging. *American Anthropologist* 93(2):383–404.

Firth, R.
1963   *We, the Tikopia: A Sociological Study of Kinship in Primitive Polynesia*. 2d ed. abr. Boston: Beacon.

Fischer, M. M. J.
1986   Ethnicity and the Post-Modern Arts of Memory. In *Writing Culture*, ed. J. Clifford and G. E. Marcus, pp. 194–233. Berkeley: University of California Press.

Fogelson, R. D.
1982   Person, Self, and Identity: Some Anthropological Retrospects, Circumspects, and Prospects. In *Psychosocial Theories of the Self*, ed. B. Lee, pp. 67–109. New York: Plenum.

Fortes, M.
1959   *Oedipus and Job in West African Religion*. Cambridge: Cambridge University Press.
1973   On the Concept of the Person among the Tallensi. In *La Notion de personne en Afrique noire*, ed. G. Dieterlen, pp. 283–319. Paris: Centre National de la Recherche Scientifique.

Freeman, J. M.
1984   *Untouchable: An Indian Life History*. Stanford: Stanford University Press.
1989   *Hearts of Sorrow: Vietnamese-American Lives*. Stanford: Stanford University Press.

Friedman, J.
1993   The Past in the Future: History and the Politics of Identity. *American Anthropologist* 94(4):837–859.

Fujii, J.
1974   The Kalihi Most People Never See. *Honolulu Star-Bulletin*, 30 June.

Furuto, S. M.
1991   Family Violence among Pacific Islanders. In *Handbook of Social Services for Asian and Pacific Islanders*, ed. N. Mokuau, pp. 203–215. Westport, Conn. Greenwood Press.

Gallimore, R., J. W. Boggs, and C. Jordan
1974   *Culture, Behavior, and Education: A Study of Hawaiian-Americans*. Sage Library of Social Research 11. Beverly Hills, Calif.: Sage.

Gallimore, R., and A. Howard, eds.
1968   Studies in a Hawaiian Community: Na Makamaka o Nanakuli. In *Pacific Anthropological Records* 1. Honolulu: Bernice P. Bishop Museum.

Geertz, C.
1973   *The Interpretation of Cultures*. New York: Basic Books.
1983   *Local Knowledge*. New York: Basic Books.
1984   'From the Native's Point of View': On the Understanding of Anthropological Understanding. In *Culture Theory: Essays on Mind, Self, and Emotion*, ed. R. A. Shweder and R. A. LeVine, pp. 123–136. Cambridge: Cambridge University Press.
1988   *Works and Lives: The Anthropologist as Author*. Stanford: Stanford University Press.

Goldman, I.
1970   *Ancient Polynesian Society*. Chicago: University of Chicago Press.

Goodenough, W. H.
1965   Personal Names and Modes of Address in Two Oceanic Societies. In *Context and Meaning in Anthropology*, ed. M. E. Spiro, pp. 265–276. New York: Free Press.

Goodman, M. E.
1967   *The Individual and Culture*. Homewood, Ill.: Dorsey.

Handler, R., and J. Linnekin
1984   Tradition, Genuine or Spurious. *Journal of American Folklore* 97(385): 273–290.

Handy, E. S. C.
[1927] 1971   *Polynesian Religion*. New York: Kraus Reprint.

Handy, E. S. C., and M. K. Pukui
1972   *The Polynesian Family System in Ka-'u, Hawai'i*. Tokyo: Charles E. Tuttle.

Handy, E. S. C., M. K. Pukui, and K. Livermore
1934   *Outline of Hawaiian Physical Therapeutics*. Bernice P. Bishop Museum Bulletin 126. Honolulu: Bernice P. Bishop Museum.

Hannerz, U.
1986   Theory in Anthropology: Small Is Beautiful? The Problem of Complex Cultures. *Comparative Studies in Society and History* 28(2):362–367.

Hanson, A.
1991   Reply to Langdon, Levine, and Linnekin. *American Anthropologist* 93(2):449–450.

Hasager, U., and J. Friedman, eds.
1994   *Hawai'i: Return to Nationhood*. Document 75. Copenhagen: International Work Group for Indigenous Affairs.

Hawaii Advisory Committee to the United States Commission on Civil Rights
1991   *A Broken Trust—The Hawaiian Homelands Program: Seventy Years of Failure of the Federal and State Governments to Protect the Civil Rights of Native Hawaiians*. Washington, D.C.: U.S. Government Printing Office.

Hawai'i. Commission on the Status of Women
1993   *Domestic Violence Report*. Honolulu.

———. Criminal Justice Statistical Analysis Center
1977   *Crime in Hawaii, 1976.* Honolulu: Criminal Justice Statistical and Analysis Center.
———. Department of Business and Economic Development (DBED)
1987   *The Data Book, 1987.* Honolulu.
———. Department of Business, Economic Development, and Tourism (DBEDT)
1994   *Data Book, 1993–1994.* Honolulu.
———. Department of Health, Research, and Statistics Office
1973   *Research and Statistics Report No. 1.* Honolulu: Hawaii State Department of Health, Research, and Statistics Office.
———. Department of Planning and Economic Development (DPED)
1976   *The Data Book.* Honolulu.
1985   Research and Economic Analysis Division, *Racial Statistics in the 1980 Census of Hawaii.* Statistical Report 180. Honolulu.
———. Department of Social Services and Housing, Corrections Division.
1972–73a Characteristics of Adult Residents in Hawaii's Correctional Facilities, Fiscal Year 1972–1973. Mimeograph report.
1972–73b Characteristics of Juvenile Residents in Hawaii's Correctional Facilities, Fiscal Year 1972–1973. Mimeograph report.
———. Housing Authority
1974–75 *Composite Report.* Honolulu.
1988   *Composite Report, July, 1987–June, 1988.* Honolulu.
———. Office of Hawaiian Affairs (OHA)
1986   *Population Survey/Needs Assessment.* Final Report. Honolulu: OHA.
1994   *The Native Hawaiian Data Book.* Honolulu: OHA.
1996   *Native Hawaiian Data Book, 1996.* Honolulu: OHA.
Hawaiian Association of Asian and Pacific Peoples (HAAPP)
1974   *A Shared Beginning: An Asian and Pacific Perspective on Social Conditions in Hawaii.* Statewide Mental Health Conference. Honolulu.
Hecht, J.
1977   The Culture of Gender in Pukapuka: Males, Female and the *Mayaki-tanga* 'Scared Maid.' *Journal of the Polynesian Society* 82(2): 183–206.
Heelas, P., and A. Lock, eds.
1981   *Indigenous Psychologies: The Anthropology of the Self.* London: Academic.
Heen, E. L.
1936   The Hawaiians of Papakolea: A Study of Social and Economic Realism. Master's thesis. University of Hawaii.
Heighton, R. H. Jr.
1971   Hawaiian Supernatural and Natural Strategies for Goal Attainment. Ph.D. diss., University of Hawaii.
Higginbotham, N.
1985   The Cultural Accommodation of Mental Health Services for Native Hawaiians. In *Contemporary Issues in Mental Health Research in the Pacific Islands*, ed. A. B. Robillard and A. J. Marsella, p. 94–126. Honolulu: Social Science Institute, University of Hawaii.

Hingston, A.
1908   Polynesia. In *Women of All Nations*, vol. 2, ed. T. A. Joyce and N. Thomas, p. 36–69. London: Cassell.

Howard, A.
1971   Households, Families and Friends in a Hawaiian-American Community. Working Paper 19. Honolulu: East-West Center.
1974   *Ain't No Big Thing: Coping Strategies in a Hawaiian American Community*. Honolulu: University Press of Hawaii.

Howard, A., R. H. Heighton Jr., C. E. Jordan, and R. G. Gallimore
1970   Traditional and Modern Adoption Patterns in Hawaii. In *Adoption in Eastern Polynesia*, ed. V. Carroll, p. 21–51. ASAO Monograph no. 1. Honolulu: University of Hawaii Press.

Hunt, T. L.
1990   Review of *Before the Horror: The Population of Hawai'i on the Eve of Western Contact*, by D. E. Stannard. *Pacific Studies* 13(3):255–263.

Ii, J. P.
1959   *Fragments of Hawaiian History*. Ed. D. Barrére. Trans. M. K. Pukui. Honolulu: Bishop Museum Press.

Ito, K. L.
1978   Symbolic Conscience: Illness Retribution among Urban Hawaiian Women. Ph.D. diss., University of California, Los Angeles.
1982   Illness as Retribution: A Cultural Form of Self-Analysis among Urban Hawaiian Women. *Culture, Medicine and Psychiatry* 6(4): 385–403.
1983   *Ho'oponopono* and the Ties That Bind: An Examination of Hawaiian Metaphoric Frames, Conflict Resolution and Indigenous Therapy. Paper presented at the Conference on Talk and Social Inference, Pitzer College, Claremont, Calif., October.
1985a   *Ho'oponopono*, 'To make right': Hawaiian Conflict Resolution and Metaphor in the Construction of Family Therapy. *Culture, Medicine and Psychiatry* 9:201–217.
1985b   Affective Bonds: Hawaiian Interrelationships of Self. In *Person, Self, and Experience*, ed. G. M. White and J. Kirkpatrick, p. 301–327. Berkeley: University of California Press.
1987   Emotions, Proper Behavior (*Hana Pono*) and Hawaiian Concepts of Self, Person, and Individual. In *Contemporary Issues in Mental Health in the Pacific Islands*, ed. A. B. Robillard and A. J. Marsella, p. 45–71. Honolulu: Social Science Research Institute, University of Hawaii.

Johnston, P.
1996   OHA's Trust Share Targeted at Legislature. *Ka Wai Ola O OHA* 13(3): 1.

Judd, H. P.
1930   *Hawaiian Proverbs and Riddles*. Bulletin 77. Honolulu: Bernice P. Bishop Museum.

Kaeppler, A. L.
1985   Hawaiian Art and Society: Traditions and Transformations. In *Transformations of Polynesian Culture*, ed. A. Hooper and J. Huntsman, pp. 105–131. Auckland: Polynesian Society.

References

Kamakau, S. M.
1964   *Ka Poʻe Kahiko: The People of Old.* Ed. D. B. Barrére. Trans. M. K. Pukui. Bishop Museum Special Publication 51. Honolulu: Bishop Museum Press.

Kameʻeleihiwa, Lilikalā K.
1992   *Native Land and Foreign Desires.* Honolulu: Bishop Museum Press.
1996   *He Moolelo kaao o Kamapuaʻa* [A legendary tradition of Kamapuaʻa, the Hawaiian pig god]: *An Annotated Translation of an Hawaiian Epic from Ka leo o ka lalui, June 22, 1891–July 23, 1891.* Honolulu: Bishop Museum Press.

Kanahele, G. H. S.
1985   *Kū Kanaka Stand Tall: A Search for Hawaiian Values.* Honolulu: University of Hawaii Press and Waiaha Foundation.

Kapferer, B.
1979   Mind, Self, and Other in Demonic Illness: The Negation and Reconstruction of Self. *American Ethnologist* 6(1):110–133.

Kardiner, A.
1939   *The Individual and His Society.* New York: Columbia University Press.

Kealoha, S.
1996   Native Hawaiian Vote Lead by "Gadoots." *Ka Wai Ola O OHA* 13(9):14.

Keesing, R. M.
1982   *Kwaio Religion.* New York: Columbia University Press.
1984   Rethinking *Mana. Journal of Anthropological Research* 40:1437–1456.
1987   Anthropology as Interpretive Quest. *Current Anthropology* 28(2):161–176.
1989   Creating the Past: Custom and Identity in the Contemporary Pacific. *Contemporary Pacific* 1:19–42.
1991   Reply to Trask. *Contemporary Pacific* 3:168–177.

Keesing R. M., and R. Tonkinson, eds.
1982   Reinventing Traditional Culture: The Politics of *Kastom* in Island Melanesia. Special Issue. *Mankind* 13(4).

Kelly, M.
1980   Land Tenure in Hawaii. *Amerasia Journal* 7(2):57–73.

Kennedy, J. G.
1977   *Struggle for Change in a Nubian Community: An Individual in Society and History.* Palo Alto, Calif. Mayfield.

Kent, N.
1983   *Hawaii: Islands under the Influence.* New York: Monthly Review Press.

Keyes, C. F., ed.
1981   *Ethnic Change.* Seattle: University of Washington Press.

Kirch, P. V.
1984   *The Evolution of Polynesian Chiefdoms.* Cambridge: Cambridge University Press.

1990   Review of *Before the Horror: The Population of Hawai'i on the Eve of Western Contact*, by D. E. Stannard. *Contemporary Pacific* 2(2):394–396.

Kirkpatrick, J.
1983   *The Marquesan Notion of Person*. Ann Arbor: UMI Research Press.

Knauft, B.
1984   Ethos of Harmony in a Violent New Guinea Society. Paper presented at the Eighty-third Annual Meeting of the American Anthropological Association, Denver.

Kondo, D. K.
1990   *Crafting Selves: Power, Gender, and Discourses of Identity in a Japanese Workplace*. Chicago: University of Chicago Press.

Korbin, J. E.
1978   Caretaking Patterns in a Rural Hawaiian Community: Congruence of Child and Observer Reports. Ph.D. diss. University of California, Los Angeles.
1990   *Hana 'Ino*: Child Maltreatment in a Hawaiian-American Community. *Pacific Studies* 13(3):7–22.

Kuschel, R.
1988   Cultural Reflections in Bellonese Personal Names. *Journal of the Polynesian Society* 97(1):49–70.

Lakoff, G., and M. Turner
1989   *More Than Cool Reason: A Field Guide to Poetic Metaphor*. Chicago: University of Chicago Press.

Lebra, T. S.
1983   Shame and Guilt: A Psychocultural View of the Japanese Self. *Ethos* 11(3):192–209.

Lee, B., ed.
1982   *Psychosocial Theories of the Self*. New York: Plenum.

Lee, D.
1959   *Freedom and Culture*. Englewood Cliffs, N.J.: Prentice-Hall.

Lee, D. D.
1976   *Ethnic Structures in Hawaii*. Hawaii Department of Health, Research, and Statistics Office, Population Report 6. Honolulu: Hawaii Department of Health, Research, and Statistics Office.

Lemert, E. M.
1962   Stuttering and Social Structure in Two Pacific Island Societies. In *Human Deviance, Social Problems, and Social Control*, 2d ed., pp. 197–206. Englewood Cliffs, N.J.: Prentice-Hall.

LeVine, R. A.
1984   Properties of Culture: An Ethnographic View. In *Culture Theory*, ed. R. A. Shweder and R. A. LeVine, pp. 67–87. Cambridge: Cambridge University Press.

Lévi-Strauss, C.
1978   *The Origin of Table Manners: Introduction to a Science of Mythology*. London: Jonathan Cape.

Levy, R. I.
1973   *Tahitians: Mind and Experience in the Society Islands*. Chicago: University of Chicago Press.

1974 Tahiti, Sin and the Question of Integration between Personality and Sociocultural Systems. In *Culture and Personality: Contemporary Readings*, ed. R. A. LeVine, pp. 287–306. New York: Aldine.

1983 Introduction: Self and Emotion. *Ethos* 11(3):128–134.

1984 Emotion, Knowing, and Culture. In *Culture Theory: Essays on Mind, Self, and Emotion*, ed. R. A. Shweder and R. A. LeVine, pp. 214–237. Cambridge: Cambridge University Press.

Lienhardt, G.

1985 Self: Public, Private. Some African Representations. In *The Category of the Person*, ed. M. Carrithers, S. Collins, and S. Lukes, pp. 141–155. Cambridge: Cambridge University Press.

Lind, A. W.

1930 The Ghetto and the Slum. *Social Forces in Hawaii* 9:206–215.

1939 Social Disorganization in Hawaii. *Social Process in Hawaii* 5:6–10.

1967 *Hawaii's People*. 3d ed. Honolulu: University of Hawaii Press.

Linnekin, J.

1983 Defining Tradition: Variations on the Hawaiian Identity. *American Ethnologist* 10(2):241–252.

1985 *Children of the Land: Exchange and Status in a Hawaiian Community*. New Brunswick, N.J.: Rutgers University Press.

1990 *Sacred Queens and Women of Consequence: Rank, Gender and Colonialism in the Hawaiian Islands*. Ann Arbor: University of Michigan Press.

1991a Text Bites and the R-Word: The Politics of Representing Scholarship. *Contemporary Pacific* 3:172–177.

1991b Cultural Invention and the Dilemma of Authenticity. *American Anthropologist* 93(2):446–449.

Lutz, C. A.

1985 Ethnopsychology Compared to What? Explaining Behavior and Consciousness among the Ifaluk. In *Person, Self, and Experience: Exploring Pacific Ethnopsychologies*, ed. G. M. White and J. Kirkpatrick, pp. 35–79. Berkeley: University of California Press.

1988 *Unnatural Emotions*. Chicago: University of Chicago Press.

Lutz, C., and G. M. White

1986 The Anthropology of Emotions. *Annual Review of Anthropology* 15:405–436.

MacCormick, C., and M. Strathern, eds.

1980 *Nature, Culture, Gender*. Cambridge: Cambridge University Press.

Malo, D.

1971 *Hawaiian Antiquities*. Trans. N. B. Emerson. 2d ed. Honolulu: Bishop Museum Press.

Marcus, G. E., and D. Cushman

1982 Ethnographies as Text. *Annual Review of Anthropology* 11:25–69.

Marcus, G. E., and M. M. Fischer

1986 *Anthropology as Cultural Critique: An Experimental Moment in the Human Sciences*. Chicago: University of Chicago Press.

Marsella, A. J., G. DeVos, and F. Hsu, eds.
1985   *Culture and Self.* New York: Tavistock.
Maruyama, M.
1988   *All I Asking for Is My Body.* Honolulu: University of Hawaii Press.
Mauss, M.
1967   *The Gift: Forms and Functions of Exchange in Archaic Societies.* New York: Norton.
1985   A Category of the Human Mind: The Notion of the Person, the Notion of Self. In *The Category of the Person,* ed. M. Carrithers, S. Collins, and S. Lukes, pp. 1–25. Cambridge: Cambridge University Press.
McGregor-Alegado, D.
1980   Hawaiians: Organizing in the 1970s. *Amerasia Journal* 7(2):29–55.
Meltzer, B. N., J. W. Petras, and L. T. Reynolds
1975   *Symbolic Interactionism: Genesis, Varieties and Criticism.* London: Routledge & Kegan Paul.
Meyers, F. R.
1979   Emotions and the Self: A Theory of Personhood and Political Order among Pintupi Aborigines. *Ethos* 7(4):343–370.
Middleton, J.
1973   The Concept of the Person among the Lugbara of Uganda. In *La notion de personne en Afrique noire,* ed. G. Dieterlen, pp. 491–509. Paris: Centre Nationale de la Recherche Scientifique.
Nash, J., ed.
1992   *I Spent My Life in the Mines: The Story of Juan Rojas, Bolivian Tin Miner.* New York: Columbia University Press.
Native Hawaiians Study Commission
1983a   *Report on the Culture, Needs, and Concerns of Native Hawaiians Pursuant to Public Law 96–565, Title III, vol. 1.* Washington, D.C.: U.S. Government Printing Office.
1983b   *Claims of Conscience: A Dissenting Study of the Culture, Needs, and Concerns of Native Hawaiians, vol. 2.* Washington, D.C.: U.S. Government Printing Office.
Newton, F. N.
1973–75   Fieldnotes, Vols. 1–6. University of California, Los Angeles, Department of Psychiatry, Kona Project files.
1978   *Aloha* and Hostility in a Hawaiian-American Community: The Private Reality of a Public Image. Ph.D. diss., University of California, Los Angeles.
Norbeck, E.
1977   A Sanction for Authority: Etiquette. In *The Anthropology of Power,* ed. R. D. Fogelson and R. N. Adams, pp. 67–76. New York: Academic Press.
Nordyke, E. C.
1977   *The Peopling of Hawaii.* Honolulu: University Press of Hawaii.
1989a   *The Peopling of Hawai'i.* 2d ed. Honolulu: University of Hawaii Press.

1989b   Comment. In *Before the Horror: The Population of Hawai'i on the Eve of Western Contact,* by D. E. Standard, pp. 105–113. Honolulu: Social Science Research Institute, University of Hawaii.

Obeyesekere, G.
1992   *The Apotheosis of Captain Cook: European Mythmaking in the Pacific.* Princeton: Princeton University Press.

Ogan, E.
1984   History, Political Economy, and Hawaiian Identity. *American Ethnologist* 11(1):189–190.

Okamura, J. Y.
1980   Aloha Kanaka Me Ke Aloha 'Aina: Local Culture and Society in Hawaii. *Amerasia Journal* 7(2):119–137.

Oliver, D.
1974   *Ancient Tahitian Society.* 4 vols. Honolulu: University Press of Hawaii.

Ortner, S. B.
1973   On Key Symbols. *American Anthropologist* 75(5):1338–1346.
1984   Theory in Anthropology since the Sixties. *Comparative Studies in Society and History* 26(1):126–166.

Ortner, S. B., and H. Whitehead, eds.
1981   *Sexual Meanings.* Cambridge: Cambridge University Press.

Paglinawan, L. K.
1972   *Ho'oponopono* Project II: Development and Implementation of *Ho'oponopono* Practice in a Social Work Agency. Manuscript report to Hawaiian Culture Committee, Liliuokalani Trust, Queen Liliuokalani Children's Center.

Parish, S. M.
1991   The Sacred Mind: Newar Cultural Representations of Mental Life and the Production of Moral Consciousness. *Ethos* 19(3):313–351.

Peterson, J.
1975   Status and Conflict: An Ethnographic Study of an Independent Hawaiian Church. Ph.D. diss., University of Hawaii.

Poole, F. J. P.
1982   The Ritual Forging of Identity. In *Rituals of Manhood*, ed. G. Herdt, pp. 99–154. Berkeley: University of California Press.
1985   Coming into Social Being: Cultural Images of Infants in Bimin-Kuskusmin Folk Psychology. In *Person, Self, and Experience*, ed. G. M. White and J. Kirkpatrick, pp. 183–242. Berkeley: University of California Press.

Pukui, M. K., and S. H. Elbert
1971   *Hawaiian Dictionary: Hawaiian-English, English-Hawaiian.* Updated and combined 3d and 1st eds. Honolulu: University Press of Hawaii.
1986   *Hawaiian Dictionary.* Rev. and enlarged ed. Honolulu: University of Hawaii Press.

Pukui, M. K., S. H. Elbert, and E. T. Mookini
1976   *Place Names of Hawaii.* Rev. and enl. ed. Honolulu: University Press of Hawaii.

Pukui, M. K., E. W. Haertig, and C. A. Lee
 1972   *Nānā I Ke Kumu (Look to the Source).* Vol. 1. Honolulu: *Hui Hanai*, Queen Liliuokalani Children's Center.
 1979   *Nānā I Ke Kumu (Look to the Source).* Vol. 2. Honolulu: *Hui Hanai*, Queen Liliuokalani Children's Center.

Quinn, N.
 1991   The Cultural Basis of Metaphor. In *Beyond Metaphor: The Theory of Tropes in Anthropology,* ed. J. W. Fernandez, pp. 56–93. Stanford: Stanford University Press.

Rabinow, P.
 1977   *Reflections on Fieldwork in Morocco.* Berkeley: University of California Press.

Ramenofsky, A. F.
 1990   Review of *Before the Horror: The Population of Hawai'i on the Eve of Western Contact,* by D. E. Stannard. *Pacific Studies* 13(3): 263–269.

Read, K. E.
 1995   Morality and the Concept of the Person among the Gahuku-Gama. *Oceania* 25(4):233–282.

Reinecke, J. E.
 1940   Personal Names in Hawaii. *American Speech* 15(4):345–352.

Reisman, P.
 1977   *Freedom in Fulani Social Life.* Chicago: University of Chicago Press.

Ritchie, J., and J. Ritchie
 1989   Socialization and Character Development. In *Developments in Polynesian Ethnology,* ed. A. Howard and R. Borofsky, pp. 95–135. Honolulu: University of Hawaii Press.

Rocha, B. A.
 n.d.   One View of Hawaiian Mental Health. Unpublished paper.

Rodgers, S., ed.
 1995   *Telling Lives, Telling Stories: Autobiography and Historical Imagination in Modern Indonesia.* Berkeley: University of California Press.

Rogers, G.
 1977   'The Father's Sister Is Black': A Consideration of Female Rank and Powers in Tonga. *Journal of the Polynesian Society* 86(2): 157–182.

Rosaldo, M. Z.
 1980   *Knowledge and Passion: Ilongot Notions of Self and Social Life.* Cambridge: Cambridge University Press.
 1983   The Shame of Headhunters and the Autonomy of the Self. *Ethos* 11:135–151.
 1984   Toward an Anthropology of Self and Feeling. In *Culture Theory: Essays on Mind, Self, and Emotion,* ed. R. A. Shweder and R. A. LeVine, pp. 137–157. Cambridge: Cambridge University Press.

Rosaldo, R.
 1989   *Culture and Truth: The Remaking of Social Analysis.* Boston: Beacon.

References

Sahlins, M.
1981   *Historical Metaphors and Mythical Realities: Structure in the Early
         History of the Sandwich Islands Kingdom.* ASAO Special Publications
         1. Ann Arbor: University of Michigan Press.
1985   *Islands of History.* Chicago: University of Chicago Press.
1989   Captain Cook at Hawaii. *Journal of the Polynesian Society*
         98(4):371–423.
Sangren, P. S.
1988   Rhetoric and the Authority of Ethnography. Includes Commentary.
         Current Anthropology 29(3): 405–435.
Scheff, T. J.
1984   The Taboo on Coarse Emotions. *Review of Personality and Social Psy-
         chiatry* 5:146–169.
Schmitt, R. C.
1968   *Demographic Statistics of Hawaii, 1778–1965.* Honolulu: University of
         Hawaii Press.
1989   Comment. In *Before the Horror: The Population of Hawai'i on the Eve
         of Western Contact*, by D. E. Stannard, pp. 114–121. Honolulu: Social
         Science Research Institute, University of Hawaii.
Scholte, B.
1987   The Literary Turn in Contemporary Anthropology: A Review of *Writ-
         ing Culture* by James Clifford and George E. Marcus. *Critique of An-
         thropology* 7(1):33–47.
Schön, D. A.
1979   Generative Metaphor: A Perspective on Problem-Setting in Social Pol-
         icy. In *Metaphor and Thought*, ed. A. Ortony, pp. 254–283. Cambridge:
         Cambridge University Press.
Shook, E. V.
1985   *Ho'oponopono.* Honolulu: East-West Center, Institute of Culture and
         Communication.
Shore, B.
1989   *Mana* and *Tapu.* In *Developments in Polynesian Ethnology*, ed. A.
         Howard and R. Borofsky, pp. 137–173. Honolulu: University of Hawaii
         Press.
Shostak, M.
1983   *Nisa: The Life and Words of a !Kung Woman.* New York: Vintage.
Shweder, R.
1985   Menstrual Pollution, Soul Loss, and the Comparative Study of Emo-
         tions. In *Culture and Depression*, ed., A. Kleinman and B. Good, pp.
         158–199. Berkeley: University of California Press.
Shweder, R. A., and E. J. Bourne
1982   Does the Concept of the Person Vary Cross Culturally? In *Cultural
         Conceptions of Mental Health and Therapy*, ed. A. J. Marsella and G.
         M. White, pp. 97–137. Dordrecht: Reidel.
Shweder, R. A., and R. A. LeVine, eds.
1984   *Culture Theory: Essays on Mind, Self, and Emotion.* Cambridge: Cam-
         bridge University Press.

Simonson, D., et al.
 1981   *Pidgin to da Max*. Honolulu: Bell Press.
 1982   *Pidgin to da Max Hana Hou*. Honolulu: Peppovision.
Smith, J.
 1974   *Tapu Removal in Maori Religion*. Memoirs of the Polynesian Society
          no. 40. Wellington: Polynesian Society.
 1981   Self and Experience in Maori Culture. In *Indigenous Psychologies: The
          Anthropology of the Self*, ed. P. Heelas and A. Lock, pp. 145–159. Lon-
          don: Academic Press.
Smith, R. J.
 1990   Hearing Voices, Joining the Chorus: Appropriating Someone Else's
          Fieldnotes. In *Fieldnotes: The Makings of Anthropology*, ed. Roger
          Sanjek, pp. 356–370. Ithaca: Cornell University Press.
Solomon, R. C.
 1984   Getting Angry: The Jamesian Theory of Emotion in Anthropology. In
          Culture Theory: Essays on Mind, Self, and Emotion, ed. R. A. Shweder
          and R. A. LeVine, pp. 238–254. Cambridge: Cambridge University
          Press.
Sontag, S.
 1979   *Illness as Metaphor*. New York: Vintage.
Spiro, M. E.
 1984   Some Reflections on Cultural Determinism and Relativism with Spe-
          cial Reference to Emotion and Reason. In *Culture Theory*, ed. R. A.
          Shweder and R. A. LeVine, pp. 323–346. Cambridge: Cambridge Uni-
          versity Press.
 1993   Is the Western Conception of the Self "Peculiar" within the Context of
          the World Cultures? *Ethos* 21:107–153.
Stannard, D. E.
 1989   *Before the Horror: The Population of Hawai'i on the Eve of Western
          Contact*. Honolulu: Social Science Research Institute, University of
          Hawaii.
 1990   Response. *Pacific Studies* 13(30):284–301.
Steiner, F.
 1967   *Taboo*. Baltimore: Penguin (Pelican).
Stewart, C. S.
 1970   *Journal of a Residence in the Sandwich Islands during the Years 1823,
          1824, and 1825*. Honolulu: University of Hawaii Press.
Strathern, M.
 1981   Self-Interest and the Social Good: Some Implications of Hagen Gen-
          der Imagery. In *Sexual Meanings*, ed. S. B. Ortner and H. Whitehead,
          pp. 166–191. Cambridge: Cambridge University Press.
 1987   Out of Context: The Persuasive Fictions of Anthropology. Includes
          Commentary. *Current Anthropology* 28(3):251–281.
Straus, A. S.
 1977   Northern Cheyenne Ethnopsychology. *Ethos* 5(3):326–357.
 1981   The Structure of the Self in Northern Cheyenne Culture. In *Psychoso-
          cial Theories of the Self*, ed. B. Lee, pp. 11–128. New York: Plenum.

References

Tobin, J.
1994   Cultural Construction and Native Nationalism: Report from the Hawaiian Front. *boundary 2* 21(1):111–133.

Trask, H.
1984–85   Hawaiians, American Colonialization, and the Quest for Independence. Special issue: The Political-Economy of Hawaii. *Social Process in Hawaii* 31:101–136.
1986   Review of *Children of the Land* by J. Linnekin. *Hawaiian Journal of History* 20:232–235.
1991   Natives and Anthropologists: The Colonial Struggle. *Contemporary Pacific* 3:159–167.
1993   *From a Native Daughter: Colonialism and Sovereignty in Hawai'i.* Monroe, Maine: Common Courage Press.
1994   *Kūpa'a 'Āina*: Native Hawaiian Nationalism in Hawai'i. In *Hawai'i: Return to Nationhood*, ed. U. Hasager and J. Friedman, pp. 15–32. Document 75. Copenhagen: International Workgroup for Indigenous Affairs.

U.S. Department of Commerce, Bureau of the Census.
1983a   *1980 Census of Population, General Population Characteristics, Hawaii.* Washington, D.C.: GPO.
1983b   *1980 Census of Population and Housing, Census Tracts, Honolulu, Hawaii.* Washington, D.C.: GPO.
1990   *Census of Population and Housing: Population and Housing Characteristics of Census Tracts and Block Numbering Areas, Honolulu, Hawaii MSA.* Washington, D.C.: GPO.

Valeri, V.
1985   *Kingship and Sacrifice: Ritual and Society in Ancient Hawaii*, trans. P. Wissing. Chicago: University of Chicago Press.

Vancouver, G.
1798   *A Voyage of Discovery to the North Pacific Ocean and Round the World.* Vol. 3. London: G. G. and J. Robinson and J. Edwards.

Wagner, R.
1981   *The Invention of Culture.* Rev. and exp. ed. Chicago: University of Chicago Press.

Watson, K. A.
1975   Transferable Communicative Routines: Strategies and Group Identity in Two Speech Events. *Language and Society* 4:53–72.

Watson-Gegeo, K. A., and S. T. Boggs
1977   From Verbal Play to Talk Story: The Role of Routines in Speech Events among Hawaiian Children. In *Child Discourse*, ed. S. Ervin-Tripp and C. Mitchell-Kernan, pp. 67–90. New York: Academic Press.

White, G. M.
1985   Premises and Purposes in a Solomon Island Ethnopsychology. In *Person, Self, and Experience: Exploring Pacific Ethnopsychologies*, ed. G. M. White and J. Kirkpatrick, pp. 328–366. Berkeley: University of California Press.

1990   Emotion Talk and Social Inference: Disentangling in Santa Isabel, Solomon Islands. In *Disentangling: Conflict Discourse in Pacific Societies*, ed. K. A. Watson-Gegeo and G. M. White, pp. 53–121. Stanford: Stanford University Press.

1991   *Identity through History: Living Stories in a Solomon Islands Society.* Cambridge: Cambridge University Press.

White, G. M., and J. Kirkpatrick, eds.

1985   *Person, Self, and Experience: Exploring Pacific Ethnopsychologies.* Berkeley: University of California Press.

Whittaker, E.

1986   *The Mainland Haole: The White Experience in Hawaii.* New York: Columbia University Press.

Wierzbicka, A.

1993   A Conceptual Basis for Cultural Psychology. *Ethos* 21:205–231.

Wikan, U.

1990   *Managing Turbulent Hearts: A Balinese Formula for Living.* Chicago: University of Chicago Press.

1995   The Self in a World of Urgency and Necessity. *Ethos* 23:259–285.

Yamamoto, E.

1979   The Significance of Local. *Social Process in Hawaii* 27:101–115.

Yamanaka, L. A.

1996   *Wild Meat and the Bully Burgers.* New York: Farrar, Straus & Giroux.

1997   *Blu's Hanging.* New York: Farrar, Straus & Giroux.

Yanagisako, S. J.

1977   Women-Centered Kin Networks in Urban Bilateral Kinship. *American Ethnologist* 4(2):207–226.

Index

Index

The Anthropology of Contemporary Issues

A SERIES EDITED BY

ROGER SANJEK